Lexical Meaning

The ideal introduction for students of semantics, *Lexical Meaning* fills
the gap left by more general semantics textbooks, providing the teacher
and the student with insights into word meaning beyond the traditional
overviews of lexical relations. The book explores the relationship between
word meanings and syntax and semantics more generally. It provides a
balanced overview of major theoretical approaches, along with a lucid
explanation of their relative strengths and weaknesses. After covering the
main topics in lexical meaning, such as polysemy and sense relations,
the textbook surveys the types of meanings represented by different word
classes. It explains abstract concepts in clear language, using a wide range
of examples, and includes linguistic puzzles in each chapter to encourage
the student to practice using the concepts. "Adopt-a-word" exercises give
students the chance to research a particular word, building a portfolio of
specialist work on a single word.

M. LYNNE MURPHY is Senior Lecturer in Linguistics in the School of
English at the University of Sussex.

CAMBRIDGE TEXTBOOKS IN LINGUISTICS

Lexical Meaning

Lexical Meaning

M. LYNNE MURPHY

University of Sussex

CAMBRIDGE UNIVERSITY PRESS
Cambridge, New York, Melbourne, Madrid, Cape Town, Singapore,
São Paulo, Delhi, Dubai, Tokyo, Mexico City

Cambridge University Press
The Edinburgh Building, Cambridge CB2 8RU, UK

Published in the United States of America by Cambridge University Press, New York

www.cambridge.org
Information on this title: www.cambridge.org/9780521677646

First published 2010

Printed in the United Kingdom at the University Press, Cambridge

A catalogue record for this publication is available from the British Library

Library of Congress Cataloguing in Publication data
Murphy, M. Lynne.
Lexical meaning / M. Lynne Murphy.
   p.   cm. – (Cambridge textbooks in linguistics)
Includes bibliographical references and index.
ISBN 978-0-521-86031-4 (hardback) – ISBN 978-0-521-67764-6 (paperback)
1. Semantics.   2. Lexicology.   I. Title.   II. Series.
P325.M824   2010
401′.43 – dc22   2010024388

ISBN 978-0-521-86031-4 Hardback
ISBN 978-0-521-67764-6 Paperback

for Phil

Contents

List of figures

Preface: using this book

Lexical semantics is approached by students of linguistics at various points in their undergraduate and graduate curricula, and this book is intended to suit anyone who has had some introduction to linguistics, but who has not yet studied lexical semantics in any depth. Given such a broad audience, it is inevitable that at some points in the text some readers will consider the material difficult and others will consider it a bit basic. My aim is to present problems of word meaning in all their messy glory – showing where there are interesting problems to be solved and considering multiple viewpoints on those problems. The big questions of how meanings work have been pondered for centuries, but the answers remain elusive, since how these questions can be answered depends upon the background assumptions about the nature of language, meaning, and mind that different approaches bring to them. In order to limit the range of background assumptions, this book is biased toward componential theories that are compatible with generative approaches to grammar. For readers who already have some general knowledge about linguistic theories, this book demonstrates how those approaches tackle issues of word meaning. Readers for whom these theories are not yet familiar will discover how their perspectives vary when it comes to the lexicon and meaning. If this leaves you wanting more information about the theories generally, the "Further reading" section near the end of each chapter plots out a proposed course of reading to broaden and deepen your knowledge of these subjects.

Adopt-a-word

Two types of exercise are provided at the end of each chapter. The general exercises provide problems to think about and new data with which to practice the concepts introduced in the chapter. In addition to these, each chapter has some "Adopt-a-word" assignments. These assignments allow you to explore the concepts introduced in the text through the perspective of a single word. We will cover a variety of topics and theoretical perspectives in a limited number of pages, but if you specialize in a particular word, you will be able to explore those topics in some depth and build on the knowledge you gain from chapter to chapter, rather than just flitting from one topic to the next. While you may cover a lot of linguistic ground, you will follow a coherent theme – the study of a particular word.

You may choose a word that interests you for Adopt-a-word, or, if you have no word in mind, you can choose one of the adoptable words at the end of this preface.

If you would like to choose your own word, keep the following in mind:

- Ideally, your word should be established enough to have been covered in standard dictionaries, otherwise it will be difficult to do some of the assignments.
- Your word should have three to seven senses in such a dictionary – anything more and you may find yourself writing a book rather than a short essay for any particular assignment.
- Be sure to consider words other than nouns, particularly verbs and adjectives.
- In my own course, I have disallowed certain swear words – not out of any sense of prudishness, but because there has been enough interest in these words that whole books have been written on them, and thus there is little left for the student to discover on her own.
- While the words I suggest below are from English, you can do Adopt-a-word assignments with words from any language with which you are sufficiently familiar (or have sufficient resources to study).

Until chapter 8, most assignments will suit most words, but after that point we start looking at particular types of meanings. So, for example, if your word is a noun and never used as a verb, it is unlikely that the assignments in chapter 10 will be relevant to it, but the ones in chapter 8 will be particularly interesting to do. If you do not adopt a particular word for the whole of the course, then the Adopt-a-word assignments can still be done with different words in different chapters – choose from any of the words at the end of the preface.

A note for instructors

The Adopt-a-word scheme lends itself well to portfolio assessment, since it results in a group of assignments with a coherent theme. The portfolio can be comprised of the best three or so of the student's written assignments. This can be especially useful for developing a course that is strong on writing and revision, as required in many universities. The Adopt-a-word scheme also ensures that students are doing active and original research from the outset of their lexico-logical study. You can customize the assignments to the level and requirements of your course by including additional requirements, such as the number or type of bibliographic sources to be used. The Adopt-a-word assignments also make good topics for small-group discussions. Additional Adopt-a-word assignments can also be invented for broader lexicology courses for issues like morphology, etymology, usage controversies, social variation, acquisition, and so forth.

Some words for adoption

These words have been tried and tested in Adopt-a-word courses. Some of these may be more interesting for students of British English than of American (or other) English, or vice versa. Before making a final decision, do a little research on the word in order to see if it suits you and your dialectal interests.

adult	*band*	*blond(e)*
buff	*bug*	*camp*
care	*clap*	*cool*
dark	*dice*	*diet*
fiddle	*flow*	*fret*
fringe	*funk*	*gamble*
glamo(u)r	*gray/grey*	*guess*
guy	*hip*	*kit*
lad	*lodge*	*log*
mad	*meat*	*mint*
moist	*pants*	*partner*
poor	*punk*	*purse*
sad	*sneak*	*spin*
stuff	*talent*	*tattoo*
text	*true*	*wave*
wild	*zero*	*zip*

Acknowledgments

I am very grateful to colleagues and students for their generosity in giving feedback on various parts of the manuscript that led to this book. Many thanks to: Lynne Cahill, Seongsook Choi and her students, Richard Coates, Vyv Evans, Cliff Goddard, Georgia Green, Melanie Green, Sascha Griffiths, Ray Jackendoff (who provided some interesting examples for chapters 8–10), Steven Jones, Anu Koskela, Diana McCarthy, Carita Paradis, Roberta Piazza, Elena Tribushinina, Christian Uffmann, Max Wheeler, Anna Wierzbicka, the students on Approaches to Meaning (in English), Language and Linguistics, Semantics and Structure of English II at Sussex University, and the anonymous reviewers of the proposal and manuscript. The usual disclaimers apply; I hope that I have done well by the comments given to me.

Anu Koskela, who at various times has been my co-teacher on most of the semantics courses at Sussex, deserves special mention. She has provided and facilitated many kinds of feedback on the work presented here, and has also contributed the drawings in chapters 3, 4, 8, and 11, and the Wittgenstein/Wierzbicka exercise in chapter 3. I thank her for her generosity and her intellectual and visual precision.

Thanks to the Department of Linguistics and English Language at Sussex for the leave time that got this book started and the general support of my colleagues there.

I cannot fail to acknowledge Arden Lily Murphy Viner, whose arrival in this world (dramatic as it was) terrifically slowed down the completion of the manuscript – but, boy, was she worth it. Lots of love and gratitude to her dad and my partner, Phil, who was instrumental in the finishing of this book, in spite of the obvious distractions.

Typographical conventions

*	marks ungrammatical examples.
#	marks semantically or pragmatically anomalous (odd) examples.
? or ??	marks examples that are grammatically or semantically difficult to process or subject to an atypical interpretation. These are slightly "better" than examples marked by #. The more ?s, the more questionable the example is.
italics	signal a "metalinguistic" use of an expression – that is, use of the expression to refer to itself as an expression, rather than in its normal sense. For example, the word *water* is italicized when it refers to the word *water* and not when it refers to actual water.
'single'	Single quotation marks enclose a gloss (description of the meaning) of an expression or of aspects of an expression.
SM CAPS	Small capital letters signal reference to a concept, ontological category (see chapter 7), or semantic component.

PART I

Meaning and the lexicon

1   The lexicon – some preliminaries

Key words: LEXICAL SEMANTICS, LEXICON, LEXIS, MENTAL LEXICON, LEXEME, CONVENTIONAL, (NON-)COMPOSITIONAL, ARBITRARY, LEXICAL UNIT, WORD, IDIOM, COLLOCATION, OPEN/CLOSED CLASS, LEXICOGRAPHY, CORPUS, NATIVE SPEAKER INTUITION

1.1   Overview

In order to set the stage for exploring lexical semantics, this chapter defines basic terms and ideas in the field, particularly the notions of LEXICON, LEXEME, and WORD. It then describes and evaluates four methods for investigating the lexicon: dictionaries, corpora, intuition, and experimentation.

1.2   What is a lexicon?

Word meanings are notoriously difficult to pin down – and this is well demonstrated in defining the basic terminology of lexical semantics. **Semantics** is the study of linguistic meaning, but it will take the next three chapters to discuss what *meaning* might mean in any particular theory of semantics. The *lexical* in *lexical semantics* refers to the **lexicon**, a collection of meaningful linguistic expressions from which more complex linguistic expressions are built. Such lexical expressions are often, but not always, words, and so **lexical semantics** is often loosely defined as 'the study of word meaning,' although the word *word*, as we shall see, is not the most straightforward term to use.

While many of the details of the structure and content of the lexicon are discussed in detail in later chapters, some general discussion of what the lexicon is and what it contains must come first. A **lexicon** is a collection of information about words and similar linguistic expressions in a language. But which information? Which expressions? What kind of collection? Whose collection? We'll cover these issues in the following subsections, but first we must acknowledge the polysemy (the state of having multiple meanings) of the word *lexicon*. **Lexicon** can refer to:

- a dictionary, especially a dictionary of a classical language; or
- the vocabulary of a language (also known as **lexis**); or
- a particular language user's knowledge of her/his own vocabulary.

For our purposes, we can disregard the first meaning and leave the study of such dictionaries to students of classical languages. The last two definitions are both relevant to the study of lexical semantics. In speaking of *the lexicon*, different scholars and theories assume one or the other or the interrelation of both, as the next subsection discusses.

1.2.1   Where is the lexicon?

Some traditional approaches to the lexicon generally make claims about the vocabulary of a language, its **lexis**. Taking this perspective on vocabulary, the lexicon is "out there" in the language community – it is the collection of anything and everything that is used as a word or a set expression by the language community. Other linguistic perspectives, including those discussed in this book, focus on vocabulary "in here" – in the mind of a language user. The term **mental lexicon** is used in order to distinguish this more psychological and individualistic meaning of *lexicon*.

Clearly though, we have to take into account the fact that the "out there" and "in here" lexicons are interrelated; in order to communicate with each other, speakers of a language must aim to have reasonably similar ways of using and understanding the words they know – otherwise, if you said *banana*, I'd have no reason to believe that you didn't mean 'robot' or 'hallelujah.' The lexicon of the language "out there" in our culture is the lexicon that we, as individuals, aim to acquire "in here" and use. This is not the same as saying that the lexicon of a language is a union of all the lexicons of all the language's speakers. When linguists study a language's lexicon, they tend to idealize or standardize it. For instance, say there's an English speaker somewhere who, ever since being hit on the head with a mango, mistakenly uses the word *goat* to mean 'pencil.' Just because there's someone who uses the language in this way does not mean that this fact about the use of the language needs to be accounted for in a model of the English lexicon – his use is clearly a mistake. So, in order to study the lexicon of a language, one needs to have a sense of what does and does not count as part of that language. Sometimes these decisions are somewhat arbitrary, but they are not simply decisions made on the basis of what is "correct" English in some school-teacherish (that is, **prescriptive**) sense. Non-standard words and uses of words are also part of the language that we want to explain, and we can pursue interesting questions by looking at them. For example, some people use *wicked* as slang for 'especially good,' which might lead us to ask: how is it that a word's meaning might change so much that it is practically the opposite of what it originally meant?

Similarly, although mental lexicons exist in individual speakers' minds, in studying the mental lexicon we do not necessarily want to investigate any one particular speaker's lexicon (otherwise, we would have another few billion lexicons to investigate after we finish the first one). Instead, the focus is usually on an imagined "ideal" speaker of the language, which again brings us back to the notion of a language's lexicon. For an "ideal" mental lexicon, we imagine that a speaker has at her disposal the knowledge necessary to use the language's lexis.

Most current approaches to the lexicon attempt to find a balance between the "out there" and the "in here." While particular models of lexical meaning will be evaluated in this book on the basis of their psychological plausibility, part of what makes a theory psychologically plausible is whether it is consistent with (and engages with) the social facts of language acquisition and use. My continued use of the ambiguous term *lexicon* is an acknowledgment of the dual nature of the object of our study, but the terms *mental lexicon* and *lexis* are used wherever disambiguation is needed.

1.2.2 What's in a lexicon?

Having discussed the *where* of the lexicon, we move on to the *what*. The things that one knows when one knows a language can be divided into two categories: the lexical and the grammatical. A **grammar** is a system of rules or regularities in a language, and a **lexicon** is (at the very least) a collection of linguistic knowledge that cannot be captured by rules. The grammar accounts for linguistic issues like word order and regular morphological and phonological processes. For instance, our grammar tells us the difference between the sentences *Bears trouble bees* and *Bees trouble bears*, and that this is the same kind of difference as the difference between *The kangaroo ate a flower* and *A flower ate the kangaroo*. What the grammar cannot tell us is what *bear* and *bee* and *trouble* bring to the sentence. At some point in our acquisition of English, we learned that the sound [bi] and the spelling *b-e-e* are paired with a particular set of linguistic and semantic properties – like being a noun and denoting a kind of insect. The lexicon is the collection of those associations between pronunciations, meanings, and grammatical properties that had to be learned rather than produced by grammatical rules.

The lexicon is organized into **lexical entries**, much as a dictionary is organized into entries that pull together all the information on a headword (the word, typically in boldface type, at the start of a dictionary entry). Each of these lexical entries collects the appropriate information about a particular linguistic expression, called a **lexeme**. (Later we look at why it is more precise to use the term *lexeme* rather than *word* in the study of lexical meaning.) In the remainder of this subsection, we consider which expressions are lexemes and belong in the lexicon, then in §1.2.3 we'll consider what information goes in a lexeme's lexical entry. Section 1.2.4 goes into more detail on the notion of a lexeme as an abstract representation and the relationship between a lexeme (and its lexical entry) and actual uses of an expression. Let's start with this description of *lexeme*:

A linguistic form (i.e. a bit of speech and/or writing) represents a **lexeme** if that form is *conventionally* associated with a *non-compositional* meaning.

In order to make more sense of this, let's look more closely at the concepts of conventionality and (non-)compositionality, in turn.

Conventionality

Lexemes, and the information about them in the lexicon, are **conventional** – that is, these form–meaning pairings are common knowledge among the speakers of the language, and we have had to learn these particular associations of form and meaning from other members of the language community. Compare, for example, a scream with a word. If you heard someone screaming, you would not know (without further information) what they were making noise about nor why they were making noise – after all, we scream with surprise, with delight, or with horror. But if the person yelled *Spider!* or *Fire!* or *Jump!*, you'd know what they were yelling about (but perhaps still not why they were yelling about it) because those words are used by members of our speech community to signal particular things.

Non-compositionality

Lexemes are **non-compositional** – that is, the meanings of these linguistic forms are not built out of (or predictable from) the meanings of their parts. For example, the word *cat* is non-compositional because its meaning is not evident from the sounds or letters that constitute the word. It's not that the sound /t/ represents the tail of the cat or that the vowel /æ/ tells us that a cat has fur. The word *cat* and its meaning thus constitute an **arbitrary** pairing of form and meaning.

The meaning of *black cat*, however, is deducible if you know:

(a)   the word classes (adjective, noun) and meanings of the words *black* and *cat*
(b)   what it means in English to put an adjective in front of a noun.

Thus the meaning of the clause *black cat* is **compositional**; its meaning is built from the meanings of its parts. This means that *black cat* does not need to be included in the lexicon, but its non-compositional parts (*black* and *cat*) do.

Lexemes and morphological complexity

While *lexical semantics* is often loosely defined as 'the study of word meaning,' the use of *word* in this definition is misleading, since lexical semantics is more accurately described as the study of lexeme meaning, and (a) not all words are lexemes and (b) not all lexemes are words.

Here, we need to pause and define a little terminology from **morphology**, the study of word structure. **Morphemes** are the smallest meaningful units of language, so a word is one morpheme if it is not built out of smaller meaningful parts. So, for example, *language* is a single morpheme: if we try to divide it into smaller parts (like *l* and *anguage* or *langu* and *age*), we don't get meaningful parts of English. (And although we can see the word *age* in *language*, that is just accidental. *Age* is not a morpheme within *language* as 'age' is not part of the meaning of *language*.) On the other hand, *sentimentally* is composed of three morphemes: the noun *sentiment* and the suffixes *-al* (which is added to nouns to make adjectives and could be glossed as 'marked by') and *-ly* (which turns an adjective into an adverb: 'in a certain manner'). This results in a complex word that means 'in a manner that is marked by sentiment.' *Sentimentally* is thus compositionally formed from *sentiment* plus two suffixes, and since it is compositional, in that the meaning comes straightforwardly from the combination of the parts, it does not count as a lexeme on our definition. However, *sentiment* and the suffixes *-al* and *-ly* act like lexemes, in that they have conventional meanings that cannot be derived from the meanings of their parts.

Suffixes, prefixes, and other bits of language that always attach to other morphemes are called **bound morphemes**: they must be bound to another linguistic form in order to be used. Words, on the other hand, are **free morphemes**, in that they can be used without being attached to anything else. Just as words can be arranged and rearranged to make new phrases with compositional meanings, morphemes can be arranged and rearranged to make new words with compositional meanings. The first time you come across a new morphologically complex word, like *unputdownable* or *pseudoscientifically*, you will be able to understand the word if you can understand its parts.

So far, we have seen that morphemes are lexemes in that they have conventional, non-compositional meanings. But more complex expressions may also be lexemes. For example, while *greenhouse* is a **compound** noun derived from two free morphemes, its meaning is not deducible from its parts, since a greenhouse is not actually green and it is debatable whether it is a house. A series of words can also be a single lexeme, as demonstrated by the bold expressions in the following examples:

(1) a.   **Look up** that word in the dictionary!
    b.   Look up! There's a dictionary in that tree.

(2) a.   Her beloved pet is now **pushing up daisies**.
    b.   Fido was **the apple of her eye**.

In (1a), the **phrasal verb** *look up* is a single lexeme meaning 'consult,' as opposed to (1b), in which *look* and *up* each contributes its own meaning. **Idioms** like *pushing up daisies* ('dead') and *apple of one's eye* ('one's beloved') in (2) are also lexical expressions, since they are non-compositional, and thus have to be learned and mentally stored by a language speaker.

In summary, the term *lexeme* includes:

- **simple words** (free morphemes) that cannot be broken down into smaller meaningful parts, such as *cup*, *Cairo*, and *contribute*;
- **bound morphemes**, like *un-* as in *unhappy* and *-ism* as in *racism*;

- **morphologically complex words** whose meaning is not predictable from the meanings of the parts, including compounds like *greenhouse* ('a glass building for growing plants in') and *needlepoint* ('a method of embroidery onto canvas');

- **set phrases** whose meaning is not compositional, such as phrasal verbs like *throw up* ('vomit') and *give up* ('quit') and idioms like *having the world on one's shoulders* and *fly off the handle*.

Are all lexemes non-compositional?

While linguists agree that a lexicon contains conventional, non-compositional form–meaning pairings, opinions differ as to whether one's mental lexicon also contains some compositional expressions. In other words, just because we *could* understand the meaning of a complex expression from the meanings of its parts, doesn't mean that we necessarily always go through the process of composing that complex expression every time we use it. In cases like those in (3), the expressions are so well-worn that they seem like idioms, in spite of having conventional meanings.

(3) a.   happiness (happy + ness)
    b.   How are you?
    c.   It's not whether you win or lose, it's how you play the game.

Should the items in (3) be considered to be lexemes? One argument for including compositional expressions in the lexicon is that it is advantageous for a language user to have ready access to commonly used expressions. So, in a particular individual's mind it might be convenient if complex and frequent but predictable expressions, like *How are you?* or *I love you*, were stored in the mental lexicon. Having such expressions available both through grammatical assembly and through ready-made lexemes is redundant – and thus it appears to require needless extra effort to learn and store the expression in the mental lexicon. But while non-redundant models of language are more streamlined and elegant, they are not necessarily more realistic. After all, representing the same expression (or access to the same expression) in different ways or different places in one's mind could make language production and comprehension processes less likely to break down, since if one route to the expression fails, another might succeed.

Another argument for including compositional expressions in the lexicon is that some of them are particularly conventionalized – that is to say, people sometimes rely on "ready-made" compositional expressions instead of composing new ones. The extremes of such conventionalization are seen in compositional clichés like *in this day and age*, *cry like a baby*, or the example in (3c), but conventionalization of compositional expressions can be subtler too, as studies of **collocations** (particularly frequent word combinations) have shown. A case in point is example (4), which shows how the meaning 'without milk added' is indicated by different modifiers, depending on what is being modified.

(4)   *black coffee*
             black tea – however, this can also mean non-herbal tea, so people often
                prefer to say *tea without milk* or *tea with no milk*
             plain chocolate, dark chocolate
             dry cereal

Logically speaking, there is no particular reason why milkless coffee is *black* and not *plain*, nor why *dark chocolate* is not called *black chocolate* (after all, it is about the same color as black coffee). As English speakers, we've just learned that these adjectives and nouns are best used in some combinations and not others. Similarly, some nouns go with particular verbs. For example, in English one *asks* (or *poses*) a question, but one *poses* a riddle (one does not *ask* it) and one *makes* a query (one neither *asks* nor *poses* it). Such facts lead some to argue that we should be thinking of the lexicon as including larger and looser combinations than just single words and set idiomatic phrases, or that we should see the lexicon as a network of syntactic (grammatical) and semantic relations among lexemes. While these are very interesting issues, the focus in this book is particularly on the non-compositional forms (mostly words) that **must** be in the lexicon, as the emphasis on non-compositional meanings is what makes lexical semantics distinct from other kinds of semantics. Information about collocations is still of interest to us, though, as it may be used to determine differences in particular words' meanings.

1.2.3   What is in a lexical entry?

Within the lexicon, the collection of information pertaining to a lexeme is said to be its **lexical entry**, analogous to a dictionary entry. The information that must be stored about a lexeme is precisely that which is unpredictable, or arbitrary. At the very least, this means that we need to know the basics of the lexeme's form and what meaning(s) it is associated with. When speaking of a word's **form** we usually mean its pronunciation, but if we know it as a written word, then its spelling is part of its form, and if it is a part of a sign language, then its "pronunciation" is gestural rather than vocal. We only need to store in the lexicon the details of the lexeme's form that are not predictable; so, for example, we do not need to store the facts that *cat* is made possessive by adding *'s* or that the *c* in *cat* is usually pronounced with a slight puff of air – these facts are predictable by rules in the language's grammar and phonology. As we shall see in the coming chapters, theories differ in what information about meaning is (or is not) included in the lexicon. For many modern theories, meaning is not **in** the lexicon, but is a part of general, conceptual knowledge (chapter 4). That is to say, the linguistic form is represented in the lexicon, but instead of its definition being in the lexicon as well, the lexical entry "points" to a range of concepts conventionally associated with that word. Other theories (e.g. in chapter 3) view the lexicon more like a dictionary, which provides basic definitions for words.

What other information is included in a lexical entry, again, differs from theory to theory. Most would say that a lexical entry includes some grammatical information about the word, for example its **word class** (or *part of speech*: noun, verb, etc.), and the grammatical requirements it places on the phrases it occurs in. For instance, the lexical entry for *dine* includes the information that it is a verb and that it is intransitive in that it takes no direct object, as shown in (5). *Devour*, on the other hand, is recorded as a verb that is transitive, so that it is grammatical with a direct object, but not without one, as shown in (6). Asterisks (*) signal ungrammaticality.

(5) a.   We dined.
    b.   *We dined a big bowl of pasta.

(6) a.   *We devoured.
    b.   We devoured a big bowl of pasta.

We come back to these issues in chapter 7, where we consider whether the meanings of words might determine their word classes, or whether they are entirely arbitrary and need full specification in the lexicon.

We may also need information in the lexicon about which words go with which other words – for instance, the fact that *stark* collocates with *naked* but not with *nude* or the fact that the conventional antonym of *alive* is *dead* and not *expired*. We come back to some of these issues below and in chapter 6.

1.2.4   The abstract nature of lexemes

The last thing to say in this preliminary tour of the lexicon is that a lexeme is not the same as a word in real language use. Lexemes are, essentially, abstractions of actual words that occur in real language use. This is analogous to the case of phonemes in the study of phonology. A phoneme is an abstract representation of a linguistic sound, but the **phone**, which is what we actually say when we put that phoneme to use, has been subject to particular linguistic and physical processes and constraints. To take a psycholinguistic view, a phoneme is a bit of language in the mind, but a phone is a bit of language on one's tongue or in one's ear. So, the English phoneme /l/ is an abstract mental entity that can be realized in speech variously as, say, a "clear" [l] in *land*, or a "dark" [ɫ] in *calm*. The phoneme is, so to speak, the potential for those two phones.

Similarly, when we use a word in a sentence, it is not the lexeme in the sentence, but a particular **instantiation** (i.e. instance of use) of that lexeme. Those instantiations are called **lexical units**. Take, for example, the lexeme *cup*. It is associated with a range of meanings, so that we can use it to refer to:

(a)   any drinking vessel, or
(b)   a ceramic drinking vessel with a handle whose height is not out of proportion to its width, or

(c)   a hand shaped so that there is a depression in its upward facing palm, or

(d)   the part of a brassiere that covers a breast.

But in a particular use, as in sentence (7), the lexical unit *cup* is assigned just one of those meanings – in this case, meaning (b).

(7)   I prefer my coffee in cups, not mugs.

In (7), *cup* also occurs with a particular orthographic form and it is morphologically marked as a plural. So, in this case we can say that the lexical unit *cups* in (7) is an instantiation of the lexeme *cup*, which has the plural form, the standard spelling and the (b) meaning associated with that lexeme.

The lexical entry provides the information needed to use the lexeme as a lexical unit; that is, it sets the parameters of that lexeme's potential. So, as speakers or writers, we select particular lexemes to be realized as lexical units in our utterances because the parameters set in the lexical entry are consistent with what we want to do with that word – for example, for it to have a particular meaning and fill the verb slot in a sentence. As listeners or readers we recognize the lexical unit as being an instantiation of a particular lexeme and interpret the meaning of the lexeme in ways that are consistent with the lexical entry and the context in which the lexical unit occurs.

1.3   What is a word?

1.3.1   Defining *word*

While the loose definition of *lexical semantics* is 'the study of word meaning,' the focus of this textbook is more precisely lexeme meaning. Nevertheless, as a matter of fact, most of the cases discussed in this book (and most of what is traditionally considered to be lexical semantics) involve lexemes that are words rather than bound morphemes or multi-word lexemes (such as idioms). So, it is worthwhile to say a word about what words are. I have already hinted at one problem with using the term *word* as a technical term: *word* is ambiguous in that it could mean 'lexeme' as in (8) or 'lexical unit' as in (9):

(8)   Colour and color are two spellings of the same word.

(9)   There are eight words in the sentence *Jo's pet ferret hates Jo's mother's pet ferret*.

But aside from the lexeme/lexical unit ambiguity of *word*, it can be tricky to determine which lexemes count as words in a particular language. Part of the reason for this is that the notion *word* can be defined in a number of ways, including:

- **orthographically** – based on the written form
- **semantically** – based on the meaning
- **phonologically** – based on the word's pronunciation
- **grammatically** – based on positions in phrases

Ask random English speakers what a word is, and you are likely to hear definitions based on orthographic or semantic criteria. Probably the most common belief is that words are bits of language that have a space on either side of them in print. The most obvious problem with this **orthographic definition** is that it employs circular logic. The reason that we put spaces in writing is to signal the beginnings and ends of words; one must already know which bits of language are words before one can know where to put the spaces. For instance, we know to put a space between *cat* and *nip* in (10), but to run the two together in (11).

(10)   Tom saw the cat nip the baby.

(11)   Fluffy loves catnip.

Notice too that the spaces in writing do not necessarily represent spaces in speech. *Cat+nip* can be pronounced in just about the same way in sentences (10) and (11). Something other than spaces must be telling us which bits are words in these sentences. Another problem with the 'space' definition is that some orthographic systems do not put spaces between words. In writing the southeast Asian language Lao, for instance, spaces are only left at the ends of sentences. Nevertheless Lao speakers can identify the words in those sentences. If we want to talk about the bits of language with spaces on either side, we can call them **orthographic words**, but the orthographic definition doesn't get to the essence of wordhood.

Once you give up on the orthographic definition of word, you might try the **semantic definition**, which states that words represent single, complete concepts. In that case, you could tell that *cat+nip* is two words in (10) because two meanings or ideas are represented, whereas in (11) *catnip* refers to just one thing. But this definition doesn't work for a couple of reasons. First of all, how can one tell what a complete meaning is? For instance, one might think that *policeman* involves two concepts – being police and being a man – or that it is one concept involving the entire state of being a male police officer. Similarly, the same concept can be described by various numbers of words. For example, in comparing languages it is often the case that the same meaning is variously realized in different numbers of orthographic words, such as English *post office* versus Swedish *postkontor* versus French *bureau de poste*. The "semantic" definition of word thus leads us either to the illogical conclusion that these expressions meaning 'post office' must involve different numbers of meanings, since they involve different numbers of words, or to the conclusion that some languages have more spaces in their words than others. While the second conclusion might be true, we can do better than this definition.

A **phonological word** is a unit of language that is subject to the language's particular word-based phonotactic constraints (i.e. which sounds can go next to which other ones) and phonological processes (e.g. variations in pronunciation of, say, the first consonant in a word or the main vowel in a word). For example, in English no word begins with the phoneme /t/ followed by /n/, so the first time you heard the word *catnip*, you didn't have to consider the possibility that what you heard was two words, *ca* and *tnip*. A more general signal of phonological wordhood in English is that a phonological word has no more than one main stress. For long words, like *homeostasis*, there may be more than one stressed syllable, but there is one that is more stressed than the others: *homeoSTAsis*. So, we can tell that *cat nip* in (10) is two words because the two syllables are stressed evenly, but *catnip* in (11) is a candidate for wordhood because it has main stress just on *cat*. Phonological tests of wordhood do not, however, always coincide with our semantic and grammatical intuitions and our orthographic practice concerning word boundaries. For instance, because function words are usually not stressed in English, there is only one phonological word in the two-syllable form *a cat* – even though it is two orthographic words and arguably two semantic units. Phonological tests for wordhood are also entirely language-specific – for example, the stress test in English would not work for French, Chinese, or Norwegian. Thus the concept of PHONOLOGICAL WORD is not terribly useful as a means of defining *word* in general, across languages.

Even though we have so far discussed words as form–meaning associations, the notion of wordhood can be considered to have more to do with grammar than with written/spoken form or meaning. A **grammatical word** is an expression that is uninterruptible,[1] 'movable,' and that has a part of speech that can be identified on the basis of its morphological inflections and its distribution in phrases. To return to the *cat+nip* example, *catnip* is a noun, but *cat nip* in (10) has no single part of speech. It is not even a phrasal constituent (i.e. a complete part unto itself) in that sentence, as can be determined by various tests of constituency. For example, *cat nip* cannot be replaced by a single word that refers to the same thing in (10), whereas the noun *catnip* in (11) can be replaced by the pronoun *it*. Grammatical words cannot be split up within a sentence. Thus if we make the sentences in (10) and (11) into cleft sentences by moving a noun into an *it is/was* clause, we have to move *cat* separately from *nip* in the first case, but must move *catnip* as one unit, as (12) and (13) show.

(12) a.   It was the cat that Tom saw nip the baby.
     b.   *It was the cat nip that Tom saw the baby.

(13) a.   *It is cat that Felix loves nip.
     b.   It is catnip that Felix loves.

---

[1] Infixes create apparent counterexamples to the "uninterruptible" criterion. Infixes are bound morphemes that are inserted at particular points within words. In English the only infixes look rather word-like, as in *abso-bloomin-lutely*. (Most other examples are not uttered in polite company!) We can tell that *bloomin'* is an infix here because if it were not, we'd have to believe that there are two English words, *abso* and *lutely* (and we have little other evidence to support that), and because only a small subclass of morphemes can be inserted in this place. For instance, *abso-completely-lutely* is not possible at all. Other languages have greater numbers and ranges of infixes, so the uninterruptibility criterion should more precisely be stated as 'uninterruptible by other words.'

Furthermore, *cat nip* can be interrupted but *catnip* cannot, as shown in (14) and (15), respectively.

(14)   Don't let the cat unintentionally nip the baby.

(15)   *Felix loves catwonderfulnip.

Using the grammatical or phonological criteria for wordhood, some expressions usually written with spaces within them count as words. These are **compound words** whose orthographical representations have not caught up with their lexical status. For example, we can tell that *ice cream* is a word because it has main stress on *ice*, it can be replaced in a sentence by *it*, we cannot put other words or morphemes in the middle of it (**ice minty cream*), and so forth.

1.3.2   Open-class and closed-class words

Words are often classified into two categories: **open class** and **closed class**. The open class includes nouns, most kinds of verbs, and (in English and many other languages) adjectives. The term *open class* alludes to the fact that new words can be added to those categories. For instance, if we have a new invention to name, we can invent a new noun to name it. New verbs are also often added to the language; one needs only look at the evidence of verbs that have recently been made from nouns, like *impact* and *spam*. The category of open-class words overlaps with that of **content words**, that is, words that are particularly meaningful and can refer to things or situations or properties (etc.) in the world. It also overlaps with the category of **lexical words**, that is, the sorts of words that need to be included in a model of the lexicon because they have conventional meanings that are non-compositional. The open classes are marked by the range and richness of the meanings that they encode.

On the other hand, the closed classes contain **function words** or **grammatical words**; that is, words that have grammatical functions rather than rich meanings. The closed classes include pronouns (*you, them*), modal verbs (*could, must*), determiners (*a, the*), prepositions (*of, in*), and conjunctions (*and, but*). New members of these classes are not added to the language very often. Instead they tend to gradually evolve from lexical words in a process called **grammaticalization**. For example, the lexical verb *go* means 'to move (toward a goal).' But its progressive form *be going (to)* has evolved into a grammaticalized prospective (future) marker, as in *She's going to love her gift*. The 'movement' meaning of *go* has been bleached out of the grammaticalized version and so the *going* in *be going to* can be considered to be a function word, rather than a content word.

The closed classes represent a more restricted range of meanings, and the meanings of closed-class words tend to be less detailed and less referential than open-class words. Compare, for example, members of the open noun class, like *ecstasy, jackhammer, mechanic*, and *authoritarianism*, with closed-class pronouns like *it, she*, and *them*. The nouns encode plenty of detail so that you know immediately what they designate, while the pronouns give you only a few hints: for example, whether they are referring to animate or inanimate things or to males or females. Other closed-class words such as *the*, *of*, and *but* are even harder to define because they are not used to refer to things in the world at all. A useful diagnostic is that open-class words typically can be used meaningfully on their own. For example, *chocolate*, *grumpy*, and *moo* can be seen to be meaningful in their own right because we could use each on its own to describe something we have experienced or as answers to questions, as in (16):

(16)   *What do you want?*   Chocolate.
         How do you feel?   Grumpy.
         What do you want the cow to do?   Moo.

In contrast, it is hard to think of a context in which a closed-class word like *of* or *the* or *could* would be used on its own, since those words act as the glue that holds sentences together rather than the contributors of meaning in a sentence.

You might object that *of* could be used on its own as the answer to a question like *What is a two-letter word that starts with 'o'?* But notice that in that answer we would not be using *of* to mean whatever *of* means; we would be using it to be the name of the word *of*. This is a **metalinguistic** use of the word – use of the word to refer to itself. In writing, metalinguistic use of words is marked by putting quotation marks around the word (as done outside linguistics) or underlining or italicizing it, as is done in this and other linguistics texts. Those typographical markings are necessary to point out that the word is being used as a representation of itself.

Since closed-class words play important roles in grammar, they tend to be studied as part of non-lexical rather than lexical semantics. Lexical semanticists typically concentrate on the lexical, open-class words, which make particularly rich semantic contributions to their phrases. Whether grammatical words are represented in the lexicon, just as lexical words are, is another matter that divides theoretical opinion. Psycholinguistically and neurolinguistically speaking, there is evidence that grammatical words are stored and processed separately from lexical words. For example, grammatical words and lexical words tend to be the victims of different types of speech errors, and people with aphasia (language loss due to brain injury) often lose the ability to use grammatical words while their lexical abilities remain more or less intact, or vice versa.

That being said, the idea that some word classes are semantically contentful and others are not is oversimplistic. Members of the preposition category, for example, vary considerably in how semantically rich they are. While *of* is a good example of a grammatical preposition with little semantic content (in phrases like *the publication of this book*), other prepositions, like *above* or *outside*, have more semantic content and can be used to describe various kinds of relations between two things. From a semantic point of view, it is often more interesting to consider what semantic contributions words make to sentences rather than to consider their word class, as members of different word classes can carry similar meanings. For example, the preposition *above* makes a similar contribution in sentence (17a) as the adjective *superior (to)* does in (17b) or that the noun *superior* does in (17c), or that the verb *top* contributes in (17d).

(17) a.   The manager is **above** the other employees in the organizational chart.
   b.   The manager is **superior** to the other employees in the organizational chart.
   c.   The manager is the other employees' **superior** in the organizational chart.
   d.   The manager **tops** the other employees in the organizational chart.

While one can find differences in the meanings of these sentences and the bold words in them, the bold words have in common that they all indicate a 'higher than' relation, despite the fact that they belong to different word classes. Chapter 2 explores what meanings are and what types of meanings exist.

1.3.3   Lexicalization

Whereas grammatical words come into being via grammaticalization, lexical words are the result of **lexicalization**, the assignment of a lexeme to a meaning in a particular language. *Lexicalization* can refer either to the process by which a meaning comes to have a form associated with it, or to the existence of such a form–meaning association. In the latter case, we can say that different languages **lexicalize** the world differently, meaning that different languages pick out different parts of human experience to name. For example, English has different words for toes and fingers while Italian doesn't lexicalize these body parts separately, calling both *dita*. Speakers of either language can, of course, talk about these parts of the body together or separately; for instance, in English we can say *fingers and/or toes* or *digits* if we don't want to discriminate between the two, and Italian speakers can use *dita del piede* ('digits of the foot') to refer specifically to toes and not fingers. One could say that what is different about the two languages in this case is that by lexicalizing one meaning rather than another, the language prioritizes a particular view of the body.

1.3.4   Where do words come from?

New lexicalizations can arise either through the addition of new words to the language or through semantic change in old words. We'll look at the latter case in chapter 5. **Neologisms**, or new words, come about in a number of ways, including:

- **Coining** – A new word is invented from previously meaningless sounds. Sometimes words are invented that resemble in sound what they symbolize. Such cases of **onomatopoeia** (from the Greek roots for 'name' and 'make') include *bang* for the sound a gun makes and *cuckoo* as the name of a bird that makes that sound. More rarely, words are just created out of thin air, though this mostly happens for proper names. For example, the brand name *Kodak* and the US state name *Idaho* were coined because someone liked the look and sound of them.[2]

- **Derivation** – Affixes (such as prefixes or suffixes) are added to a word to make a new word, such as *disobey* from *obey*, *resignation* from *resign* or *teacher* from *teach*. This type of affixation changes the word class (part of speech) and/or the meaning of the base word. (This is opposed to **inflection**, in which affixes are used to change a word's grammatical subclass – for instance the tense of a verb or the number of a noun. Inflection is not a word-formation device, in that it does not create a new lexeme, but creates an instantiation of an existing lexeme.)

- **Compounding** – Two existing words are joined to make a new word that combines their meanings, as in *backlash* or *bluebell*.

- **Blending** – Parts of two words are combined in a way that combines their meanings. For example, *brunch* takes its *br* from *breakfast* and its *unch* from *lunch*, and *urinalysis* comes from *urine* + *analysis*. These are sometimes called **portmanteau words**.

- **Clipping** – The new word is created by shortening an existing word – for example, *fax* from *facsimile* or *flu* from *influenza*. Such cases may not at first involve the introduction of a new meaning into the lexicon, but the original and clipped forms may gradually drift apart in meaning. For instance, *fax* came to be used as a verb (*I faxed her the contract*), but *facsimile* does not have that use.

- **Borrowing** – A word or phrase from one language is adopted by a different language. For example, *chauvinism* was borrowed into English from French. Frequently, borrowed words undergo some changes in form and meaning in the new language. In the case of *chauvinism*, the original French *chauvinisme* has lost its final <e>, and its meaning has changed over time so that it is less likely in English to refer to 'patriotism' (particularly loyalty to Napoleon) as it first did in French, and more likely to refer to 'sexism.'

- **Calque**, or **loan translation** – A concept is imported from another language and the name for it is literally translated. For example, when French needed a word for 'skyscraper,' the English word was translated into French as *gratte-ciel* ('scrapes sky'). English, in turn, translated the French *marché aux puces* ('market of the fleas') into *flea market* when it needed a term for that kind of market.

- **Acronyms** – A new word is created from the initials of a phrase. These may be "true" acronyms, which are pronounced as they are spelt, such as *laser* (from *light amplification by simulated emission*

---

[2] George Eastman coined the name *Kodak* for his company. Many people believe that *Idaho* is a Native American word, but this is a myth. Someone invented it and then claimed it was Native American, in order to give it some credibility (see www.idahohistory.net/ES2_idahosname.pdf).

of radiation), or **alphabetisms**, which are pronounced as a series of letters – for example *DIY* for 'do it yourself.'

- **Backformation** – A word is created by removing perceived affixes from an existing word. In this case, the original word looks as if it was derived from a simpler word, but it wasn't. For example, *orientation* existed in English as a noun derived from the verb *orient*. But since we are used to seeing verbs with *-ate* and related nouns that end in *-ation* (like *narrate/narration* and *evaluate/evaluation*), some English speakers perceived *-ion* as the suffix on *orientation* and "back-formed" the verb *orientate*.

Our concerns in this book are more to do with how new meanings come into the language rather than new word forms – since the latter is more a subject for a morphology course. But as we can see above, new word forms are often created because we wish to lexicalize meanings that have not yet been lexicalized in our language.

1.4   How to research words and their meanings

There are four ways to research word meaning. One is to make use of already existing research on word meanings, namely **dictionaries** and other lexicographical products. The other three methods can be used both in creating new dictionaries and in determining the accuracy of existing ones. These are **corpus methods**, **introspection**, and **experimentation**. All four are discussed in turn in this section.

1.4.1   Dictionaries

Dictionaries of various types can be useful starting points if one is interested in the meaning of a particular word or set of words. Standard desk dictionaries include information on the word's orthography, pronunciation, meanings, and word class. They may also include information on the word's historical roots, or **etymology**, and lists of related words, such as morphological derivations, synonyms, and antonyms. Some dictionaries provide information on usage, including the dialect or sociolect that the word belongs to, its level of formality (**register**), and any prescriptive rules about how the word "should" or "should not" be used in particular contexts. Finally, some dictionaries also include examples of the word's use in quotations or invented examples and/or further encyclopedic information about whatever the word refers to. Learners' dictionaries, monolingual dictionaries written for learners of the language, tend to include more grammatical information and examples, but often skip the less common uses of words – for example, the word's meaning/use in a particular profession or a particular game. Some learners' dictionaries also give information about the word's frequency of occurrence in speech and writing. Thesauruses are dictionaries organized on semantic rather than alphabetical principles, and show meaning relations among words.

People often talk about "the dictionary" as if there is only one, saying things like *I looked it up in the dictionary* or *That's not in the dictionary*. This phrasing reflects an assumption that all dictionaries give the same information, and it may even imbue them with a certain mystical quality – note how people speak of THE *dictionary*, much as they would speak of THE *Bible* or THE *Koran*. The definite article *the* before *dictionary* implies that there is one version of the language that is represented in the same way in anything that is called *dictionary*. However, any particular dictionary gives its own snapshot of the language, as there is no way that a single book or CD-ROM – or even a shelf full of them – could do justice to the myriad ways in which the language and its words are used . . . and have been used in the past and will be used in the future.

Puzzle 1–1

The following two definitions are taken from very similar dictionaries; both the *Collins Concise Dictionary of English* (CCDE) and the *Concise Oxford Dictionary* (COD) are desktop dictionaries of standard British English produced in the 1990s. See how many differences you can spot between their entries for **gratuity** (see end of chapter for answers):

gratuity /grətjuːɪtɪ/ *n. pl.* **-ties 1**. a gift or reward, usually of money, for services rendered; tip. **2**. *Mil.* a financial award granted for long or meritorious service. (CCDE)

gratuity /grətjuːɪtɪ/ *n.* (*pl.* **-ies**) money given in recognition of services; a tip [OF *gratuité* or med.L *gratuitas* gift f. L *gratus* grateful] (COD)

As well as representing different information about particular words, different dictionaries include different words. For example, of the words that begin with the letters *n-i-d*, both CCDE and COD include four words, but only one of those words is in both dictionaries: CCDE has *Nidaros, nidicolous, nidifugous*, and *nidify*, while COD has *nide, nidificate, nidify*, and *nidus*. The moral of this story is that if you use a dictionary as a research aid for lexical semantics, you get only a partial picture of a language's lexicon or of any particular lexeme in it, for several reasons. **Lexicographers** (dictionary writers) must fit the information that they have about a word into a finite space and prepare the information in a finite amount of time. Thus lexicographers constantly make conscious and subconscious choices about what information should be left out of their dictionaries. These decisions depend in part on the purpose of the dictionary and the audience it is aimed at. Most everyday dictionaries focus on representing the "standard" language, so they tend not to include much slang, regional usage, or jargon. The methods that dictionaries use to collect information (see the discussion of corpora, below) heavily bias them toward the written rather than the spoken standard. And since the language constantly changes, dictionaries cannot keep up with all of the newest words and word senses. Even well-worn uses of words are often left out, simply because you can probably figure them out for yourself, based on the meanings that *are* listed in the dictionary. For example, neither COD nor CCDE includes the meanings that one would normally attribute to *apple* in Puzzle 1–2.

Puzzle 1–2

What are the meanings of *apple* in the following examples?

a.   The **apple** cake is much nicer than the banana one.
b.   That **apple** air freshener is a bit overwhelming.
c.   The **apple** in that painting is very realistic.

Using several dictionaries can enable you to expand the amount of information you have about a word, but the spatial limitations and objectives of particular dictionaries constrain the amount of information you find in them. (And never forget: dictionaries can contain errors and go out of date!) Furthermore, dictionaries are **descriptive** works. They can give you information about how a word is or was used in a language, but they do not try to explain why and how the uses of the word are constrained. That is the job of lexical semantics.

1.4.2   Corpus research

Modern dictionaries are typically based on lexical semantic research method number two: corpus research. A **corpus** (plural: **corpora**) is a collection of linguistic material that can be searched, usually using specialized computer software. Corpora vary wildly in their size, breadth and depth of coverage. Some, like the British National Corpus, are aimed at being representative of the language at large, and so they include texts of written works and transcripts of spoken language from a number of different genres; for example, newspapers, novels, speeches, and informal conversations. Others are created with more specific interests in mind. For example, one might use a corpus of Shakespeare's works in order to identify patterns in his writing that could help to identify other potential works by Shakespeare. Or, one could create a corpus of writing by non-native English speakers, in order to determine what types of mistakes are common to these writers so that one can devise better teaching methods. Thanks to rapid progress in computing in recent decades, corpus linguistic research is now very common.

One tool for use in corpus studies is concordance software, which searches a corpus for a particular word or phrase plus some number of words on either side of the search word and organizes them so that the collocates of the search word are clear. For example, (18) shows a partial result for searching for the form *high* (plus four words before and five after) in James Russell Lowell's 1864–65 essay *Abraham Lincoln*, using Essex University's W3 corpus software:

(18)

proverb (if a little	**high,**	he liked them none the
his fitness for the	**high**	place he so worthily occupies
had an air of	**high-**	breeding to join in the shallow
one moment capable of	**higher**	courage, so they are liable
that there was anything	**higher**	to start from than manhood;
memory of a grace	**higher**	than that of outward person, and
of the day to	**higher**	and more permanent concerns.
have elected him. No	**higher**	compliment was ever paid to
intensity from those	**higher**	ideas, those sublime traditions
to circumstances,the	**highest**	reason or the most brutish
much of justice, the	**highest**	attainable at any given moment

Such searches allow us to see the particular contexts in which particular words occur, which can help to determine aspects of their meaning. In the above case, we can see that *high*, at least in Lowell's essay, is much more frequently used in some metaphorical sense than in the literal sense of 'being a fair distance from the ground.' To take another example, corpus research has revealed that the verb *budge* is almost always negated in real language use, as in *it wouldn't budge* (Sinclair 1998). This gives a starting point for exploring the semantic differences between *budge* and expressions with similar meanings, like *move* and *give way*.

What one can discover from using a corpus is limited by several factors. First is how big and representative, or **balanced**, the corpus is. For instance, does it overrepresent certain genres? Does it include spoken language? How well has it been edited to weed out transcription or typographical errors? For less frequent words or meanings, one needs a particularly large corpus in order to ensure that enough data about the word is found. For example, the word *budge* occurs only about three times in every million words (Dahl 1979 – spoken American), so one would need a corpus of about seven million words in order to find 20 examples of it – and that is still a small amount of data to base one's conclusions on.

Second is the matter of what linguistic information has been added to the corpus and what software is available for use with it. Some corpora include extra grammatical information, such as word class, associated with each word in the corpus. In this case, we say that the corpus is **tagged** with grammatical information. Tagged corpora can be used in order to research groups of words from the same word classes or groups of grammatical contexts. For example, if we wanted to determine which English nouns are modified by *high* and which ones by *tall*, we could search for *high*+[noun] and *tall*+[noun] and compare the results. We would find, for example, that chimneys and people are often described as *tall*, while cliffs and collars are *high*. The next step would be to ask ourselves what the meanings of the *high* nouns had in common with each other that made them differ from the *tall* nouns. The corpus cannot tell us that; that's what semanticists are for.

And then we have the problem that not everything about meaning is plainly evident from a corpus. For example, if a word has several meanings (as most do) it can be difficult in many contexts to determine which of those meanings is in use in a particular bit of corpus material. Furthermore, a corpus can tell you part of what is possible in a language, but it cannot tell you what is impossible in the language – it can only tell you what does and what does not occur in a particular corpus.

1.4.3   Semantic intuitions

Corpus methodology thus needs to be supplemented by introspection, that is, **native speaker intuition** – the judgment of a native speaker of a language as to what words mean, what sentences are meaningless or ungrammatical, which words or phrases mean the same thing, which contradict each other, and so forth. Often the native speaker in question is the linguist doing the research, but one can study languages other than one's own by interviewing native speakers and asking for their judgments of the words or phrases (so long as you two have a means of communicating with each other, that is). This is necessary if you are studying the semantics of a language other than your native tongue. Non-native English speakers using this book might find it useful to consult native English speakers who can check your intuitions about word meanings and uses. (Just be sure to check with your instructor before consulting with anyone in reference to work that you will submit for a credit on your course.)

Puzzle 1–3

Try doing a bit of introspective research on adjectives that can be modified by measure phrases, by asking yourself (or another English speaker):

Can one say *six centimeters long*?
What does it mean when someone says *The string is six centimeters long*?
Does it mean that the string is long?
Can one say *six centimeters short*?
If so, does it mean the same thing as *long* in *The string is six centimeters long*?
If not, what is the difference?
Can one say *30 degrees warm*, *Twelve kilos heavy* (and so forth)?
What generalizations can you make about adjectives that can or cannot be modified using measure phrases?

While they have been a mainstay of linguistic research, native speaker judgments have come under serious scrutiny, not least due to the advent of corpus linguistics, which often demonstrates that word combinations or uses that have been judged impossible by native speakers can sometimes be found in the writing or speech of native speakers of the language. Thus, the intuitive method and the corpus method can provide checks and balances on each other.

What neither method does is answer the question *Why?* For example, if we determine that *long*, *short*, and *warm* occur or do not occur with different types of measure phrases, then we have discovered something interesting, but the more interesting thing to do is to determine what patterns can be found in this information and to try to explain these patterns by providing a theory of adjective meaning that accounts for the differences in how these adjectives "behave" in the language.

1.4.4   Experimentation

The last kind of evidence that is used in studying lexical semantics is psycholinguistic experimentation, which more particularly reveals the nature of the mental lexicon and of meanings as stored in the mind. This can involve asking a group of people for their intuitions about word meaning, as was done in a famous experiment by William Labov (1973). Labov showed pictures of vessels of various shapes to a number of English speakers and asked them to say what they would call those objects. Using such an experiment, one can discover where the boundaries of a word's applicability are – or one might find (as Labov did) that no such boundaries are easily discerned (see §3.4). For example, a vessel that is sometimes called *a bowl* might be cup-like enough that it is sometimes called *a cup*.

Other experiments take more indirect routes to finding out about meanings. For example, lexical priming experiments determine the ease with which subjects identify words after they have seen (or heard) words that are more or less semantically related to that word. Such experiments have determined that, for instance, people recognize that *banana* is a word faster if they have recently seen the word *apple*. This leads to the hypothesis that the two words are somehow linked in the mental lexicon such that **activating** one of them enables easier access to the other – by **priming** the mental pathway to it. A wide range of often-ingenious experiments has provided much insight into the mental lexicon.

But, as with any method, caution must be used in planning, executing, and interpreting psycholinguistic experiments. While we have identified an "ideal speaker" as the subject of mentalistic studies of lexical semantics, there is no ideal speaker to experiment upon. We could try to develop models of an individual's mental lexicon by doing a series of experiments on a single subject, but the results are unlikely to give a clear picture of the subject's lexical knowledge, since our view will be hampered by performance factors like the subject's state of alertness or his preoccupations at any particular moment. Instead, experimenters usually test a range of individuals (while controlling for particular variables like age, sex, and educational level), but since no two individuals have the same vocabulary and no two have acquired their vocabularies in the same way, the picture that emerges is of an average speaker more than an ideal one. Interpreting experimental results is laden with uncertainties. For example, does *apple*'s lexical priming of *banana* indicate that the two lexemes are related in the mind, or simply that their meanings (irrespective of their forms) are related in the mind? Does the fact that two subjects draw different boundaries for a word's meaning mean that the two have different understandings of the word, or that the meaning of the word is not fixed in anyone's mind?

Puzzle 1–4

Imagine an experiment in which you asked several people to look at pictures of various pieces of outerwear and assign them one of two names: *coat* or *jacket*. In this experiment, everyone agreed that pictures A, E, and F should be called *coats* and pictures B and D should be called *jackets*, but people gave different answers about C and G, some calling both *jackets*, some calling both *coats*, and some considering C a *coat* and G a *jacket*. What hypotheses about the meanings of these (and similar) words would you propose on the basis of these results? What further experimentation could you do in order to choose among these hypotheses?

1.5   Structure of this book

This book is divided into three parts. In chapters 1 through 4, we look at the question of what meaning is and give the basics of several theories of meaning. This provides a basis for discussing the more contemporary theories' approaches to various lexical semantic issues in later chapters. Part II (chapters 5–6) considers relations among meanings and among words. Part III starts with a discussion of the relation between meaning and word classes (chapter 7), then turns to particular semantic issues for nouns (chapter 8), verbs and other predicates (chapters 9 and 10), and adjectives (chapter 11).

1.6   Further reading

While much vocabulary has been introduced and defined in this chapter, I have taken for granted that the reader knows the meanings of grammatical terms like *noun* and *verb*. Readers who would like some support on these terms should consult a dictionary of linguistic terms such as Trask (2000) or Crystal (2003). Good reference grammars of English are (in ascending order of difficulty) Biber *et al.* (1999), Quirk *et al.* (1985), and Huddleston and Pullum (2002).

Larry Trask's (2004) essay "What is a word?" goes over the various definitions of word (and their pros and cons) in further detail. On the argument that compositional (as well as non-compositional) items must be included in the lex-icon, chapter 6 of Ray Jackendoff's *Foundations of Language* (2002) is good place to start. This position is central to the theory (or set of theories) called Construction Grammar – see, for example, Fillmore, Kay, and O'Connor (1988) and Goldberg (1996). The division of vocabulary into open and closed class has also become controversial. For another perspective, see chapter 1 of Leonard Talmy's *Toward a Cognitive Semantics*, vol. I (2000).

This chapter introduced a fair amount of morphological terminology, which is indispensible in the discussion of lexicology. Some useful introductions to mor-phology are Heidi Harley's *English Words* (2006), Geert Booij's *The Grammar of Words* (2007), and Francis Katamba and John Stonham's *Morphology* (2006).

Howard Jackson's *Words and Meaning* (1988) provides a dictionary-based perspective on lexical semantics, and so is a good source on how dictionaries work. An excellent source on the methods of dictionary making is Sidney Lan-dau's *Dictionaries: The Art and Craft of Lexicography* (2001). For an overview of English dictionaries and lexicographical practice, see Henri Béjoint's *Modern Lexicography* (2000).

A good guide for beginning to use corpora is Michael Stubbs' *Words in Phrases* (2002). Charles Meyer's *English Corpus Linguistics* (2002) gives more detail on how to make a corpus. Reeves *et al.* (1998) summarize various experimental psycholinguistic methods of learning about the mental lexicon and give a few experiments to try out for yourself. John Field's *Psycholinguistics: A Resource Book for Students* (2003) gives some of the basics of psycholinguistic approaches to the lexicon.

1.7   Answers to puzzles

1–1

As one would expect, much is similar about the two dictionary entries. The presentation of the headword (in bold) and the pronunciation are exactly the same, and they both indicate that it is a noun with a spelling change in the plural. But here we see our first little difference: CCDE shows how the last syllable (*ty* → *ties*) changes in the plural, whereas COD shows us just the letters that are different in the plural. The definitions of the general sense of the word (sense 1 in CCDE) are very similar, with both noting the synonym *tip*, but according to COD a gratuity is made of money, whereas CCDE leaves open the possibility that it might take some other form – for example, a bottle of wine or box of chocolates given to one's hairdresser or letter carrier. The most obvious difference is that CCDE records a specific military use of the word as a second sense. Either the writers of COD did not come across this meaning, or (more likely) they considered it to be just a specific type of gratuity that is covered by the definition they have given. Finally, COD gives a detailed etymology of the word, while CCDE gives none, although it does give etymologies for other words.

1–2

(a)   = containing/made with apples;
(b)   = scented like apples;
(c)   = an image of an apple.

1–3

Answering these questions, you should discover that:

(a)   when one says *6 centimeters long*, it means *6 centimeters in length* – the thing that is measured is not necessarily long (it might be short);

(b)   *6 centimeters short* is a bit different. It might sound like a wrong or humorous way of saying *6 centimeters long*. If you can say it with a straight face, then the usual interpretation of *The string is six centimeters short* would be that it is six centimeters *too* short, not that the string measures six centimeters in total. For instance, it needs to be a meter, but it is only 94 centimeters long.

(c)   Some other positive single-dimension and time adjectives can occur with measure phrases, like *6 meters tall, 6 meters wide, 6 hours late, 6 years old*, but not (in English) adjectives from other semantic fields such as temperature (**30 degrees warm*), weight (**30 kilos heavy*), or multi-dimensional size (**30 acres big*) – unless they are interpreted as 30 units *too* warm/heavy/ big.

1–4

These results suggest at least two hypotheses. One is that different people have different understandings of these words – that is, there are different varieties of the language (dialects or idiolects) in which *coat* and *jacket* mean slightly different things. The other hypothesis is that there is no firm division of meanings between *coat* and *jacket* and that people are just picking one or the other for the difficult cases because the experiment requires them to. Perhaps if left to their own devices they would call G both *coat* and *jacket*, or perhaps it is the context (e.g. what kind of weather it is worn in) that determines whether it is called *coat* or *jacket*. The first hypothesis holds that the language differs among people, but the second holds that the language is probably the same, but the meaning of the words is not easily delimited. One way to assess which hypothesis is more likely would be to test the same group of people again and see if their answers are consistent with their previous answers. (It would be good to alter the order of the pictures or to include some pictures other than the ones they had seen before, so that they have to think anew about the problem rather than just remembering what they did before.) If their answers are consistent, then the "different varieties" hypothesis is not ruled out, but if their answers are different each time they take the test, it suggests that the boundaries between the two words' meanings are not absolute and firmly fixed in mind.

(1.8) Exercises

Adopt-a-word

See the Preface for further information about Adopt-a-word and words that you can adopt.

A. Using your adopted word, contrast the everyday notion of WORD to the lexicological notion LEXEME. What is the difference between saying that *X is a word* and *X is a lexeme*? Are both concepts useful? Do they serve different purposes? Another way of framing this essay would be to ask, "What is a word, and why is that question difficult to answer?" Make your adopted word the illustrative focus of your argument.

B. Compare and contrast two dictionaries' entries for your word. You might consider the following issues: How much do they vary in the amount of information provided? Do they give an appropriate amount of information for the type of dictionary? Do they cover the same range of meanings (do they do it in the same or different ways)? Do they accurately describe how the word is used/what it means (in your experience)? Some ideas for planning your essay:
  • The dictionaries should be as similar as possible, differing in just one major way – for example, same publisher but for different audiences (e.g. learner versus native speaker), or two learners' dictionaries by different publishers.
  • Read the dictionaries' front matter (the introductory essays and guides) for information about their range of coverage, research methods, and style.

General exercises

1. For each of the following, demonstrate how to use the orthographical and grammatical criteria for determining how many words there are in each expression. If your answer differs for the two criteria, explain why there are more or fewer words according to the grammatical criterion. If you think that there is more than one possible answer for a particular example, explain why.
   a. homework
   b. Everybody sing!
   c. four-wheel-drive vehicle
   d. couldn't
   e. United Kingdom
   f. give up

2.   Look again at the expressions in exercise 1. Is the number of lexemes in any of these different from the number of grammatical words? Explain why or why not and discuss any problem cases.

3.   Assume, for the sake of this exercise, that lexemes are always non-compositional. In the following sentences, identify the lexical units that occur. Next, determine how many different lexemes there are in each sentence. State how this differs from the number of morphemes in the sentence. If you think there is more than one possible answer for any sentence, explain why. (Remember that lexemes/lexical units may be bigger or smaller than words.)
a. Mobile homes are susceptible to hurricane damage.
b. The new treatment is a shot in the arm for burn victims.
c. I'm looking over a four-leaf clover that I overlooked before.

2   What do we mean by *meaning*?

Key words: PRAGMATICS, INFERENCE, ENTAILMENT, DENOTATION, CONNOTATION, SOCIAL MEANING, AFFECT, SENSE, REFERENCE, REFERENTIAL THEORY, EXTENSION, IMAGE THEORY

2.1   Overview

While the last chapter defined the *lexical* in *lexical meaning*, in this chapter we start to consider the meaning of *meaning*. While the term *meaning* is used in many ways inside and outside the discipline of linguistics, the semantic approach in this book is particularly concerned with denotative meaning. The next section compares denotative meaning to other meaning types and looks at the questions lexical semanticists ask and why they ask them. After that, we look at how to define denotative meaning, focusing on defining the difference between what a word refers to and what a word "means."

Before we go any further, however, it is important to acknowledge that it is rare for a word to have a single meaning. For instance, *shoe* can refer to an object that protects the foot, but it can also be a verb that means 'to put shoes onto,' or a noun that designates a part of a brake mechanism, or part of the idiom *put yourself in someone else's shoes*, in which case some might argue that *shoes* means 'situation.' This is to say that the word *shoe* is **polysemous**, that is, multi-meaninged. Polysemy is a major issue in lexical semantics, but before going into the issue of multiple meanings, we want to look first at the nature of meanings. This means that we will turn a (mostly) blind eye to polysemy until chapter 5 and ignore, for the sake of argument and illustration, meanings of words that are other than the one presently being discussed.

2.2   The boundaries of lexical semantics

As Puzzle 2–1 demonstrates, *mean* is polysemous, and a single thing or word can "be meaningful" in many different ways. This section distinguishes semantic kinds of meaning from pragmatic ones and denotative meaning from connotative and social meaning.

Puzzle 2–1

Show that *means* means something different in each of the following sentences by substituting another word or phrase for each instance of *means*.

(a)   *Happiness* means 'the state of being happy.'
(b)   Happiness means never having to frown.
(c)   *Happiness* means *gladness*.
(d)   *Happiness* means what I'm feeling right now.
(e)   *Glädje* means *happiness* in Swedish.
(f)   *Happiness* means something more ordinary than *ecstasy*.

2.2.1   Semantics vs. pragmatics

Lexical semantics involves the study of lexical words (and other lexemes) and how they lexicalize particular meanings. The first thing we need to do before going any further is to delimit the realm of lexical meaning – that is, what aspects of meaning count as "lexical semantics," and what aspects do not. As an exercise, think about what *shoe* describes in example (1) before reading any further.

(1)   Cinderella was going to be late for the ball because she couldn't find her other shoe.

After reading this sentence, you can imagine the scenario and say a lot about the missing shoe. It seems to be one half of a pair of shoes. It belongs to Cinderella, so it is probably of a style that is appropriate to a woman. Since not being able to find it is causing her to be late for a ball, it might be a shoe that she intends to wear to the ball, and since balls are dressy occasions, it is probably a dressy shoe. If you know the story of Cinderella, you might expect that this shoe is a glass slipper.

You do not know any of these things from the word *shoe*, however. This is information that the **context** provides. We assume quite a bit about the shoe in question based on what the sentence tells us and on what we know in general about shoes (that people wear them, that they come in pairs, that women and men wear different styles), about balls (that they are dressy occasions), and about Cinderella (that she is female and that a glass shoe was pivotal to her fate), among other things. This information about the shoe in the sentence is not part of what *shoe* itself brings semantically to the sentence, but a series of **inferences** we have made based on the information available to us in the context. Such inferences are part of the realm of **pragmatics**, the study of context-bound meaning. While some theories make less of a distinction between context-bound and context-independent meaning than others, all the information that arises from these inferences is **defeasible**; that is, able to be cancelled out by further information, as it is in (2).

(2)   The mare was almost ready to pull the carriage, but Cinderella was going to be late for the ball because she couldn't find her other shoe. She had three of them piled on the table in the blacksmith's shop, but where was that fourth one?

In this case, the mention of a mare (a female horse) changes our expectations about interpreting *shoe* at the end of the sentence. In this case, the *her* in *her shoe* is not necessarily Cinderella – it could be the horse. And once we know from the next sentence that there are three other shoes and that the action is taking place in a blacksmith's shop, we're ready to dismiss the possibility that the shoe is one that Cinderella would wear and thus we do not make any of the inferences about the shoe being dressy or made of glass.

In both (1) and (2), then, we make pragmatic inferences about the shoe based on our knowledge of the context. Contextual information can include the **co-text**, the rest of the linguistic material surrounding the word, plus **background knowledge** (sometimes called **encyclopedic** or **world knowledge**) about shoes and balls, and knowledge about the discourse situation at hand – for instance, whether we are hearing about the shoe in the context of a news report or a fairy tale, in which case we would more readily believe that it might have magical properties. Where we are provided with less contextual information, as in (1), we rely on inference in order to fill in the gaps in our mental picture of the situation. In cases in which we have been given more information, we use inferences to make the connections between the bits of information we have (e.g. if a mare, a shoe, and a blacksmith's shop have been mentioned, then the shoe is probably a horseshoe). In studying lexical semantics, we are interested in the question of what the word *shoe* brings to this and other sentences, rather than in how much we can figure out about the actual shoe that is relevant to this particular context.

In other words, semanticists are usually less interested in the pragmatic inferences that we can glean from bits of language and more interested in semantic **entailments** – that is, what conclusions necessarily follow from that particular use of the word. For example, that we call something a *shoe* entails that it is footwear. At this point, I am oversimplifying matters – pragmatic inferences like *It must be a pretty shoe if Cinderella would wear it* and semantic entailments like *If it is a shoe, then it is footwear* are the extremes of a range of different kinds of inferences. In between are inferences like *if it's a shoe, it's (probably) not made of liver*, and one of the questions we need to ask is whether the information that's necessary for that kind of inference is part of the meaning of the word *shoe* or not. (These issues are discussed in chapter 3.)

For the meantime, let's look a bit more carefully at the nature of the logical relation of entailment. Entailment is a relation between **propositions**, that is to say, statements that can be true or false. The entailment relation can be phrased as an *if A then B* statement joining two such propositions. If *A* is true, then *B is* *necessarily true* as well. Starting from the assumption that we can single out a 'footwear' meaning of the noun *shoe* (and ignore verb or adjective meanings of *shoe* and those to do with car brakes, etc.), we can ask: "Which of the following statements expresses an entailment?" In other words, is any of these sentences necessarily and always true?

(3)   If it is a shoe, then it is made to be worn on a foot.

(4)   If it is a shoe, then it is made for humans to wear.

(5)   If it is a shoe, then it is made of leather.

(6)   If it is a shoe, then it is size 10.

For a statement like these to be an entailment, the *then* statement must always be true when the *if* statement (*it is a shoe*) is true. So, in order to judge whether these sentences are entailments, we have to ask: "Can it ever be the case that something that is a shoe is *not* made to be worn on a foot/made for humans to wear/etc.?" You have probably already determined that (3) is the only entailment here, since there exist shoes that are not for humans (e.g. horseshoes), not leather (e.g. canvas shoes), and not size 10 (e.g. size 9 shoes). So, if something is a shoe, it is *necessarily* footwear, but it may also have other properties that are incidental, rather than necessary (entailed) properties of *shoe*-ness.

Puzzle 2–2

Which of the following (unfortunately morbid) statements express entailment relations? Treat X and Y as placeholders for any noun phrase – that is, consider whether these statements are true, no matter which noun phrases X or Y might be replaced with.

(a)   If X kills Y, then Y dies.
(b)   If X assassinates Y, then Y dies.
(c)   If X shoots Y, then Y dies.
(d)   If X shoots Y, then Y is hit by a bullet.
(e)   If X drowns, then X dies.
(f)   If X drowns, then X is submerged in water.

2.2.2   Dimensions of meaning

In addition to pragmatic meaning, which is context-dependent, words come with lexical types of meaning – that is, meaning that is specific to the word and must be recorded as part of its lexical entry. The most important of these is denotative meaning, and so our task here is to differentiate that from other types.

Denotative (sometimes also called **conceptual** or **cognitive**) **meaning** involves the relation between a word and the things (or properties or actions or concepts) that it refers to. A word's denotative meaning is its "literal" meaning, the kind of meaning that is most directly represented in dictionary definitions of a word. In knowing the denotative meaning of a word, you know what the word can and cannot refer to, and you know what other words it is semantically related to or not, and hence what entailments it forces in particular contexts. For instance, because I know the meaning of the word *pet* I know that odors cannot be called *pets* but certain animals can, and I know that *pet* and *dog* can in certain circumstances be the same thing. That is to say that *pet* and *dog* have different denotative meanings which happen to overlap to some degree, so that they sometimes, but not always, can be used to refer to (or **denote**) the same thing.

Besides denotative meaning, words can also have **connotative meaning**, or **connotation**. Use this term with caution, as it has a technical meaning in semantics that only partly coincides with its use in everyday speech. Connotations are semantic associations that a word has, which are not strictly part of the denotative meaning of the word. For instance, *feline* and *cat* and *kitty* can all denote the same things, yet they are quite different in their connotations, as can be seen in (7):

(7) a. A feline jumped out of the tree.
   b. A cat jumped out of the tree.
   c. A kitty jumped out of the tree.

Feline sounds more scientific and less domestic, so you might assume that the feline in (7a) is some kind of wildcat that might be found in a zoo. On the other hand, you might picture the kitty in (7c) as something small and cute. But, denotatively speaking, the sentences in (7) could all be true if any cat jumped out of the tree, no matter its size, appearance, or disposition. The assumptions one makes based on the choice of one of those words or the other are just assumptions, just connotations. Connotations are often included in dictionary definitions, but we need to be careful here not to confuse connotations, which are loose associations, with denotative meaning, which indicates what the word can and cannot refer to. If someone tells you about a feline they saw, they are not lying if the animal they're talking about is a common housecat, even if their choice of the word *feline* led you to believe that it was not.

The last dimension of meaning we'll consider is **social meaning**, which is what an expression can tell you about the person who is saying it and the social situation they are in. If someone says *howdy* to you rather than *hello*, you might figure out a number of things about that person: perhaps they are American, perhaps they are from a rural area, perhaps they feel friendly toward you and feel that the situation is informal. Again, these are just assumptions that you are making – if an English person calls a lift *an elevator*, you can hardly accuse him of lying about his nationality just because he used the American word. A particular subtype of social meaning is **affect**, which indicates the speaker's feelings or attitude toward the thing that they are talking about. Compare the cases in (8):

(8) a. That artist was a drunk.
   b. That artist was an alcoholic.

If someone said (8a) you would get the feeling that they do not approve of the artist's drinking habits, and perhaps do not approve of the artist at all, but (8b) sounds more sympathetic to the artist's condition. Of course, it gets tricky at times to separate some of the non-denotative aspects of meaning. In the case of (8) we could also say that *drunk* and *alcoholic* have different connotations – we might associate loud, anti-social behavior more with *drunk* than with *alcoholic*, for example. The issues of connotation and affect are often intertwined, since if you want to express disapproval, you'll probably use words that have unfavorable connotations. In general, we can contrast both connotation and social meaning with denotative meaning, since neither connotation nor social meaning affect the logical (entailment-related) relations that a word enters into. From now on, when we talk about *meaning*, we'll be focusing on denotative meaning.

2.2.3   Questions lexical semanticists ask

In the Cinderella story above, we understood the denotative meaning of *shoe* to be something like 'a covering for the foot that is hard enough at the bottom to prevent injury to the foot.' We would have to look more deeply at sentences that include *shoe* and more broadly at a number of other contexts in order to figure out if this definition of *shoe* truly represents what *shoe* means. We would need to ask:

*   What kinds of things can we refer to with the word *shoe*?
*   How should we express the particular qualities that a shoe has?
*   What is entailed by the sentence *That is a shoe*?

Asking and attempting answers for those questions gets us as far as lexicographers (dictionary makers) go in searching for the meanings of words. In writing a dictionary definition, they try to isolate what the word can signify and then to paraphrase the criteria for using that word to refer.

But writing dictionary definitions is ultimately a circular exercise because one uses words to express the meanings of other words. As semanticists, we want to go deeper into word meaning than this and determine what meanings are made of, how they are related to one another, what are possible and impossible meanings, and how meanings might be stored in the mind. These issues are discussed in later chapters. Nevertheless, it is still useful to be able to paraphrase meanings using words. Such paraphrases, also called **glosses**, are indicated in single quotation marks. One must keep in mind, however, that these glosses are not themselves the meanings of the words (as they are represented in our minds) – they are descriptions of the meanings of the words.

2.3   The nature of denotative meaning

So, we're studying denotative meaning. This of course raises the question of what denotative meanings are made of. We'll go about answering this question by starting with some problematic views of what meaning is, and seeing what we can learn from their mistakes. Part of the reason to go through these past approaches is because they coincide with many folk theories of what meaning is and what words are for, and so it's good to dispel a few misconceptions before getting too far into semantics.

2.3.1   Referential Theory: its problems and lessons

The first approach to set aside is **Referential Theory**, but in doing so we'll introduce some valuable concepts that show what a good theory of meaning needs to be about. Discussions of Referential Theory come from the tradition of philosophy of language. In this theory, the meaning of a word is the set of things that it can refer to (or "point out") in the world, that is, the set of its **referents**, or **denotata**. Such a set is called a word's **extension**. For instance, the extension of *Paris, France* includes exactly one city {PARIS}, while the extension of *semanticist* contains all the semanticists that exist: {B. ABBOTT, K. ALLAN, E. BACH, J. BARWISE, P. BENNETT, M. BIERWISCH, ...}. Thus, *cucumber* "means" the set of cucumbers in the world, and *jump* "means" the instances of jumping in the world, and *happy* "means" the set of things in the world that are happy. Certainly, sometimes we use the word *mean* in a referential way. For example, if someone asks you what *philtrum* means, you can point to the groove between your upper lip and your nose and say, "It means this thing." But that doesn't work for every kind of expression. Before reading any further, make a list of words that you think would be problematic for a theory that equates meaning with reference.

Your list might include words like *of* and *the*, which would be meaningless in Referential Theory since they identify nothing in the world. However, such words are not really a fair test of a lexical semantic theory, since they can be said to have grammatical functions rather than meanings (see §1.3.2). Most lexical semantic theories that we'll consider don't account for the semantics of function words in the same way as they account for content words. You may also have listed words for abstract things, like *love* or *democracy*. But if *love* and *democracy* actually exist (and I'm pretty sure that at least one of them does), then Referential Theory accounts for them. So, the word *love* "points to" whatever love there is in the world, regardless of the fact that it may be hard to see or touch. The real problem for Referential Theory is the existence of expressions that don't point to anything real. Take, for example, the expressions *Tooth Fairy*, *goblin*, and *happy cucumber* (i.e. a cucumber that is happy), and let's assume (if you don't already believe so) that none of these things actually exists. If none of them exists, then each of them has the null set for an extension:

Tooth Fairy	REFERS TO	{}
goblin	REFERS TO	{}
happy cucumber	REFERS TO	{}

Thus, according to Referential Theory, *Tooth Fairy*, *goblin*, and *happy cucumber* all mean the same thing, since they have the same extensions. But we know that when English users say *Tooth Fairy*, they use that phrase instead of *happy cucumber* precisely because those two expressions *do* mean different things. So, the first blow to Referential Theory is its wholly unsatisfactory treatment of expressions for non-existent entities.

The other major problem that Referential Theory faces is the fact that language users do not always intend that expressions with the same extension should be understood to be synonyms. A classical example is *Phosphorus* and *Hesperus*, the Latin names for the Morning Star and the Evening Star. Since these two words both refer to the planet Venus, Referential Theory holds that the two words mean the same thing. But the Romans who used these words believed that Hesperus and Phosphorus were two different stars, so from their point of view, they did not mean the same thing. Because Referential Theory is just about the relationship between language and the world, there is no room in it for points of view, and it can only say that *Hesperus* and *Phosphorus* are synonyms.

2.3.2   Sense vs. reference

The lesson we learn from Referential Theory is that, as the philosopher Gottlob Frege pointed out, meaning is not equivalent to referents or extensions. Instead, there must be a more abstract notion of meaning, called *sense* (a translation of the German *Sinn*). A **sense** (also called **intension** – note that this is different from *intention*) is some abstract representation of what the referents of a word have in common, in other words the qualities that something needs to have in order for us to apply a certain label to it. So, the sense of *dog* tells us how to tell which things to call *dog* (i.e. four-legged mammals that bark) and which things we should not call *dog* (everything else). The **Law of Denotation** states that the "bigger" a word's sense (i.e. the more conditions that it places on what counts as a referent for that word), the smaller its extension will be. Compare *dog* and *poodle*, for instance. There is a certain set of qualities that a thing must have in order for it to count as a *dog*. In order to count as a poodle, a thing has to have all the dog qualities, plus some more qualities (curly hair, for instance). So, since the sense of *poodle* has more restrictions on what it can denote than *dog*'s sense has, there are bound to be fewer things called *poodle* in the world than things called *dog*.

Separating sense from reference allows us to account for the fact that *goblin* and *happy cucumber* mean different things. Although neither refers to anything, we know that their senses would point out different things in the world if they did exist. Senses also allow us to identify different meanings of expressions that just happen to refer to the same thing, like *Hesperus* and *Phosphorus*. Even though both words end up referring to the same thing, they come to that reference in different ways – one by pointing out a star that shines in the morning, and the other by pointing out one that shines in the evening.

Puzzle 2–3

If sense and reference are different sorts of things, then it is possible that there are linguistic expressions that have senses but no referents or referents but no senses. See if you can complete the table below by thinking of examples that fulfill the criteria stated for each row and column. So, for example, in the bottom right-hand corner, you need to fill in an expression that has neither a sense nor any referents (i.e. an empty extension). You can find examples for boxes 1 and 3 in this section. The other two are quite tricky, since they concern expressions that have no senses. Give it a try and check the answers if you get stuck.

	has a sense	has no sense
has at least one referent	1.	2.
has no referent	3.	4.

Usually when people talk about *meaning* (as in *The meaning of that word can be found in the dictionary*), they refer to the word's sense rather than its extension, and from now on we can take the phrase *lexical meaning* to refer to the senses of lexemes. But this raises the question of how a sense would be represented in a mental lexicon. The next two chapters examine theories of meaning that constitute serious attempts to answer that question. But first let's look at a common folk theory of how senses are represented in the mind in order to demonstrate why a more sophisticated approach is needed.

2.4   Are senses "images in the mind"?

While *goblin* and *unicorn* may be identical in terms of their empty extensions, you have no trouble knowing that the two name entirely different things. If you ever met a unicorn, you would know very well that *goblin* or *Tooth Fairy* or *happy cucumber* would not be accurate descriptions of it. Part of the way that you would recognize a unicorn if you met one is that you probably have a picture in your mind of what a unicorn looks like. Thus it is tempting to think of word senses as pictures in the mind. This approach is called the **Image Theory** of meaning. However, there are many reasons that this theory cannot be right. Pause a moment to think of some before reading on.

One of the reasons that senses cannot be "pictures in the mind" is that pictures are necessarily more specific than meanings should be. If I imagine a unicorn, it's a white one, its horn is long and straight and it's the size of a pony. Now, if I saw a purple animal that looked like a stallion with a swirly horn growing out of the center of its forehead, I would say *Look! It's a unicorn! They're real!* In that case, the thing that I am calling a unicorn does not actually look much like the picture in my head. If the picture in my head can differ from the thing that the word refers to, then why wouldn't an albino rhinoceros count as a unicorn in my mind? After all, an albino rhino is similar to the unicorn picture in my head – it is a white animal with a horn on its head. The problem is that there's nothing in the picture that tells me which are the "important" parts of a unicorn – that having a horn and being horse-like are necessary but that being white is less so. The sense of a word must indicate the **essence** of what it is to count as a unicorn or a rhinoceros, and a picture captures much more than that essence without sorting out what is essential and what is not.

Another reason that senses cannot be pictures is that there are plenty of words for unpicturable things, which are nevertheless meaningful words that can mean different things. If meanings consist of pictures, then what would be the meaning of *air* or *time* or *semantics*? You might envision *time* as a clock, but in that case how would you know the difference between the meaning of *time* and the meaning of *clock*?

In the end, Image Theory does little to further our understanding of how we go about the business of meaning when we use words, but examining this theory has pointed out that theories of word meaning need instead to focus on the essential properties that allow the word to refer to particular things and not others.

2.5   Meaning and concepts

A mental lexicon, as discussed in chapter 1, is an individual's collection of knowledge concerning words, while, as we saw earlier in this chapter, our minds also store large collections of world knowledge. Lexical semantics can be seen as spanning these two realms. For example, when you read the word *beanbag*, you subconsciously search your lexicon for a word that's spelled that way, then link that form to the conventional meaning of *beanbag* (as you understand it), and to your **concept** of a beanbag – that is, your understanding of what a beanbag is and the knowledge you have about beanbags. **Concepts** are part of our world knowledge, and we use words to communicate about those concepts. My concept of *beanbag* includes information about what beanbags are made of, what they are used for, what sizes they typically come in and so forth.

Not all concepts are lexicalized – that is, not all concepts have a name. For example, I have a concept of the dip in a saucer in which a teacup can fit, but I don't know a name for it. Concepts can also be invented ad hoc, that is, we assemble new concepts depending on our needs – for instance, you may at some point in your life need a concept to represent the category of THINGS TO PACK FOR A TRAIN JOURNEY TO SIBERIA – and in that case, you will form that concept – but you are unlikely to lexicalize such a temporarily relevant concept (see Barsalou 2009). These points show that there is a mismatch between words and concepts – some concepts are associated with particular words, and others are not.

So, we have an inventory of words (the lexicon) that represent concepts that we have in our world knowledge. A basic question for semanticists is: what is the nature of the relationship between words and concepts?

A **lexical meaning**, or **sense**, can be thought of as whatever it is that connects the word form to the appropriate concept. There are a few ways of envisioning this relation. Some approaches, like the main one we'll consider in the next chapter, hold that the meaning of a word is represented in its lexical entry. In this case, the lexical entry for *beanbag* would include some sort of definition of *beanbag*, which is consistent with but separate from one's BEANBAG concept. In order to support such a theory, one must show that the definitional information about what *beanbag* can denote is separable from the broader knowledge in the BEANBAG concept, including the knowledge of what you might do with a beanbag. The other extreme is to see meanings and concepts as being the same things. In this case, one holds that the word *beanbag* connects to everything one knows about beanbags, and doing lexical semantics involves making models of how concepts are structured. In between these extremes is the idea that some semantic information is represented in the lexicon – for example, any information that contributes to the grammaticality of sentences – but other conceptual knowledge contributes to our understanding of what the word can denote. We'll look at these issues as we review more theories of meaning in the next two chapters.

2.6   Summary and conclusions

In this chapter we have seen first that there are many aspects to meaning, but that the exploration of denotative meaning is the heart of lexical semantics.

We also looked at two theories of what meaning is and saw that while these theories might initially seem appealing, they present serious problems in accounting for the full range of lexical word meanings. The important thing we learned from them, however, is that we need a good theory of intensional meaning, or sense, and of how senses are represented in the mind. One of the questions raised for semanticists is where meaning is situated – in the lexicon, as part of conceptual knowledge, or some combination of the two. In the next two chapters, we explore the idea that word meanings are built from smaller meaning components, starting first with the idea that meaning can be precisely determined by such components.

2.7   Further reading

While I've described three dimensions of meaning (denotative, connotative, and social), other authors have noted more dimensions, some of which are more relevant to sentential than to lexical meaning. Geoffrey Leech (1981, chapter 2) discusses seven such dimensions. For more on non-denotative meaning, see Keith Allan's (2007) pragmatic account.

Referential theory is discussed most in the philosophical literature. Frege's "Über Sinn und Bedeutung" (usually translated as "On sense and reference" or "On sense and nominatum") can be found in many collections, including A. P. Martinich (ed.), *The Philosophy of Language* (2005). Overviews of philosophy of language, including discussion of Referential Theory, can be found in the *Internet Encyclopedia of Philosophy* (see Wolf 2006), Lycan (1999) and Morris (2007). Image Theory is less discussed in the literature, but Jean Aitchison (2003) discusses it briefly (calling it "Snapshot theory").

2.8   Answers to puzzles

2–1

(a)   can be defined as
(b)   results in
(c)   is a synonym of
(d)   refers to
(e)   can be translated as
(f)   connotes [or, is associated with]

2–2

(a), (b), and (e) are entailments. We can use this fact to determine that the notion of 'dying' must be part of the meanings of the words *kill*, *assassinate*, and *drown*.

(c) is not an entailment – while Y might die if X shoots Y, Y might also survive. We can conclude from this that *shoot* just refers to the act of shooting at something else and hitting it, not that that shooting necessarily causes death.

(d) also seems not to be an entailment, since not all acts of shooting involve bullets. Instead, X might shoot Y with a laser or an arrow, for example. Note, however, that we often understand 'bullets' when we hear *shoot*. For instance, on a news report, we might hear 'A soldier has been shot.' In this case, we expect that a bullet is involved because that's the most usual type of shooting in this day and age, and if something more atypical happened, like laser shooting, we assume that the newscaster would have mentioned it. One might argue in this case that *shoot* has more than one meaning – that it has a 'fire at and hit with a missile' meaning and a 'fire at and hit with a bullet' meaning. (You may find that your dictionary records these as two separate meanings.)

(f) is not an entailment, as to drown is to die by inhaling water, and this doesn't have to involve being submerged in it. We might assume when we hear about a drowning that submersion happened, and therefore we might be surprised if a recently drowned corpse appears to be dry, but this is just a pragmatic inference, not an entailment.

2–3

1.	Any common noun, verb, or adjective that refers to something in the real world has a sense and a referent: e.g. *dog, bark, cucumber, intellectual* . . .
2.	Many philosophers/semanticists (e.g. Mill 1867, Kripke 1972) argue that proper names, such as *Phillip, Paris*, and *Big Ben*, have referents but not senses. This is because proper names act simply as "pointers" to the things that they name, the names themselves are not meaningful. You might object that *Phillip* means 'lover of horses' – after all, it says so in baby name books. But that's not really the meaning of the name – it's just part of its history. When Phillip's mother named him *Phillip*, she didn't first have to ascertain that he indeed loved horses. Similarly, even though we know that Phillip is a boy's name, 'boyness' isn't part of its meaning either, since I could name my daughter or my bicycle *Phillip*. Not every one agrees that proper names have no senses. Another popular view (e.g. Kneale 1962, Geurts 1997) holds that proper names have senses that represent the meaning of *Phillip* as 'the individual that we call *Phillip*.'
3.	Items like *goblin, unicorn*, and *happy cucumber* have a sense but no extension.
4.	It is difficult to find expressions with neither sense nor extension because languages don't usually bother to have words that are completely meaningless – what would be the communicative point? True nonsense goes in this category, such as *falalalala*, which is the refrain of a Christmas song, but means nothing at all. You might also put function words like *of* in this box, because it could be said that they don't so much have senses as functions (see §1.3.2), although some linguists would disagree with you.

2.9   Exercises

Adopt-a-word

A.   Use a thesaurus to find synonyms for your word, and use these to illustrate the notions of denotation, connotation, and social meaning by determining whether the synonyms differ from your word on one or more of these aspects of meaning.

B.   Discuss what your word "means" according to Referential and Image Theories, and use this evidence in order to critique these theories.

General

1.   Horn (2001) discusses **metalinguistic negation**, in which an utterance is negated not to deny the denotative meaning expressed, but to object to the

way in which it is phrased. For example, someone might say *I'm not a drunk – I'm an alcoholic!* in order to protest being described as *drunk* because of the connotations associated with the word *drunk*. In other words, they are denying the connotations or affect of the term, not its denotative meaning. Find and describe two more examples of metalinguistic negation involving denial of the connotations or affect of a term, rather than its denotation.

2.   Determine whether the following statements express entailments. If so, discuss what the entailment tells us about the denotative meaning of *teacher*. If not, discuss whether it expresses a typical pragmatic inference that may arise when using the word *teacher* and whether this reflects any connotation or social meaning for *teacher*. (Use (f) to compare *teacher* with another verb+*er* noun. Is the verb+*er* combination **compositional** in the sense described in chapter 1?)
a. If X is a teacher, then X is paid to teach.
b. If X is a teacher, then X is female.
c. If X is a teacher, then people learn from X.
d. If X is a teacher, then X has taught.
e. If X is a teacher, then X teaches.
f. If X is a thinker, then X thinks.

3.   For each of the following, explain why it is necessary to distinguish the sense and referent(s) of the expressions.
a. the chair I'm sitting on
b. people who have been to Mars
c. William Shakespeare
d. the most famous English playwright
e. the author of *Romeo and Juliet*

3 Components and prototypes

Key words: COMPONENT, CLASSICAL THEORY, DEFINITION, ENCYCLOPEDIC INFORMATION, DECOMPOSITION, NECESSARY AND SUFFICIENT CONDITIONS, SEMANTIC FEATURE, SEMANTIC PRIMITIVE, REDUNDANCY RULES, PROTOTYPE

3.1   Overview

This chapter introduces componential approaches to meaning and some of the more serious challenges to such approaches. In componential approaches, word senses are built out of constituent parts – that is, word senses are complexes of simpler meaning components. One type of componential approach is the Classical Theory of meaning, which defines words on the basis of necessary and sufficient conditions. After looking at general properties of classical componential approaches, we turn to Katz's groundbreaking work in the classical style from the 1960s and 1970s. Then we examine some psychological evidence about the nature of meanings – that senses have "fuzzy boundaries" and display "prototype effects." This kind of evidence invalidates the classical notion that all senses are based strictly on necessary and sufficient conditions. Yet as we see in chapter 4, other componential approaches have risen to these challenges. This chapter provides some of the vocabulary that we need for discussing the more contemporary theories.

3.2   Senses as definitions: Classical Theory

The last chapter concluded that meanings of words must represent the "essence" of what it is that unites the things (or events or properties, etc.) that the word denotes. Since classical times, it has been common to try to express these essences as collections of semantic properties. In other words, meanings of words are considered to consist of elements of meaning that are "smaller" and less complex than the meaning of the word. So, for example, we might consider that the noun *girl* is composed of the elements FEMALE, HUMAN, and CHILD or that the verb *to drop* involves submeanings CAUSE, GO, and DOWN. In general, such sublexical elements of meaning are called **semantic components**, although in particular theoretical approaches they might be called by different terms, like **semantic features** or (with a more specific meaning, which we'll see below) **semantic primes** or **primitives**. Analyzing meanings in terms of such components is thus called **componential analysis**, and the theories that represent meaning using these semantic "building blocks" are gathered under the general term **componential approaches**.

Building meanings out of smaller parts is a familiar concept from the discussion of **compositional** meaning in chapter 1. Recall that we said that an expression's meaning is compositional if the meaning of the whole expression can be determined from the meaning of its parts and the language's rules for arranging the parts into the whole. So, the meaning of *the big book that Andrew read* is composed of the meanings of the six lexical units in that phrase and the grammatical relations among them (so, we know, for example, that *big* modifies *book* and not *Andrew* in this case). Componential views of lexical meaning can be said to be **decompositional** in that they go beyond the visible parts of a word (its morphemes) and decompose the meaning into smaller semantic components.

Individual componential theories often differ in the collections of components that they employ and may have different kinds of rules for combining them. This chapter takes a somewhat historical view of componential approaches in order to introduce some of the basic concepts underlying them and in order to show general strengths and weaknesses of such approaches. In the next chapter, and the rest of the book, we explore some contemporary componential approaches and compare their perspectives on a number of semantic phenomena.

The notion that word senses are built from simpler semantic constituents goes back at least as far as Aristotle, and thus its most restrictive form is often referred to as the **Classical Theory** of meaning. We can think of the Classical Theory as employing a "dictionary metaphor" with regard to how senses are represented in the lexicon. A basic assumption underlying this metaphor is that lexemes can be **defined**, that is, that a lexeme's sense can be restated in some way that provides a reasonably clear distinction between what a word denotes and what it does not denote. Take, for example, the first sense definition for *actress* in the *Encarta World English Dictionary* (1999):

(1)   **actress** *n*. **1**. a woman or girl who acts in plays, movies, or television.

This definition gives us a clear means to determine whether or not someone is an actress. That is, in order to be truthfully called an *actress*, a thing must meet the following conditions:

(a)   an actress is a woman or girl, and
(b)   an actress acts in plays, movies, or television.

The definition lists the **necessary and sufficient conditions** for the denotation of *actress*. The conditions in the definition are **necessary** in that neither can be left out; in order to be an actress one must be a human female *and* one must act.

They are **sufficient** in that together those two conditions on reference are all that are needed to distinguish actresses from non-actresses. Either condition alone would be insufficient, however, since condition (a) denotes female non-actresses like the Queen of England and myself and (b) denotes acting non-actresses like Johnny Depp and Michael Caine.

As well as providing necessary and sufficient properties of actresses, the definition in (1) avoids possible properties of actresses that are not necessary – that is, which do not determine whether someone is an actress or not. For example, while some actresses are famous, not all are; therefore, fame is not a necessary property of being an actress. Even a property that *is* true of all actresses may not be a necessary property. For example, imagine that all actresses in the world happen to have a sixth toe on their left foot – that still does not mean that having an extra toe is a necessary part of being an actress. You do not need to have seen Julia Roberts' feet before deciding whether she's an actress.

These other possible properties of actresses, like being famous or having atypical feet, have no role to play in the Classical Theory, which makes a distinction between **definitional** properties, which contribute to a word's sense, and **encyclopedic** knowledge about the word and its **denotata** (referents). The fact that acting can be a pathway to fame is encyclopedic knowledge that allows us to deduce that actresses may be famous. We may also have stereotypes of actresses as being thin, rich, beautiful, or abnormally toed, but these again are considered irrelevant to the business of meaning in the Classical Theory. In other words, the Classical Theory takes the position that only the necessary conditions are included in the sense of a lexeme. As applied to linguistic theories, like the one in the next section, this assumption is often used to differentiate linguistic knowledge (definitions) from general world knowledge (encyclopedia). On this view, the mental lexicon contains definitions that allow words to then be mapped onto the concepts that they represent. The concepts, in turn, represent much richer, encyclopedic information about the words' referents. As we shall see, it can be very difficult to determine where the boundary between the definitional and the encyclopedic lies, and thus the more modern approaches in the next chapter take different positions on the location of that boundary and whether the boundary really exists.

3.2.1   A componential metalanguage

One of the strengths of a componential approach is its specification of a precise **metalanguage** used for describing senses. A metalanguage is a system for describing a language that does not rely on the language itself. There are two reasons for not wanting to rely on English, for example, in describing the semantics of English. First, using the whole of the English language to define the whole of the English language just gets you going around in circles. Second, we are aiming for a semantic methodology that can account for any language, so we do not want to use English to describe English and Maori to describe Maori.

Using English to describe Maori, or vice versa, could also be misleading, as there may be meanings in one that do not translate well into the other.

Thus, in doing semantic analysis we use a metalanguage, a code for representing the meanings that a language represents. Different semantic theories employ their own particular metalanguages. Like a natural language, a metalanguage needs a vocabulary and a grammar. The vocabulary of a componential semantic metalanguage is the inventory of semantic elements, or **components**, that can be combined and recombined to constitute new senses. Those components that cannot be further defined through the metalanguage are deemed to be semantic **primitives**, the most basic building blocks of meaning.

In general, componential approaches work toward having an inventory of primitives that is both:

- **restrictive**: there are as few primitives as possible,

and

- **versatile**: any particular primitive contributes to a range of different lexical meanings.

The grammar of the metalanguage restricts the ways in which semantic components can be combined and determines the relations between components within a meaning. The simplest grammar for a componential metalanguage would be an unordered list of simple properties, as in (2):

(2)   *woman*   [FEMALE, HUMAN, ADULT]
        girl   [FEMALE, HUMAN, CHILD]

To reduce the number of components needed and to make them more versatile, though, we could replace features like ADULT and CHILD with **binary features**, as shown in (3). These features are "binary" in that they have two possible values, + or −, and the feature is not complete unless it has one of those values.

(3)   *woman*   [+FEMALE, +HUMAN, +ADULT]
        girl   [+FEMALE, +HUMAN, −ADULT]
        child   [+HUMAN, −ADULT]
        puppy   [+CANINE, −ADULT]

It is important to note that although the features here are represented as English words (in small capitals), they are not particularly English features. It would be as accurate to call them Δ, □, and Ø, or Spanish HEMBRA, HUMANO, and ADULTO, as to call them FEMALE, HUMAN, and ADULT. Our aim is to come up with a semantic metalanguage that is **universal** – that is, it can be applied to any language. We use English words just because that makes it easier for us to remember which meaning components they stand for. Thus, the description of *woman* in (3) could also be said to be a semantic analysis of Spanish *mujer* or Swedish *kvinna*, since they do not differ much, semantically speaking, from English *woman*.

We can see in examples (2) and (3) that one advantage of a componential theory is that it shows how senses are related to one another. For example, we can see in (3) that *girl* is a kind of *child* and that *puppy* and *child* have [−ADULT] status in common, but that they do not denote the same things. We see more about these relations in chapter 6.

Puzzle 3–1

Are the features HUMAN and CANINE, as used in example (3), primitive features? Are there smaller components that they might be broken down into?

Binary features like those in (3) are sometimes used because of the analogy with the binary features used in phonetics, such as [+VOICED] and [−VOICED] to distinguish /b/ and /p/, respectively. However, they are a bit simplistic. After all, a feature specification like [+CANINE] is a bit odd, as there are no particular lexemes that require the feature [−CANINE]. A slightly more sophisticated system would involve features that could be specified by a range of values, with different sorts of values for different sorts of features. So, for example, there could be a feature SPECIES that would be specified with values such as CANINE, HUMAN, FELINE, and so forth. Thus the metalanguage of such a system involves a list of features (or **attributes**) with a list of values that each feature can take, as in Table 3.1. In (4), some of the examples from (3) are rewritten in this system, in a structure called an **attribute-value matrix** (AVM).

Table 3.1 *Some attributes and their values*

Attribute	Values
SPECIES	{HUMAN, CANINE, FELINE, BOVINE ... }
SEX	{MALE, FEMALE}
ADULT	{YES, NO}

(4)   *woman*

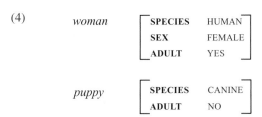

puppy

The use of AVMs is common in a range of lexical semantic theories, especially those that have been designed to interact with particular generative syntactic approaches (see chapter 4).

Puzzle 3-2

ADULT works as a binary (+/− or 'yes/no') feature for the examples we have seen so far, in that a child is a non-adult, a woman is an adult, and a puppy is a non-adult. But looking beyond these examples, are there English words that would not be well served by a simple +/−ADULT binary feature? That is, do we make finer lexical distinctions in age?

3.2.2   Redundancy rules

Another key characteristic of the grammars of many componential metalanguages is the use of **redundancy rules**. Such rules establish a hierarchy of features, such that if a semantic representation includes feature *y*, then it goes without saying that it includes feature *x*. So, for example, since *puppy* has the SPECIES value CANINE, it inherits the information that puppies are animals and, more specifically, mammals, and that they are living things and physical objects, as shown in (5). The redundancy rules, then, provide a sort of "family tree" of features, so that it is always the case that the value CANINE is found in the meanings of mammal names and not bird names, for example. This economy measure simplifies the componential representation of words that are lower on the family tree, since you do not have to define 'mammal' within the representation of the meaning of *puppy*.

(5)

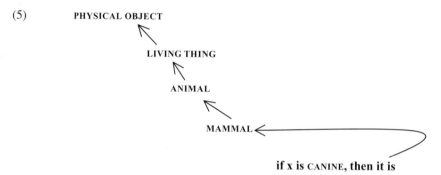

3.2.3   Componential approaches: main points

A last general point to make about componential approaches is that just as lexemes can be decomposed into semantic components, so can larger compositional expressions. Thus, componential approaches provide a truly **compositional semantics** (see chapter 1), in that more complex expressions are always built from lexical meanings, which in turn are built from smaller components.

Before turning to look at more specific componential approaches, let's summarize the key assets of componential approaches generally:

- Componential approaches reduce complex meanings to a finite set of semantic "building blocks."
- These components (if well devised) can be applied to any language.
- Definitions that are expressed as semantic components clearly distinguish what is and is not denoted by an expression.
- The combinability and recombinability of semantic components allow for the generation of a potentially unlimited number of meanings, and for the integration of lexical and phrasal semantics.
- Similarities in the componential representations of different words determine their semantic relations to one another.
- Redundancy rules reduce the number of components that need to be written in a semantic representation, as they guarantee that senses that have certain components will also be understood to have other components.

3.3   An early componential approach – Katz

For historical reasons, it is worthwhile to look at the componential theory developed by linguistic philosopher Jerrold Katz and his colleagues (Katz and Fodor 1963, Katz and Postal 1964, Katz 1972). This approach can be considered the precursor to the approaches in the next chapter, in that it was the first serious attempt to integrate semantic and syntactic aspects of language within the then-new generative approach to linguistics.

3.3.1   Sense as definition: Katz's approach

This approach also most directly develops the "dictionary metaphor" for lexical semantics. First, it assumes that there is a mental dictionary. In other words, the componential definitions Katz posits are assumed to be part of a mental lexicon that is separate from general conceptual knowledge – thus Katz maintains the dictionary/encyclopedia distinction. Second, Katz's componential definitions are structured much like traditional dictionary definitions, which are typically composed of two parts: genus and differentiae. The **genus** of a definition indicates what general category the defined thing belongs to, while the **differentiae** tell us how the defined thing is different from all the other things in the genus category. For the definition of *actress*, the genus is indicated here in parentheses and the differentiae in square brackets.

(6)   **actress** *n.* (a woman or girl) [who acts in plays, movies, or television]

Following the dictionary metaphor, Katz's version of the genus/differentiae distinction is his distinction between **semantic markers** and **distinguishers**, shown in (7). (I have made the distinguisher a bit more specific here to avoid the circularity involved in defining *actress* using *act*.)

(7)   **actress₁** (Human) (Female) [who plays a character in an artistic performance]

In this theory, semantic markers (in parentheses) are the components of meaning that are responsible for the semantic relations among words in the language. So, *actress* is seen as part of the classes of HUMAN things and FEMALE things, and therefore is similar to words like *lady* and *policewoman*, but cannot ever refer to the same things as *filly* or *man* do, since *filly* lacks the marker (Human) and *man* lacks (Female). The distinguisher in square brackets distinguishes actresses from all other types of female humans.

3.3.2   From words to phrases: projection and selectional restrictions

In order to integrate the lexical meaning with phrasal meaning, Katz and Fodor (1963) introduced the notion of **projection rules**, by which the semantic components of a lexeme "project" up the phrasal tree to give the meanings of phrases and, eventually, the whole sentence. For example, the phrase *the talented actress* can be represented as in (8). Here the markers and distinguishers at the bottom of the tree for *the*, *talented*, and *actress* are combined at the higher levels of the tree to give the meanings of the phrase. Note that this theory treats grammatical words like *the* in the same way as it treats lexical words. (Evaluative) in this example is a marker used for certain adjectives.

(8)

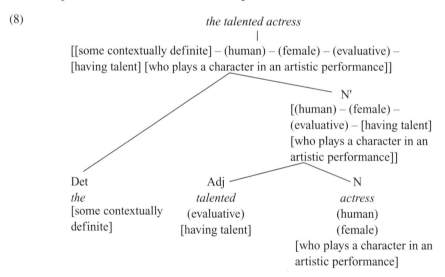

Not all words combine with one another in semantically sensible ways, however. Katz *et al.* employed the notion of **selectional restrictions** to account for the oddness of phrases like *happy cucumber* or *wary sausages*. These are restrictions that are specified in a word's lexical entry, and state for an adjective what kinds of semantic markers must be present in the noun it modifies and for a verb what kinds of semantic markers its objects or subjects must have, and so forth. Thus *wary sausages* and *happy cucumber* are odd because *wary* and *happy* both specify that they must go with a noun that has the marker (Sentient). *Happy actress* works because *actress* has the marker (Human), and by redundancy rules, this includes the marker (Sentient).

3.3.3   Evaluating Katz's approach

Several problems with the Katzian approach became clear by the mid-1970s. One problem is the distinction between markers and distinguishers. While Katz and Fodor held that the semantic relations among words and words' selectional restrictions are dependent just on the markers, Bolinger (1965) pointed out that the information in distinguishers also has a role to play in determining which words can go together. For example, Katz and Fodor described *bachelor* as (Male) (Human) [never married], and so it should be the properties (Male) and (Human) alone that determine which other words *bachelor* is consistent with. In Bolinger's example *the bachelor's legitimate daughter*, however, it is *bachelor*'s distinguisher that tells us that *bachelor* ([never married]) and *legitimate daughter* (i.e. daughter from a married union) contradict each other. If markers and distinguishers do not have different jobs to do, then it is hard to defend the position that a semantic theory needs both.

Another problem for Katz's approach is whether it is really possible to distinguish "definitional" and "encyclopedic" meaning, as section 3.4 discusses.

3.4   Against the classical approach: prototypes

A problem with Katz's approach and classical-type approaches in general became clearer in the 1970s when a series of experiments showed that word meanings are not usually as precise as "necessary and sufficient conditions" make them out to be. Instead, meanings are often imprecise and context-specific.

Word meanings may have **fuzzy boundaries**, meaning that a word's denotation may be hard to specify exactly. This was demonstrated in a famous experiment by William Labov (1973), in which he showed people pictures like the ones below, and asked them to give the name of the object. He found that there were some pictures that everyone would call a *cup* or a *bowl* or a *vase*, but others were harder to classify.

Items that are difficult to categorize, like (b) in figure 3.1, might be categorized differently in different contexts. For example, if (b) had coffee in it, you would probably call it *a cup*, but if it had ice cream in it, you would probably call it *a bowl*. If (a) had ice cream in it, however, you might very well call it *a cup with ice cream in it*, demonstrating that both the shape of something and its function

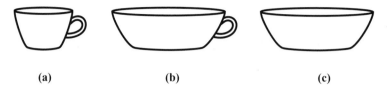

(a)   (b)   (c)

Figure 3.1 *Experimental stimuli in the style of Labov (1973)*

determine whether it is a *cup* or a *bowl*. In the cases of more "central" members of their categories, like (a) and (c), shape seems more important than function, but when something is at the edges of a category, then other issues, like function (what you use it for) and context (where you find it), may play a bigger role in determining whether it belongs to the category or not. In the classical tradition, the fact that ice cream usually goes in bowls is considered encyclopedic information that has nothing to do with the meaning of *bowl*. Labov's experiment hints that such so-called encyclopedic information cannot be dismissed as irrelevant to denotation.

A series of experiments by psychologist Eleanor Rosch and colleagues in the 1970s demonstrated that some categories seem to be organized around "typical" members of categories. By this point, Battig and Montague (1969) had shown that people tend to give similar answers when asked to list members of categories such as *fruit* and *furniture*. Stop for a moment and think what you would put in a list of five types of furniture.

Chances are that *chair*, *table*, and maybe *bed* are on your list. Certainly, those are very common types of furniture, so it is perhaps not surprising that they come to mind. But a lot of other names for common furniture items don't come as quickly to mind – for example, *bookcase* and *stool*. Rosch (1973, 1975) asked subjects to rate items in lists of furniture, fruit, and so forth on a scale of 1 (very typical of the category) to 7 (not typical of the category at all). She found that people tended to rate the same items in a similar way, and that their notions of what is typical correlate with the frequency and order of items listed in Battig and Montague's experiment.

In another experiment, Rosch (1973) presented subjects with a series of examples and asked them to say whether or not the thing belonged to some category, such as BIRD or FRUIT. She timed their responses and found that people were very quick to decide that robins and sparrows are birds and that they are not vegetables, but they were slower in deciding that penguins, chickens, or ducks are birds. These kinds of experimental results reveal **prototype effects**; that is, the more central something is to a category, for example the more typically "birdy" a bird is, the more strongly and immediately it is associated with the name of that category. The flipside of this is what happened when subjects were asked whether or not a bat is a bird. They generally answered correctly that bats are not birds, but just as the "yes, it's a bird" answer took longer for penguins than for robins, it took longer to say "no, it's not a bird" for bats than for elephants. It seems that bats have enough bird-like characteristics to make one have to ponder a bit longer about whether or not to count them as birds, but in the end subjects determined that they were not "birdy" enough to be called *bird*.

Well-known prototype effects include the following, most of which we have already seen:

- **Frequency**: When asked to list members of a category, prototypical members are listed by most people.
- **Priority in lists**: Prototypical examples are among the first that people list.
- **Speed of verification**: People are quicker to recognize more proto-typical members of a category as being members of that category.
- **Generic v. specialized names**: More prototypical members of the category are more likely to be called by a generic (or "basic level" – see §6.2.2) name of the category, rather than by more specialized names. For example, if a robin (a typically "birdy" bird) swooped down on your picnic and stole your sandwich, you might say *Hey, that bird took my sandwich!* (rather than *that robin*). But if a duck (a less "birdy" bird) did the same thing, you would be more likely to say *Hey, that duck took my sandwich!* (rather than *that bird*).

One way of approaching prototype effects would be to assume that there are still necessary conditions for being a bird (like having two legs and feathers) that can be distinguished from non-necessary but typical features like being able to fly. We might say then that being feathered and bipedal are **core features** of *bird*, and that the other features like flying, singing, and living in trees are **peripheral features** that account for the prototype effects but don't make or break an animal's birdhood. However, identifying core features can be difficult, if not impossible. Imagine that a group of birds living near a toxic waste dump began having chicks without feathers, and this was such an evolutionary advantage for these birds (no more feathers that pick up toxic waste) that an entire species of featherless birds arose. Notice that I have still called them *birds*. In this scenario, feathers seem to be a peripheral feature of *bird*, rather than a core feature – which raises the question of whether we can really say with any certainty that any features are core features.

The philosopher Ludwig Wittgenstein (1958) made this point with the example of *game*. One might try to define *game* as 'an activity with a set of rules in which people compete for fun.' But not all games are competitive; for example, playing peek-a-boo with a baby. And not all of them are just for fun; for example, armies use war games to train troops. We could try to redefine *game* as 'a structured human activity in which one tries to reach certain goals,' but that does not differentiate games from computer programming or following a recipe. So, it seems impossible to make any list of necessary and sufficient conditions for being a game, nor do there seem to be any real core features beyond being an activity. Features of games include having rules, involving competition, being done just for fun, and so forth, but not every game has to have all of these features; they just need to have a "family resemblance" to each other. You can tell that something is a game because it is similar enough to other things that are called *games*, just like when I'm with my brothers and people exclaim, "I can tell you're all Murphys!" We do not all have blond hair or our mother's nose, but we each have different combinations of a number of such shared properties so that we are perceived as belonging to the same MURPHY category.

Although the discussion here, like the bulk of the research in this area, has focused on nouns, fuzzy boundaries and prototype effects are issues for other grammatical categories as well. Take for example the verb *to walk*. There are more and less typical examples of walking, with things like power-walking and limping being among the less typical.

Nevertheless, we need to be careful with the notions of fuzziness and prototypes, as not all meanings have fuzzy boundaries and not all prototype experiments have proved to be reliable. Words like *hypotenuse* have precise sense boundaries. Either a line in a triangle is opposite a 90° angle or it is not, and only if it is do we call it a *hypotenuse*. There's no such thing as a prototypical hypotenuse, as each one is as typical as the next one. *Odd* as in *odd number* is similarly precise – an integer is either *odd* or it's not. Still, on some tests it seems to show prototype effects. For example, if you ask someone for an example of an odd number, they are much more likely to say *three* than to say *3,450,671*. But this should not lead us to conclude that *odd* is defined by prototype (and that the prototype resembles *three*) – it just shows that some kinds of numbers are easier to recall and more helpful to give as examples than others.

While the existence of prototype effects and categorization by family resemblance creates serious problems for definition by necessary and sufficient conditions, it does not mean that componential approaches have to be abandoned altogether. What must be rejected is the notion that definitional (linguistic semantic) and encyclopedic (world knowledge) aspects of meaning can be easily separated. In the next chapter, we look at some contemporary componential approaches that have engaged with the problem of prototype effects.

3.5   Summary

This chapter introduced the notion of semantic components and semantic primitives and looked at how they are used in classical, dictionary-like approaches to meaning. Such approaches hold that a word's sense is composed of a set of necessary and sufficient conditions. They are appealing because they structure meaning in ways that are familiar from dictionaries and because they use theoretical notions that are familiar from other aspects of linguistics (such as using features). However, they are seriously challenged by evidence of fuzzy meaning and prototype effects and by examples like *game* for which no lists of universally necessary and sufficient conditions have been devised.

3.6   Further reading

Most general semantics textbooks (e.g. Löbner 2002, Saeed 2003) provide introductions to the issues in this chapter. Laurence and Margolis (1999) discuss the pros and cons of classical, prototype, and other approaches. Newmeyer (1986) provides a history of the Katzian approach, including discussion of other setbacks that the theory faced. Wittgenstein discussed family resemblances in his *Philosophical Investigations* (1958). Rosch (1978) provides a good overview of her experiments and their relevance. Taylor (2003) follows the prototype ideas from that point onward, and gives further critique of the Classical approach.

3.7   Answers to puzzles

3–1

Features like CANINE and HUMAN could be broken down further, presumably, into features such as ANIMATE, MAMMAL, QUADRUPED/BIPED, etc., but it is questionable whether there is a set of psychologically plausible, necessary and sufficient conditions that can differentiate species. For example, the set QUADRUPED, FURRY, and DOMESTICATED might differentiate dogs from humans, but does not differentiate dogs from cats. Other features that we might use to differentiate dogs and cats either are not necessary for all dogs/cats (e.g. being a certain size, having a particular face/snout proportion) or are not readily usable by language users (e.g. their chromosomal makeup or parentage). We came back to this problem in §3.4.

3–2

The distinction between *child* and *baby* clearly indicates that there is more to age than binary distinctions. Both are [+YOUNG] or [−ADULT], but something more is needed to indicate their differences in age. A solution to this might be to posit an AGE feature with a range of values {INFANT, YOUNG, ADOLESCENT, ADULT, ELDERLY}, which could be used to distinguish a range of age-specific descriptions like *baby*, *child*, *youth*, *teenager*, *adult*, and *senior*.

3.8   Exercises

Adopt-a-word

While most of the examples in this chapter are nouns, the issues discussed here can apply to other lexical categories too. For example, there is a fuzzy boundary between the verbs *walk* and *jog*, but one could as well attempt a list of necessary and sufficient conditions that distinguish the two words. So don't be afraid to try these exercises with verbs or adjectives.

A.   Craft a list of necessary and sufficient conditions for your word, using just a simple list of properties (that is, don't worry about binary features or AVMs). After making the best list of conditions that you can, critique your analysis by pointing out any cases that demonstrate the fuzziness of the word's meaning.

B.   Adapt Labov's or one (or more) of Rosch's experiments to determine the prototypical characteristics associated with your word. Perform the experiment on at least eight people and compare their results.

General

1.   Develop a list of features (these can be expressed as short phrases) to distinguish the meanings within the following set of words. After doing this, show whether redundancy rules might be used to show relations among the features.

   book, magazine, dictionary, publication, newspaper, paperback

2.   Do question 1, but make the Katzian distinction between markers and distinguishers. Discuss how you determined which components should be markers rather than distinguishers and whether this decision was clear-cut.

3.   As mentioned in this chapter, Wittgenstein claimeds that *game* cannot be defined by necessary and sufficient conditions. Here is an excerpt of his argument:

   Consider for example the proceedings that we call 'games.' I mean board-games, card-games, ball-games, Olympic games, and so on. What is common to them all? . . . –Are they all 'amusing'? Compare chess with noughts and crosses. Or is there always winning and losing, or competition between players? Think of patience. In ball games there is winning and losing; but when a child throws his ball at the wall and catches it again, this feature has disappeared. Look now at the parts played by skill and luck; and at the difference between skill in chess and skill in tennis. Think now of games like ring-a-ring-a-roses; here is the element of amusement, but how many other characteristic features have disappeared! And we can go through the many, many other groups of games in the same way; we see how similarities crop up and disappear.   (Wittgenstein 1958:31–32)

   Wittgenstein's discussion had an important role in making linguists rethink the idea that word meanings can be defined by necessary and sufficient conditions. However, Wierzbicka (1990:357) maintains that a definition of *game* that identifies the properties common to all kinds of games is possible: according to her, the following features are essential for the concept of *game*:

(1) human action (animals can play, but they don't play games); (2) duration (a game can't be momentary); (3) aim: pleasure; (4) "suspension of reality" (the participants imagine that they are in a world apart from the real world); (5) well-defined goals (the participants know what they are trying to achieve); (6) well-defined rules (the participants know what they can do and what they cannot do); (7) the course of events is unpredictable (nobody can know what exactly is going to happen).

Discuss whether you think Wierzbicka's definition is adequate. Note any examples of games that seem to lack any of the properties that Wierzbicka has listed and consider whether there are other kinds of activities that this definition also applies to, but that would be incorrectly included in the category GAME.

4   Modern componential approaches – and some alternatives

Key words: CONCEPTUAL SEMANTICS, (LEXICAL) CONCEPT, GENERATIVE LEXICON, QUALIA, NATURAL SEMANTIC METALANGUAGE, SEMANTIC PRIME, EXPLICATION

4.1   Overview and questions

While the Classical-style componential approaches of the last chapter were too inflexible to account for fuzzy meaning, various current componential approaches have broken down the traditional barrier between lexical and conceptual representations of meaning, thus confronting more directly the relation between linguistic semantics and general cognition, as well as interfacing with current theories of grammatical structure. This chapter gives overviews of three componential approaches: Jackendoff's Conceptual Semantics, Pustejovsky's Generative Lexicon, and Wierzbicka's Natural Semantic Metalanguage. Particular applications of these approaches are discussed in more detail in later chapters. The purpose of this chapter is to draw out the main motivations of these approaches and their chief similarities and differences. After looking at these componential approaches, we briefly consider two non-componential alternatives: meaning atomism and image schemas.

Given the semantic concepts discussed in previous chapters, here are some questions to keep in mind while reading about each of these approaches:

1.   What is the vocabulary and grammar of the componential metalanguage? (See §3.2.1.)
2.   Does the theory identify universal semantic primitives? (Recall §3.2.1.)
3.   Can phrasal meanings be built out of word meanings? That is, does this theory of word meaning contribute to a compositional model of phrasal meaning? (Recall §1.2.2 and §3.2.3.)
4.   Are the components linguistic or conceptual in nature? That is, are they part of a "mental dictionary" of the language, or are they part of how we conceptualize the world – something above and beyond

language? In other words, do the components belong to linguistic knowledge or world/encyclopedic knowledge? (Recall §2.5.)

5. Does the approach confront the problem of prototype effects? How? (See §3.4.)

Puzzle 4–1

Use the following table to keep track of the similarities and differences among the approaches covered in this chapter. The numbers in the first column refer to the numbers of the questions listed above. The answers for the Katzian approach in chapter 3 are filled in as a model.

Question	Katz's approach (chapter 3)	Conceptual Semantics	Generative Lexicon	Natural Semantic Metalanguage
2. universal primitives	not entirely (distinguishers do not rely on primitives; they're language-specific)	2.	2.	2.
3. compositionality	yes	3.	3.	3.
4. linguistic or conceptual?	linguistic	4.	4.	4.
5. prototypes	no	5.	5.	5.

4.2   Jackendoff: Conceptual Semantics

Ray Jackendoff's componential approach, **Conceptual Semantics** (CS; 1976, 1983, 1990, 1997, 2002), like the Katzian approach, fits within the generative tradition in linguistics. But as its name hints, the semantic components in CS are conceptual in nature (see §2.5). Jackendoff's goal is to investigate:

> how linguistic utterances are related to human cognition, where cognition is a human capacity that is to a considerable degree independent of language, interacting with the perceptual and action systems as well as language.   (Jackendoff 2006:355)

CS has no mental dictionary in the Classical/Katzian sense; that is, there is no store of word meanings that is separate from the store of concepts about the things the words might refer to. Instead, **lexical concepts**, that is, concepts that are represented by words, comprise a subset of concepts in general. These concepts serve as the meanings associated with word forms. For Jackendoff, then, semantics involves representing how concepts, particularly lexical concepts, are

PHONOLOGICAL   CONCEPTUAL

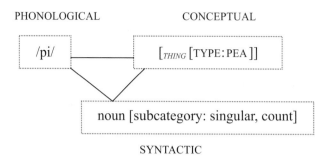

SYNTACTIC

Figure 4.1 *Lexical information about* pea

structured and how these structures interact with the formal (i.e. phonological and grammatical) aspects of language. Because Jackendoff is concerned with representing the structure of thought, not just language-specific word meanings, the components that he proposes are hypothesized to be universal.

4.2.1   The lexicon in CS

Jackendoff visualizes the lexicon as the interface of three structures: phonological, syntactic, and conceptual. For a lexical item like *pea*, then, its phonological form is part of the inventory of such forms in the phonological structure; this is linked with the NOUN category in the syntactic structure and to a semantic representation in the conceptual structure. Figure 4.1 shows the interactions of these three structures.

One effect of this tripartite arrangement is that syntactic, phonological, and semantic structures can interact in various ways. In the case of a typical lexical item, the phonological, syntactic, and conceptual information interact to give a full picture of a word, with a word class, a pronunciation, and a meaning. But other types of linguistic units might have only some of these. Consider phrases like *press the cloth flat*, *paint a wall red*, and *drink yourself silly*. While they have no words in common, they do have a structure in common; they are verb phrases made up of a verb, a noun phrase, and an adjective, in that order: [$_{VP}$V NP Adj]. They also have an element of meaning in common – in each case the verb's action causes the thing referred to by the noun phrase to have the property that is described by the adjective. Jackendoff (2002, Goldberg and Jackendoff 2004) proposes that this particular syntactic structure is linked to a conceptual representation of a **resultative** event (i.e. an action resulting in a new property). In other words, the structure [$_{VP}$V NP Adj] is meaningful in its own right, since a syntactic structure can link to a conceptual structure without necessarily involving a phonological structure. When we use such resultative structures, we integrate them with the phonological and other structures of the words that we wish to put into the structure – but the resultative meaning comes from the abstract syntactic structure. (Note that not all instances of [$_{VP}$V NP Adj] are resultatives, though – just as not every instance of the sound *bat* refers to a kind of animal. A single linguistic form might have more than one purpose. See Goldberg and Jackendoff 2004 for more discussion.)

Thus in CS, both abstract syntactic structures and phonologically realized lexical forms can be stored as linguistic structures that are associated with concepts. CS can therefore be said to expand the notion of what counts as a lexical item. Phonological forms, syntactic structures, and combinations of the two can all be meaningful in that they can be linked to conceptual structures.

4.2.2   Semantic structures in CS

Since we come back to some specific CS treatments of nouns and verbs in chapters 8–10, we focus here on some of its more general properties. CS involves a small number of major **ontological categories**, that is, categories of the type of entities that exist, such as EVENT, STATE, PLACE, AMOUNT, THING, PROPERTY, that serve as universal semantic primitives. (Chapter 7 discusses ontological categories in more detail.) Any CS analysis of a concept begins with these primitive ontological categories, which enter into a more elaborate metalanguage grammar than those we have seen so far. Because Jackendoff is interested in how sentence meanings can be built from lexical meanings, he has been very concerned with the components involved in verb senses and how these interact with other parts of a sentence, so we start with how an entire sentence meaning is structured in order to illustrate what part of the sentence meaning the verb can contribute.

The particular sentences we'll use describe EVENTS. An EVENT is a happening – it involves some kind of action or change (often described by a verb) and typically one or more participants in that event. Our examples involve physical motion events, such as those described by examples (1) and (2).

(1)   Peewee goes into the clubhouse.

(2)   Peewee enters the clubhouse.

In order to discuss these examples, we need a little preview of some of the concepts that we'll encounter in chapter 9. In each of these sentences, we have a verb: *go* and *enter* (we can ignore the agreement marker *-(e)s*, as it does not contribute to the meaning of the sentence). Each sentence also has other phrases that complete the EVENT meaning – *Peewee* and *into the clubhouse*. These phrases are the **arguments** of the verbs; that is, they are the other elements that these particular senses of the verb require in order to provide a complete description of the participants in an EVENT. We can tell that the verb requires these phrases because if we leave them out, either we have an ungrammatical sentence or we have to change to another sense of the verb in order to interpret the sentence. For instance, if we leave out *Peewee* from (1), we get example (3), which is incomplete. If we omit *into the clubhouse*, then we interpret *go* as meaning 'leave' (i.e. 'go away') rather than simply meaning 'move':

(3)   Goes into the clubhouse.

(4)   Peewee goes.

Now, Jackendoff represents motion EVENTS like 'going' and 'entering' using a semantic component GO. Like the English verbs *go* and *enter*, the component GO has two slots that must be filled by its arguments. The arguments are separated by a comma and follow GO within the parentheses in (5). There, we see that the two items that fill GO's slots must belong to the ontological categories THING and PATH. The subscripted *EVENT* in example (5) tells us what ontological type is made up of GO and its THING and PATH arguments.

(5) $[_{EVENT}$ GO $([THING], [PATH])]$

Note that GO in (5) is a semantic component named GO, not the word *go*. The component GO is part of the meaning of *go*, but also part of the meaning of many other verbs, including *enter*, *walk*, *cross*, and *turn*. The rule in (6) provides the basic template for all MOTION EVENTS, which can be filled in with details (as we'll see below) in order to represent the meaning of a range of verbs and sentences.

The PATH in (6) is further defined in terms of a predicate TO that has a slot for a PLACE. *Place*, in turn, is another ontological category that must be spelled out by another rule. Such a rule is (7), where PLACE is defined as being IN some THING (which again needs to be spelled out by another set of structures that tell us which expressions stand for THINGS).

(6) $[_{PATH}$ TO $([PLACE])]$

(7) $[_{PLACE}$ IN $([THING])]$

In other words, a PATH can be made up of a directional component TO and a PLACE, and a PLACE can be made up of a locating component IN and a THING. These are not the only EVENT, PATH, and PLACE rules that are needed – for instance, one could have a PATH *FROM* a PLACE or a PLACE *AT* or *ON* a THING, but let's stick with this short list for now.

We can use these structures and rules to describe the meanings of the sentences in (1) and (2), repeated here:

(1)   Peewee goes into the clubhouse.

(2)   Peewee enters the clubhouse.

(1) and (2) mean basically the same thing: that Peewee moves so that he goes from outside to inside a clubhouse. This could be represented as in the formula in (8), which uses the bracketing notation we saw in (5) through (7).

(8) $[_{EVENT}$GO $([_{THING}$ Peewee] $[_{PATH}$ TO $([_{PLACE}$ IN $([_{THING}$ the clubhouse])])])]$

To read the notation or write your own, keep in mind the following:

- Read the formula from left to right.
- Ontological categories are marked in italics and small capital letters. Meaning components are marked in small capitals. The parts that are written in plain font are expressions that have not been broken down into their component parts in this particular example.
- Anything within square brackets represents a member of a particular ontological category. The type of category may be listed as a subscript at the left-hand bracket. The first non-subscripted thing inside the brackets identifies the main meaning component for that item. So, the first and last square brackets in (8) enclose the GO event, the second left-bracket and the first right-bracket enclose the THING described by *Peewee*, and so forth.
- Anything within parentheses (round brackets) goes with the main component to the left of it, and fills in the "slots" for that component. For example, the first set of parentheses in (8) enclose two arguments of the GO event: the THING that goes (Peewee) and the PATH that is traveled. The PATH, in turn, has its own subparts.

Some people find it easier to visualize such semantic relations in a tree structure. The formula in (8) can be translated into the tree structure in (9), which has exactly the same information.

(9)

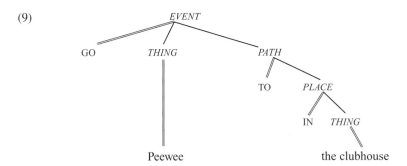

When reading or writing a tree like this, keep in mind that:

- At the top of any branch of the tree is an ontological type. These were represented by the subscripts inside the brackets in (8).
- At the very bottom should be the smallest meaning components, such as GO in the leftmost branch. However, note that we have not broken *Peewee* and *the clubhouse* down into their components here, since we are concentrating on the meaning of the verb and its relations to other parts within the sentence.
- The elements that were represented within parentheses in (8) – that is, the arguments of the main component – are represented in the

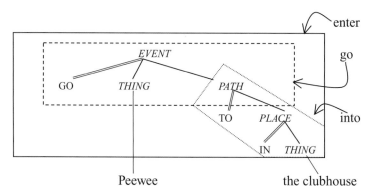

Figure 4.2 *Lexical meanings within (9)*

tree with single lines from the ontological category to the argument. The double lines go from the ontological category down to its main component – that is, the thing at the bottom of a double line in (9) is the first thing within a set of square brackets in (8).

What is interesting to us as lexical semanticists is how we can represent individual words using such componential conceptual structures. We can see this by looking at the difference in what the main verbs *go* and *enter* in (1) and (2) contribute to the full picture of the E V E N T. In Figure 4.2, the solid-line box shows the contribution of *enter* and the dashed-line box shows the smaller contribution of *go*; that is, *go* only tells us that something went along a P A T H, but *enter* tells us that a P A T H T O (rather than F R O M) and a P L A C E I N (rather than A T or O N) were involved. Because *go* does not give us specific information about the P A T H, that information has to come from elsewhere in the sentence – in this case the word *into*, whose meaning contribution is indicated by the diagonal dotted-line box.

The usual way to represent such senses is with the bracket notation, as in (10) through (12) – though these could again be translated into trees.

(10) $enter = [_{EVENT} \text{GO} ([THING], [_{PATH} \text{TO} ([_{PLACE} \text{IN} ([THING])])])]$

(11) $go = [_{EVENT} \text{GO} ([THING], [PATH])]$

(12) $into = [_{PATH} \text{TO} ([_{PLACE} \text{IN} ([THING])])]$

The rest of a sentence's meaning, then, is built up by filling in the details required by the verbs, for instance which T H I N G did the moving, and, in the case of *go*, the details of the type of P A T H involved. Note that the *go* sentence has the P A T H details to fill in, while the *enter* sentence only has to fill in what T H I N G went in another T H I N G. So, in order to express the same meaning (as in (1) and (2)), a sentence with *go* requires more words than a sentence with *enter* in order to spell out the direction of movement and the final position of the moving object inside another object.

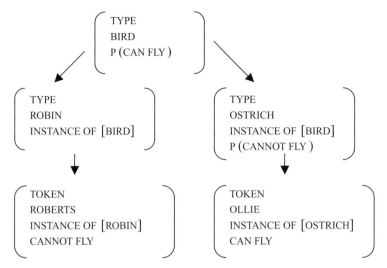

Figure 4.3 *Typical and atypical birds (Jackendoff 1983:144)*

4.2.3   Prototypicality in CS

We'll see more about CS structures in later chapters, but before moving on, it is worth noting that Jackendoff offers a way to cope with the prototype effects discussed in the last chapter. Because CS posits no distinction between linguistic meaning and non-linguistic knowledge about the things that expressions represent, it has no inherent definition/encyclopedia distinction. Jackendoff (1983) introduces **preferential** (or **P-**) **features** as a means to record typical features of categories and builds in a means to indicate exceptions to those features. Figure 4.3 gives partial componential analyses of the lexical concepts representing various THINGS.

The representations of BIRD, ROBIN, and OSTRICH indicate that these are **TYPES** of THINGS. ROBERTS and OLLIE are **TOKENS** of these TYPES, that is, individual birds that belong to the ROBIN and OSTRICH categories, respectively, as indicated by the INSTANCE-OF feature, which takes a TYPE category as its value. This acts as a redundancy device (recall §3.2.2), so that anything that is an INSTANCE OF another category inherits the features of that category. In this figure, it means that ROBIN inherits the P-feature CAN FLY from BIRD, and so we assume that if something is a robin it can fly. However, unlike other kinds of features, P-features can be overridden, as we can see for OSTRICH, which has the P-feature CANNOT FLY. This shows that if a more specific category (OSTRICH) has a P-feature (CANNOT FLY) that conflicts with that of the TYPE it is an instance of (BIRD: CAN FLY), the P-feature on the more specific category "wins." Of course, many more P-features could be included here, such as that birds usually live in trees and that robins usually have red breasts and so on, and unless there were other P-features in conflict with them, they would be inherited by anything else that is a token of those types.

Figure 4.3 also shows that Jackendoff knows some rather unusual birds; Roberts, a non-flying robin, and Ollie, a flying ostrich. The specifications of P-features again show that Roberts and Ollie are individual exceptions to their TYPES. The same mechanism would be used to allow other exceptional members of categories, such as three-legged dogs or people with twelve toes.

4.2.4   Evaluating Conceptual Semantics

In summary, CS avoids a distinction between the linguistic semantics of words and the conceptual representations of what the words represent, treating the semantics of a word as equivalent to the concept that the word is associated with. This means that it can be considered as not just a linguistic theory, but a theory of the structure of human cognition. It relies on universal primitives, reflecting ontological categories like THING and EVENT. CS is compositional, in that meanings of phrases and clauses are straightforwardly built from the senses of the words and grammatical structures involved. Nevertheless, CS rejects a strictly "necessary and sufficient conditions" approach to word senses, by incorporating means to represent "typical" and "atypical" features.

Proponents of less "formal" approaches, such as Wierzbicka (2007a, 2007b) and Goddard (1998, 2001) have criticized metalanguages like CS for being "obscure" since you need special training in order to understand them. They claim that the only way to understand semantic representations that involve strange abbreviations and brackets and subscripts is to translate them into English when we read them. If you have to do that, they say, there is little point in putting the representation into formulae in the first place. We see the flipside of that criticism in the evaluation of Natural Semantic Metalanguage in §4.4.

Wierzbicka and Goddard have also criticized the methodology of CS, in that the theory has mostly been applied to and tested on English, but it makes claims for linguistic-semantic universals. They question whether insights into the human capacity for language can be made on the basis of investigations that are so biased toward a single language.

4.3   Pustejovsky: the Generative Lexicon

James Pustejovsky's (1991, 1995) Generative Lexicon (GL) Theory shares many of the assumptions of Jackendoff's work and pays particular attention to how words come to be used and interpreted in creative ways in novel contexts. Like Jackendoff's Conceptual Semantics, GL is focused on the interface between lexical and phrasal meaning, so there is a focus on building bigger compositional meanings out of lexical parts. We explore some of these ideas further in chapters 5 and 11. Pustejovsky also accepts most of Jackendoff's ideas about the structure of linguistic knowledge, particularly that meaning is conceptual in nature.

4.3.1   Levels of semantic structure in GL

The metalanguage of GL has a relatively complex grammar, represented in AVMs (see §3.2.1). A complete AVM for a lexical sense includes four levels of analysis: Event Structure, Lexical Inheritance Structure, Argument Structure, and Qualia Structure. A lot of lexical information is included in the Qualia Structure, so we'll look at that in more detail after a quick overview of the other structures.

The **Event Structure** is most relevant to verbs, and indicates whether a verb denotes a STATE, a PROCESS, or a TRANSITION.

The **Argument Structure** indicates how many and what type of other expressions are required by the word, as well as indicating how they fit into the syntax and semantics of the sentence. For example, the argument structure for the verb *drive* indicates that it requires a driver (**x**) who needs to be an animate individual, and a vehicle to be driven (**y**), as in (13).

(13)
$$\begin{bmatrix} \textbf{drive} \\ \text{ARGSTR} = \begin{bmatrix} \text{ARG1} = \textbf{x:animate\_individual} \\ \text{ARG2} = \textbf{y:vehicle} \end{bmatrix} \end{bmatrix}$$

The **Lexical Inheritance Structure** shows how the lexeme fits into the hierarchical structure of the lexicon, for example indicating that *robin* is related to *bird* by being a TYPE of a bird. This structure does the same sort of work as redundancy rules (§3.2.2) did in Katz's approach, showing that *robin* inherits the features of *bird*, which inherits the features of *animal*, and so forth. In the GL literature, the Lexical Inheritance information is usually assumed as background information and not included in the AVM.

The information in the **Qualia Structure** defines the "essential attributes" of the word's denotata. It is composed of four types of information, each of which can be called a **quale**. This can be illustrated by looking at an example of a Qualia Structure:

(14)
$$\begin{bmatrix} \textit{novel} \\ \text{QUALIA} = \begin{bmatrix} \textbf{constitutive} = \text{narrative } (\textbf{x}) \\ \textbf{formal} = \text{book } (\textbf{x}) \\ \textbf{telic} = \text{read } (\textbf{y, x}) \\ \textbf{agent} = \text{write } (\textbf{z, x}) \end{bmatrix} \end{bmatrix}$$

(adapted from Pustejovsky 1995:78)

The Qualia Structure in (14) makes the details of a novel more specific, so that we can tell novels from other kinds of things. The **x**, **y**, and **z** in (14) are **variables**; that is, they stand in for particular entities that may be made specific in a particular sentential context. Using variables in the componential structure allows for cross-reference within the structure – the **x** in the CONSTITUTIVE quale is the same thing as the **x** in the TELIC quale, and so on. The different qualia give particular kinds of details:

- The **CONSTITUTIVE** quale indicates what the denotatum is made of, for example what kinds of parts it has and what material they are made of. In (14), it says that a novel (**x**) consists of narrative.
- The **FORMAL** quale identifies what it is that distinguishes the denotatum from other things in a larger domain – this can include things like its size, shape, color, and position. A novel, (14) tells us, is differentiated from other narratives in that it is a book. (We would have to look at the QUALIA for *book* to see more detail about what books are.) Because *novel* is identified as being a BOOK, it will be possible to use *novel* with many of the same verbs and adjectives that we can use with *book*, for instance, you can *dog-ear* a novel or say that a novel is *thick*, which you might not be able to say so naturally with some other kinds of narrative, for example an opera. (Pustejovsky's analysis here does not distinguish novels from books that are biographies, but we could add the information that novels are made of fiction in the CONSTITUTIVE quale.)
- The **TELIC** quale indicates the denotatum's purpose and function. In (14), a novel (**x**) is for someone (**y**) to read. (The entry for *read* will indicate that the reading has to be done by something animate and intelligent, so we can call **y** a *someone*, rather than a *something*.)
- Lastly, the **AGENTIVE** quale indicates factors related to the origin of the denotatum; for example, whether it is naturally occurring or an artifact, and whether a particular type of person or process created it. In this case, a novel (**x**) is something that comes about by being written by someone (**z**).

Puzzle 4–2

Using the Qualia Structure in (14) as a model, determine what kinds of information would need to be associated with each quale for the noun *lunch*.

GL uses QUALIA detail in explaining why a sentence like *Phil just finished a novel* could have two interpretations, either that Phil just finished reading a novel (relating the finishing to the TELIC properties of the novel) or that he just finished writing one (relating to the AGENTIVE quale). The combination of the senses of *finished* and *novel* interact to make these two readings possible. On the other hand, *Phil just finished lunch* can mean 'Phil has eaten lunch' or 'Phil has prepared lunch,' but not 'Phil has read lunch' because *lunch*'s QUALIA do not include any reference to reading. This involves a semantic operation called **type**

coercion, which we return to in chapter 5. The upshot of this is that GL analyzes *finish* as having a single sense that interacts with the QUALIA of its object so that *finish* can be interpreted to have a more specific meaning in context. (The other option would be to believe that our lexicon contains many different senses of *finish*, which have to do with reading, writing, preparing food, eating, etc.) Thus, rather than being like a dictionary, consisting of a static list of all the senses of a word, the Generative Lexicon instead offers dynamic means for creating new senses that are suitable to the co-text.

4.3.2   Evaluating the Generative Lexicon

GL has its origins in computational linguistics, and so many of the linguistic phenomena that have received much attention in this approach are current issues in developing natural language systems for computers. As such, some of the messier problems of semantics, particularly prototype effects and fuzzy meaning, have not been directly dealt with in GL. GL also takes no particular position on primitives – whether there are any or what they might be. Nevertheless, it is an influential theory because of its dynamic meaning creation properties, which help to account for how we "fill in" a lot of information in context – such as that *finishing a beer* involves drinking it, not reading or eating it. Many other approaches rely on pragmatic inferences, rather than lexical semantic mechanisms, to aid these interpretations.

A particularly attractive aspect of GL is the application of the four levels of structure (particularly notions like QUALIA) to nouns, verbs, and adjectives, allowing for a unified approach to lexical semantics across grammatical categories.

GL is subject to the same criticisms as raised for CS (§4.2.4) – namely, some theorists assert that the mind is unlikely to be structured in terms of such abstract and complex metalanguages. We see an alternative in the next section.

4.4   Wierzbicka: Natural Semantic Metalanguage

4.4.1   Explications

The Natural Semantic Metalanguage (NSM) theory, initially developed by Anna Wierzbicka (1972, 1996; Goddard 1998), is concerned with reducing the semantics of all vocabulary down to a very restricted set of semantic primitives, or **primes**, as Wierzbicka calls them. NSM differs from the previous theories, however, in that semantic representations (called **explications** in NSM) consist of paraphrases in a metalanguage that has vocabulary and grammar drawn from natural language, as in the representation of *happy* in (15):

(15)   X feels *happy* = sometimes someone thinks something like this:
                    something good happened to me
                    I wanted this
                    I don't want other things now
                because of this, someone feels something good
                X feels like this

The metalanguage used to represent this sense draws from a small range of semantic primitives, such as WANT, THINK, FEEL, THING, PERSON, NOT (in DON'T), and GOOD. These primitives are arranged in natural language phrases in order to **explicate** a word's sense. Because the explications can fit into natural language (unlike representations in theories that use less "natural" metalanguages), one can test NSM analyses by substituting them for the word in question in a sentence. So, for example, we should be able to rephrase (16) as (17):

(16)   The clown looks [happy].

(17)   The clown looks like [the clown thinks something like this: 'something good happened to me; I wanted this; I don't want other things now'; because of this, the clown feels something good].

The rephrased version is fairly cumbersome and we needed to add a *like* to make it work after the verb *looks*, but it still serves its purpose. If English speakers agree that (17) is a fair paraphrase of (16), then we can conclude that the analysis of *happy* in (15) is accurate.

4.4.2   Semantic primes in NSM

The semantic components (or *primes*) in NSM are required to be primitive and universal. They are primitive in that they cannot be paraphrased using only other primes – in that sense they are "indefinable." They are universal in that every prime must have an exact translation in every human language. Thus, NSM proponents assume that all languages share a core vocabulary; although the forms of the shared words will differ across languages, their meanings are the same. Goddard and Wierzbicka (1994, 2002) surveyed languages from different language families and continents, and found support for this assumption. For instance, all languages seem to have ways of expressing *I*, *you*, *someone*, *something*, *big*, *small*, *where*, and *when*. Relying on primes that are expressed in every language means that the analysis of *happy* in (15) could be translated into the core vocabulary of any other language, even if the language does not have a word that means exactly what *happy* means.

The number of primes has grown from 14 in Wierzbicka (1972) to 60 in Goddard and Wierzbicka (2002) and 63 in current work (e.g. Goddard 2010). These are shown in Table 4.1, organized into groups of semantically similar types. Table 4.1 gives the English translations, or **exponents**, of the primes, but

Table 4.1 *English exponents of NSM primes (Goddard 2010)*

I, YOU, SOMEONE, SOMETHING/ THING, PEOPLE, BODY	substantives
KIND, PART	relational substantives
THIS, THE SAME, OTHER/ELSE	determiners
ONE, TWO, SOME, ALL, MUCH/MANY	quantifiers
GOOD, BAD	evaluators
BIG, SMALL	descriptors
THINK, KNOW, WANT, FEEL, SEE, HEAR	mental predicates
SAY, WORDS, TRUE	speech
DO, HAPPEN, MOVE, TOUCH	action, event, movement, contact
BE (SOMEWHERE), THERE IS, HAVE, BE (SOMEONE/SOMETHING)	location, existence, possession, specification
LIVE, DIE	life and death
WHEN/TIME, NOW, BEFORE, AFTER, A LONG TIME, A SHORT TIME, FOR SOME TIME, MOMENT	time
WHERE/PLACE, HERE, ABOVE, BELOW, FAR, NEAR, SIDE, INSIDE	space
NOT, MAYBE, CAN, BECAUSE, IF	logical concepts
VERY, MORE	intensifier, augmentor
LIKE/WAY	similarity

linguists writing in other languages could use their languages' exponents of the primes. We can use the exponents of the primes in any language to describe linguistic expressions in any other language.

Primes like A SHORT TIME and THERE IS in Table 4.1 show that while primes must be translatable in every language, they are not necessarily represented by single words in every language – they could be represented by phrases or bound morphemes as well. Items like MANY/MUCH, which consist of two words separated by a slash, are single semantic primes with different exponents in English (called **allolexes**). That is, MANY and MUCH stand for the same unit of meaning, but they show up in the explications in one form or the other depending on what makes the explication read more naturally, since in English these words have to agree with the nouns they modify in terms of countability (see chapter 8).

In writing explications, non-prime components called **molecules** may also be used as shorthand for a longer explication, but only if it can be proven that these components *can* be broken down into primes. For example, OFTEN is frequently used in explications, but it is not considered a prime because it can be explicated using other primes, like MANY and TIME. Molecules are often marked by **M** in explications.

4.4.3   Encyclopedic information in NSM

Typical but unnecessary properties can be included in NSM representations by including components like MANY and OFTEN in the explications. For example, the explication for *cup* specifies that it is something one can drink from and that it is flat on the bottom and so forth, but also that "often they have a thin rounded part sticking out from one side which a person can hold between the fingers and thumb in one hand" (Goddard 1998:233). This allows for both teacups with handles and disposable cups without handles to be called *cup*, while still representing that having a handle is a cup-like property. Another strategy is to phrase the explication in terms of people's beliefs about the denotata, rather than a straightforward description of the denotata. Wierzbicka (1996), for instance, suggests starting the explication of *bird* with "people think things like this about creatures of this kind," and then listing properties like moving in the air, having feathers, and so forth. She says that the explication should also caution that: "some creatures of this kind cannot move in the air, but when people want to say something about creatures of this kind they say something like this: 'they can move in the air.'" Since there's no limit to how much information an explication can contain, one could add many provisos in an explication in order to specify typical, but not necessary, features of the denotata.

NSM theory makes no hard-and-fast distinction between definitional and encyclopedic aspects of meaning, and explications can rely heavily on "folk theories," that is, the rather naïve understandings that most of us have about how life, the universe, and everything work. For instance, NSM treatments of color words do not specify where on the color spectrum a particular color lies or what wavelength the color is, but instead associate the color with things in the natural world that have that color. So, for example, the explication of *green* is:

(18)   X is *green* = sometimes in some places people see many things growing
                          out of the ground
                          when people see things like X, they can think of this

4.4.4   Evaluation of Natural Semantic Metalanguage

Perhaps because it is very different from other semantic approaches, NSM has been subject to a fair amount of criticism. NSM has its roots in lexical analysis, and has been applied to a great variety of word types – everything from nouns and verbs to interjections. This contrasts with other theories, such as Conceptual Semantics, whose roots are intertwined with particular grammatical theories – and which thus have as their starting point the problem of compositionality – how to build sentence meanings. This has meant that NSM investigations of word meanings are often much deeper than those offered in other approaches, but raises the criticism that issues of compositionality have been neglected.

The use of natural language primitives is controversial for several reasons. First, natural language expressions are often imprecise and polysemous (having multiple meanings). Traditionally, semanticists have used more abstract components and more formal structures in order to have a precisely defined metalanguage that avoids the problems of imprecision and multiple meanings (see chapter 3). Because NSM primes are explicitly based on natural language expressions, they are not unambiguous – for example, Jackendoff (2007) notes that the primitive CAN is used variously to mean 'be able' and 'be possible' in NSM explications, echoing its multiple meanings in English. Because a single primitive seems to be used to express more than one sense, there is the possibility that NSM explications might be ambiguous in a way that differs from the word senses they describe.

Another question is whether these primes and the grammar for combining them are sufficient to represent precise lexical meanings. Recall the explication of *green* in (18). It is meant to indicate that *green* is the color of grass or other plants, and so when we call something *green*, it is because it reminds us of plants. But since *plant* is not a primitive, the explication instead mentions 'things that grow out of the ground in some places.' This description is vague, since it does not say which things or in what places, so it could be understood to denote things that are not green. The explication also can only go as far as saying that the property of being *green* is a visual property of these things that grow out of the ground – it has no way (unless some day COLOR is admitted into the pantheon of primitives) to indicate that *green* indicates a color. Thus, the explication in (18) could be interpreted as being about the shape or brightness of the things that grow out of the ground, rather than the hue of the color.

A particular strength of NSM is its cross-linguistic application. Researchers like Wierzbicka and Goddard have made many interesting observations regarding cultural differences, which they claim can be understood in terms of key vocabulary in the languages of those cultures whose differences can be seen through NSM explications. In other words, NSM theorists use the universal primitives found in every language in order to explicate the meanings of words that are not universal. For instance, Wierzbicka (1997) discusses the differences among English *friend* and supposed translations of *friend* in Russian and Polish, showing how different cultural assumptions about the nature of friendship are found in the meanings of those words – and how these differences can be expressed using the primes of NSM. We see more of NSM in chapter 8.

4.5   Alternatives to componential approaches

The theoretical approaches from this and the last chapter all have in common the notion that senses are built out of smaller semantic units that comprise a kind of metalanguage, and we stick with this assumption through the rest of the book. However, the nature of lexical meaning is still the subject of much debate, both in linguistics and in philosophy. Before leaving the realm of general theory, it is worth mentioning the main competitors to a componential approach to meaning.

4.5.1   Meaning atomism

One alternative to a componential view of meaning is the view that meanings have no parts. This position has been championed by philosopher Jerry Fodor (1975; Fodor *et al.* 1980), who holds that the meanings of words (i.e. lexicalized concepts) are **atomic** – they cannot be broken down into any further parts and they have no internal structure. This view argues against our intuitions that some meanings are more complex than other ones. So, the meaning atomist would think that the meaning of *actress* has nothing more to it than the meaning of *person* since neither is broken down into parts, whereas in a componential view, *actress* would have more semantic components than *person* because it describes a type of person.

One argument for the atomic position rests on the problem of creating non-circular definitions – in order to do so, one must start with a set of primitive components whose meanings do not depend on the meanings of other components. But those meanings must come from somewhere. We might conclude that they come from sensory–motor experience. For instance, RED could be a primitive, since experiencing the color red sets off particular sensors in our eyes and thus particular patterns of activity in our brains – we need not be able to define *red* in order to know what it means and to have its meaning contribute to the meaning of other words. But, Fodor *et al.* argue, the range of potential primitives in this case is too restricted to do much good in defining words like *grandmother* or *ketch* (a type of two-masted sailboat). Another argument is based on the assumption that if word meanings break down into components, then it should take longer to process sentences that have more semantically complex lexical items. In this case, it is a problem for componential analysis that it does not seem to take any longer to understand the meaning of *kill* ('cause to die') than it does to understand *die*.

Most linguistic semanticists, however, do not see these as reasons to abandon componential approaches – and certainly not reason to go as far as saying that no meanings are componential. A particular problem is Fodor's (1975) contention that atomic concepts must be innate, since they cannot be built out of existing meanings. For most scholars, it intuitively seems unlikely that people would be born with notions like *radiotherapy* or *German* already in their heads.

Atomism also entails that only a finite number of meanings/concepts exists, since the brain itself is finite. But this position is difficult to defend, since people show an unlimited ability to recognize and conceptualize new things. A compositional approach, in contrast, allows for the combination and recombination of a finite number of primitives into a potentially unlimited number of different meanings.

Finally, if meanings are atomic, then we cannot generalize about particular subclasses of meanings. In a componential approach, we can make semantic

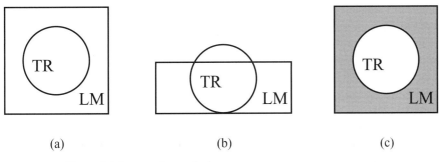

Figure 4.4 *Image schemas for* in

generalizations about 'senses that have the component H U M A N' or 'senses that have the component E V E N T,' and thus explain semantic phenomena such as the relationships among words in a language and the sensible combination of words in a phrase. Because atomic meanings have no internal structure, such generalizations cannot be made. This means that an atomistic theory cannot offer explanations for the types of phenomena discussed in this book. So, having mentioned it as an alternative view, we now set it aside for the rest of the book.

4.5.2   Meanings as image schemas

As we saw in chapter 2, it is a mistake to consider meanings simply to be "snapshots in the mind." Nevertheless, more abstract types of visual representation are common means of representing meaning within the family of linguistic approaches known as **Cognitive Linguistics**. Such approaches have been, in part, a reaction to the failings of the classical componential approach discussed in chapter 3. They have also sought to understand language and conceptualization in terms of **the embodied mind** – that is, we perceive and interact with the world through our bodies, and this body-centric experience shapes the way we think about the world and the relations within it. In taking this approach, theorists like George Lakoff and Mark Johnson have tried to abandon language-like componential metalanguages altogether. Their semantic representations are known as **image schemas**, and they have been most notably applied to the analysis of closed-class words such as prepositions and modal verbs. For instance, different senses of the preposition *in* might be represented as in figure 4.4. There, the element marked T R (which stands for T R A J E C T O R – i.e. the thing whose location is being discussed), is located 'in' with respect to the part marked L M (or 'L A N D M A R K' – i.e. the thing against which the location of the trajector is judged).

Image schema (a) in figure 4.4 could represent the use of *in* in a context like *the table in the room*. A slightly different schema, (b), would be needed for the use of *in* in *the man in the bath*, in which case the trajector (the man) would not have to be 100% enclosed by the bath. Image schema (c) would be needed for *a hole in the fabric*, and others would be needed for *in a row*, *in bed*, and *in a sandwich*, since they all describe different variations on being 'in' something. The (a) schema in figure 4.4 could serve as the basic schema – the prototype – and the other uses of *in* vary from that basic schema.

Similarly visual approaches have been taken by other cognitive linguists. They have been criticized for the inexplicitness of the theory as to how different types of linguistic and conceptual elements are to be integrated and for not offering testable hypotheses that can be disproved. Some theorists remain unconvinced that image schema can do the job of semantic representation – Goddard (1998), for example, insists that we implicitly or explicitly rely on verbal decodings of such schemata, and so they are not as independent of linguistic metalanguage as they claim to be.

Although this text makes use of insights by cognitive linguists who work in this image-schematic tradition from time to time it concentrates on componential metalanguages in particular, since the assumptions underlying image-schematic and componential approaches are different enough that it would be impractical (if I tried to discuss all the underlying differences) or misleading (if I did not) to compare the details of their treatments of particular lexical phenomena.

4.6   Summary and conclusion

This chapter has provided overviews and evaluations of three current and influential componential theories: Conceptual Semantics, Generative Lexicon Theory, and Natural Semantic Metalanguage. They differ from the Katzian Theory, discussed in chapter 3, in that they do not distinguish definitional and encyclopedic aspects of meaning. With the possible exception of Pustejovsky, they are sensitive to the need to account for prototype effects and fuzzy meaning. Still, proponents of image-schematic approaches argue that the componential approaches to fuzziness are too peripheral to these theories' treatment of meaning.

Aside from obvious differences in the forms of their metalanguages, the three theories differ in their main areas of focus. Conceptual Semantics is particularly concerned with ways in which words can be built into phrases and sentences, and GL with the problem of how words are ascribed particular senses within sentences. Natural Semantic Metalanguage theorists, however, tend to focus on the inventory of primitives in their metalanguage and on demonstrating how a wide range of linguistic and communicative phenomena can be accounted for using NSM.

Conceptual Semantics and the Generative Lexicon overlap in many ways, while Natural Semantic Metalanguage stands in contrast to these in terms of the assumptions about language and thought that inform the theories. In the following chapters, we encounter each of these theories again and consider what insights they can offer into various lexical phenomena.

4.7   Further reading

On semantic approaches generally, Laurence and Margolis (1999) describe and critique many approaches to the representation of concepts (and thus, relatedly, senses), including componential, prototype, and atomistic approaches.

Because this chapter is concerned with demonstrating some of the key features of the theories presented, it skims over many of their details. Some of these are discussed in coming chapters – for example, on ontological categories in chapter 7 and event structures in chapter 9.

For more information on the theories discussed here, Ray Jackendoff's *Foundations of Language* (2002) provides a clear discussion of the reasoning behind his own approach and compares it to the other approaches discussed here and in chapter 3. *Semantic Analysis* by Cliff Goddard (1998) is a textbook that particularly focuses on Natural Semantic Metalanguage. To see how NSM is used to describe cultural differences, see Wierzbicka's *Understanding Cultures through their Key Words* (1997). Jackendoff (2006) and Wierzbicka (2007a, 2007b) have debated their approaches to semantics in a series of articles in *Intercultural Pragmatics*, and these reveal some of the differences in the goals and assumptions underlying the two approaches.

To date there is no textbook that is primarily concerned with GL, so Pustejovsky's original work (1991, 1995) must be consulted. Unfortunately, these sources can be quite difficult.

Evans and Green (2006) and Croft and Cruse (2004) are Cognitive Linguistics textbooks with particular attention to lexical issues, including the image schema approach.

4.8   Answers to puzzles

4–1				
Questions	Katz's approach (chapter 3)	Conceptual Semantics	Generative Lexicon	Natural Semantic Metalanguage
2. universal primitives	not entirely	yes	unclear	yes
3. compositionality	yes	yes	yes	historically less central to this approach than to the others
4. linguistic or conceptual?	linguistic	conceptual	conceptual	conceptual
5. prototypes	no	yes	unclear	yes

4–2

CONSTITUTIVE: Lunch is made of food.
FORMAL: Lunch is a type of meal.
TELIC: What you do with a lunch is eat it.
AGENTIVE: Lunch comes into being when someone succeeds in cooking
                  or otherwise preparing food.

If you put these elements of LUNCH into a GL-style AVM, it should look like this:

lunch

$$\text{QUALIA} = \begin{bmatrix} \textbf{constitutive} = \text{food } \textbf{(x)} \\ \textbf{formal} = \text{meal } \textbf{(x)} \\ \textbf{telic} = \text{eat } \textbf{(y, x)} \\ \textbf{agent} = \text{cook/prepare } \textbf{(z, x)} \end{bmatrix}$$

4.9   Exercises

Adopt-a-word

A.   Using the list of semantic primes from table 4.1 and the examples from §4.5 as models, devise a Natural Semantic Metalanguage explication for your word. Test it by asking someone else to read it (leave your word off the page!) and then to guess which word you have defined. Discuss any troubles that you had in devising or testing the explications. Do they indicate weaknesses in the metalanguage?

B.   If your word is a noun, devise a **QUALIA** representation for your word, following the example in (14).

General

1.   The Conceptual Semantics tree below represents the sentences that follow. Determine which part of the tree corresponds to the bold words in the sentences, and redraw those tree parts and/or rewrite that part of the tree in bracketed notation.

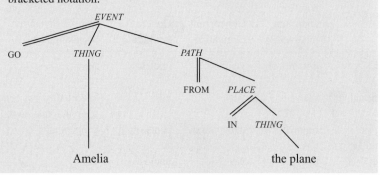

    a. Amelia **deplaned**. (Yes, this is a real word!)

    b. Amelia **went** out of the plane.

    c. Amelia **exited** the plane.

2.   Using the examples in this chapter as models, devise GL-style QUALIA structures for the following words. Discuss any problems you encounter or difficult choices you had to make in doing your analysis.

    a. dictionary

    b. sandwich

    c. poem

3.   Using the examples in this chapter as models, devise NSM-style explications for the following words, using only the semantic primes from table 4.1. Discuss any problems you encounter or difficult choices you had to make in doing your analysis.

    a. *guess* (as in *I would guess that there are 7,000 words in this chapter*)

    b. *upset* (as in *I'm upset that there's no chocolate*)

PART II

Relations among words and senses

5 Meaning variation: polysemy, homonymy, and vagueness

Key words: VAGUE, INDETERMINATE, AMBIGUITY, HOMONYMY, POLYSEMY, ZEUGMA, REGULAR (SYSTEMATIC) POLYSEMY, METONYMY, METAPHOR, MONOSEMY, COERCION

5.1   Overview

In this chapter we turn our attention to an issue we set aside earlier: the fact that in different contexts the same word form can be understood to have different semantic interpretations. For instance *book* can mean 'a collection of pages that are bound in a rigid cover' (*hand me that book*), 'the information contained in a collection of pages that are bound in a rigid cover' (*that book is depressing*) or 'reserve' (*We want to book a table for four*), and in any of its senses *book* can point to lots of different kinds of things. For example, the 'collection of pages' sense could refer to this book or to a phone book, and the 'reserve' sense of *book* can be used for booking a restaurant by phone or booking a hotel on-line. This chapter reviews three ways in which a single word form can have more than one interpretation: homonymy, polysemy, and vagueness. We'll refer to these three phenomena collectively as cases of **meaning variation**. After defining the types of meaning variation, we consider whether or not they denote completely distinct phenomena. Next we focus on polysemy (when a single word has several senses) and discuss how words come to have multiple senses and how those senses relate to one another. Finally, we consider how polysemy is treated in two theoretical approaches: the componential approach of Pustejovsky and the frame-based approach of Fillmore.

5.2   Polysemy, homonymy, vagueness

The various interpretations of a word can be related to each other in different ways, and can come about in different ways. So, under the general heading of "meaning variation" we find three distinct phenomena, starting with:

a)   If the word has one sense that is general enough that it can be applied to many different things, then the word has a **vague**, or **indeterminate**, sense.

In that case, the word can denote a variety of different things, but it gets to those things by means of a general "one sense fits all" meaning. For example, *clock* means 'a device for measuring hours' and therefore it can refer to a lot of different types and instances of clocks – digital clocks, analog clocks, alarm clocks, cuckoo clocks, and so forth.

The other two types of meaning variation arise when two uses of a word represent different senses. The state of having more than one possible sense is called **ambiguity**, and there are two types of lexical ambiguity:

b)   If two form–meaning pairings involve two different lexemes that just happen to have the same spoken and/or written form, then it is a case of **homonymy** – that is, there are two lexemes that are each other's **homonym**. For instance, the noun *kind* meaning 'type' and the adjective *kind* meaning 'considerate' are two different words that just happen to have the same spelling and pronunciation. If we want to talk just about the spoken form of the language, we can refer to **homophones**, which have the same pronunciation but not necessarily the same spelling, such as *raze* and *raise*. If we're just looking at the written language, there are **homographs**, which are spelt the same but may or may not be pronounced differently – like the musical instrument *bass* /beɪs/ and the fish *bass* /bæs/.

c)   If a single lexeme has two distinguishable senses associated with it, then we say that it is a **polyseme** or it is **polysemous**. The 'bound pages' and 'information' meanings of *book* are related to one another, so we would not want to conclude that we have two completely different words when we use the 'text' and 'tome' senses of *book*. So, we conclude that *book* is a polyseme with 'text' and 'tome' senses.

But how can you know if a word has one sense or two or five? And how can you tell if a particular word form represents one lexeme or two lexemes that just happen to look and sound exactly like each other? Let's start exploring these issues by focusing on the difference between vagueness and ambiguity before differentiating polysemy and homonymy.

5.2.1   Vagueness vs. ambiguity

If an expression is **vague** then its sense is imprecise, but if it is **ambiguous**, it has at least two separate senses. We'll look at three ambiguity tests – definition, contrast, and zeugma – and use them to show that *friend* is vague with respect to the sex of the friend, but it is not ambiguous between separate 'male friend' and 'female friend' senses.

In (1a), *friend* refers to someone male, and in (1b), it refers to someone female, so you might initially hypothesize that *friend* has two senses: 'a male person with whom one has a relationship of mutual affection' and 'a female person with whom one has a relationship of mutual affection.'

(1) a.   Ben is my friend. He's a fine fellow.
    b.   Georgia is my friend. She's a wonderful woman.

Definition test

However, the first indication that *friend* does not have two separate senses is the ease with which we can make a single definition that covers both of the cases in (1): 'a person with whom one has a relationship of mutual affection.' So, according to the definition test, *friend* is vague, not ambiguous.

Contrast tests

If *friend* is vague, then in some contexts it may refer to a person who happens to be female and in other contexts to a person who happens to be male. If this were not the case, that is, if *friend* had two gender-specific senses instead of one general sense, it would make sense to say something like (2) in order to mean (3):

(2)   # I have both friends and friends.

(3)   I have both male friends and female friends.

Compare (2) to (4), in which one can easily understand *bats* to mean two different things: a type of animal and a type of sporting equipment.

(4)   I collect things that begin with B, so I have both bats and bats.

Because the two instances of *bats* have the same form, you cannot tell whether the first or the second refers to the animal (unless you can read the mind of the person who said (4)), but you can tell that there are two distinct senses here. So because the two uses of *bat* in (4) are not simply repetitive of each other, we can say that they semantically contrast, and therefore are ambiguous. Since two meanings of *friend* do not contrast in (2), we can conclude that it is **vague**.

Another way to test whether the word has two contrasting senses is to see if (in a single situation) one can answer either "yes" or "no" to questions like (5), depending upon which way the word is interpreted. Imagine that a coach is trying to organize a team to play baseball but the equipment hasn't arrived. The coach asks:

(5)   Are there any bats here?

Chances are that the players will answer "no" without even looking into the sky to see if any small flying mammals are about. But if they did notice the bats in the sky, they could answer:

(6)   Yes, there are bats, but not bats.

On the other hand, if a child says (7) to you,

(7)   Grace and Penny are my friends. Do you have any friends?

you would not assume that there are two sex-specific senses of *friends* even though the child only referred to female friends. It would thus be strange to say:

(8)   # No, I don't have any friends [= 'female friends'], but Mark and Paul are my friends [= 'male friends'].

So, since *friend* cannot be used to contrast with *friend*, we conclude that it is vague, not ambiguous.

Puzzle 5–1

I've just claimed that there are no separate male and female senses for *friend*. Does the following dialogue prove this wrong?

Jane: Do you have a friend?
Julia: Yes, Sue is my friend.
Jane: No, I didn't mean a friend, I meant a *friend*.
Julia: Oh, yeah. Perry and I have been together for five years.

Or is there more going on here than male/female senses of *friend*?

Zeugma test

Another way to tell the difference between ambiguity and vagueness is the zeugma test. A **zeugma** (or **syllepsis**) is a sentence in which two different senses of an ambiguous word are "activated" at the same time. Zeugmas sound weird because of the inherent conflict in the word that has to incorporate both senses, as in (9) and (10).

(9)   #Man **waxes** patriotic, truck (*The Onion*, November 14, 2001)

(10)   #John had a **case** of beer and **another** of measles.

Example (9) is a satirical newspaper headline, which mocks a common headline style in which two objects of a verb are separated by a comma instead of the conjunction *and*. But in this case, the oddness of using both *patriotic* and *truck* as objects of the same instance of *wax* indicates that the verb *wax* has two senses. *To wax patriotic* uses the sense 'to speak or write in a specified manner' and goes with an adjective that describes a manner, and *to wax a truck* uses the sense 'to apply wax to' and goes with a noun for a concrete object. In (10), the use of *another of measles* highlights the ambiguity of *case*, since *another* refers back to *case*, but is meant to be interpreted using a different sense of *case* ('instance of a disease') than the first sense we come across in the sentence ('box containing a certain number of items'). The weirdness of these sentences indicates that two different senses are operating for *wax* and *case*, and thus these words are ambiguous. Compare this to the situation in (11), in which there is no problem in understanding both *one* and *another* as referring to friends, even though the referents differ in gender.

(11)   One of my friends is a policewoman and another is a fireman.

This, then, provides further evidence that there is one sense of *friend* that is vague with respect to gender – if it were not, we would have a funny zeugmatic effect here.

Puzzle 5–2

The form that a zeugma takes depends on the grammatical and semantic categories of the word in question. In the case of (9), the zeugma arose because two items (*patriotic*, *truck*) both had the same type of relation (argument) to the verb, but they required different senses of the verb in order for the verb–argument combinations to be interpretable. In other cases, pronouns or other forms that indicate co-reference, like *another* in (10), create the zeugmatic effect because they are interpreted as having a different sense from the instance of the word that they refer back to (the **antecedent** of the pronoun). For each of the following ambiguous words, try to come up with a suitable zeugma that demonstrates the difference of the senses given.

a.   *file*, verb: 'to smooth a hard material with a tool,' 'to put into a folder'
b.   *high*, adjective: 'affected by narcotic drugs,' 'significantly above the ground'
c.   *mouth*, noun: 'place where a river enters the sea,' 'opening in the lower face'

5.2.2   Polysemy vs. homonymy

Now that we have seen how vagueness differs from ambiguity, the next task is to differentiate between two sources of ambiguity: homonymy and polysemy. *Sole* in (12) is ambiguous.

(12)   Hypermart is the **sole** distributor.

There are at least three possible interpretations of *sole* in this sentence, as listed in (13).

(13)   *sole$_1$*   'the bottom surface of a shoe'
        sole$_2$ 'only'
        sole$_3$ 'a type of flatfish'

Example (12) might be saying that Hypermart distributes shoe parts ($sole_1$) or fish ($sole_3$), or it could be the only company to distribute something else ($sole_2$). Sentence (14) demonstrates that all three senses can be used without making one another redundant. This is another indication of ambiguity.

(14)   Hypermart is the $sole_2$ $sole_3$ $sole_1$ distributor.

In this case Hypermart is either the only distributor of shoe-bottoms for flatfish, or the only distributor of shoe-bottoms made of flatfish. Each *sole* makes its own contribution.

   Sole is a homonym: that is, there are three lexemes that happen to have the form *sole*. We label the the different lexemes using subscripted numbers, as in (13), in order to refer to them unambiguously in our discussion. (Note that dictionaries also use sub/super-scripted numerals to differentiate homonyms.) But why should we believe that the three senses of *sole* indicate three entirely separate lexemes that happen to be called *sole*? There are a few clues. First of all, there would be no reason for a language to develop a single word that means all these three things at once, since they have nothing to do with each other. Even if we could come up with a story for why the senses might be connected, there is historical evidence that at least the first two are not related: $sole_1$ comes from the Latin word *solea* 'sandal,' while $sole_2$ derives from a different Latin word *solus* 'alone.' These unrelated words only started to look related in English because changes over the centuries robbed them of their final syllables. The fish and the shoe-part senses have some historical origins in common, since they both come from *solea*, possibly because the fish resembles a sandal. However, since most present-day English speakers don't know about that link, it is not very relevant to their mental lexicons.

   The grammatical properties of the words provide further evidence of their separate status. $Sole_2$ is an adjective, while the other two are nouns. The two nouns have different morphological properties, making them seem even more dissimilar: the plural of $sole_1$ is *soles*, but the plural of $sole_3$ is *sole*. Thus, we can be fairly confident that the three *sole*s are homonyms, since English speakers do not seem to be using or perceiving them as a single lexeme.

   On the other hand, the other source of lexical ambiguity, **polysemy**, involves a single word with several senses. This can come about because existing senses branch out to become new senses. So, in the case of polysemy, we expect that the different senses are related in some way – you can figure out *why* the word came to have this range of senses. This can be seen in the example of *coat*:

(15)   *coat*   a. 'an outer garment with sleeves for wearing outdoors'
                      b. 'an animal's covering of fur'
                      c. 'a covering of paint or similar material'

There are three senses here, but they seem related, since they all involve an outer layer on something. The 'garment' sense came first historically, and then, by extension, people also used it to refer to other kinds of coverings. One might wonder if instead *coat* is vague and has only one general sense that means 'a covering.' In that case, the specific uses of *coat* to refer to the types of things in (15) would follow from that general sense. But notice that these senses are special: each of these kinds of things that can be called *coat* is really different from the other kinds of things that can be called *coat*. These particular senses of *coat* have become conventionalized, so that we use *coat* more readily for these things than for other types of coverings. For example, we speak naturally of *a coat of paint* but not *a coat of wallpaper* (we instead call that covering *a layer*). If it were a case of a vague 'covering' sense that's applied broadly, then we would expect it to be natural to call any covering a *coat*.

Sentence (16) demonstrates that *coat* has at least two senses:[1]

(16)   The desk has three coats on it.

If *coat* just vaguely meant 'covering' in general, this sentence would not give you enough information to form a picture of what the desk looks like with three coats on it – the coats could be tablecloths or blotter pads or anything else that one might use to cover a desk. But, without any further contextual information, the most natural way to interpret this sentence is to see a desk with three garments draped upon it. With a little more contextual prodding, we might prefer to interpret *coat* in the 'paint/varnish' sense:

(17)   The desk has three coats on it, but I still don't think it looks finished.

But if we try to understand it as having both the garment and paint senses at once, we get a zeugma effect:

(18)   # The desk has three coats on it – two parkas and one of walnut varnish.

Notice that in order to get the 'outerwear' or 'paint' senses in (16) or (17), you do not actually have to mention clothing or paint. That specific information has to be coming from the word *coat*, since there is nothing else in the sentence that indicates clothing or paint. But note that all of these senses of *coat* are still, in themselves, vague to some degree. For example, *coat* in its garment sense does not specify whether the garment in question is a fur coat or a lab coat or a raincoat.

Regular polysemy

A variety of polysemy that gets a fair amount of linguistic attention is **regular** (also called **systematic**) polysemy. This refers to word senses that are distinct, but which follow a general pattern or rule in the language. For example, words

---

[1] The 'on an animal' sense is difficult to get in this sentential context, since if a coat is separated from an animal, we tend to call it a *pelt* or a *hide*. Substitute *dog* for *desk* in this sentence, and you can see another two- or three-way ambiguity.

for containers can generally refer to both a kind of container and the contents of the container, as can be seen in (19):

(19)   **'container' sense**:   I put some sand into a box/bottle/tin/canister.
        'contents' sense: I dumped the whole box/bottle/tin/canister onto the floor.

The relation between the 'container' and 'contents' senses is completely regular, which is to say it is entirely predictable. If we invent a new kind of container, we can be certain that the name of the container will also be able to denote its contents in some situations. Other cases of regular polysemy can vary in their regularity, however. For instance, the names of dances can also name a piece of music that accompanies such dances for some cases, as shown in (20), but not so much for others, as in (21).

(20)   I'd like to hear a salsa/tango/waltz.

(21)   #I'd like to hear a break-dance/disco.

5.2.3   Interim summary – distinguishing types of meaning variation

In this section, we have identified three sources of meaning variation. If a word form is vague, then it has a general sense that can apply to various types of referents, but if it is ambiguous, then it has more than one sense and could be either a homonym or a polyseme. Figure 5.1 summarizes how to distinguish these phenomena.

While these three terms all refer to cases in which the interpretation of a form differs in different contexts, they reflect kinds of relations or properties of lexemes/senses:

- **Vagueness** is a property that a sense of a single lexeme can have, that is, the property of generality.
- **Polysemy** is a relation between senses associated with a single lexeme.
- **Homonymy** is a relation between different lexemes that are coincidentally similar in form.

Since vagueness, polysemy, and homonymy apply at different levels of consideration (single sense, single lexeme, different lexemes), it is sometimes the case that a single word form can illustrate all of these phenomena. So, the fact that *sole* is a homonym does not preclude the possibility that any of its senses might also be polysemous and that some of its senses may be vague. For instance, $sole_1$ ('bottom of shoe') is homonymous with $sole_2$ ('only'), and it is also polysemous in that it can mean both 'bottom part of a shoe' and 'bottom part of a foot.' Furthermore, the 'bottom part of a shoe' sense might be vague in some respects – for instance it does not specify the material the sole is made from, and so could be used to refer to both rubber soles and leather ones.

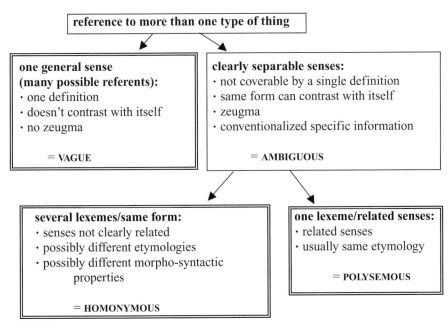

Figure 5.1 *Types of meaning variation*

5.2.4   Three categories, or a continuum?

Up to this point, we have taken a traditional view of the ways in which a form can have more than one "meaning," including some tests to tell which of these cases involve homonyms, a polyseme, or just a vague sense. These kinds of distinctions are recorded in most dictionaries: homonyms are in separate entries; polysemes have several, usually numbered senses within the word's entry; and vague senses are defined in suitably general ways. But in reality it is often difficult to judge whether two interpretations of a word form constitute a case of homonymy or polysemy or vagueness. Polysemes are supposed to have related senses, but different people have different views of what is related and how related two senses have to be in order to be "related enough" for polysemy. Dictionaries tend to rely on etymological criteria to determine which lexemes are homonyms, but (as already mentioned) historical facts are not always relevant to mental lexicons, since you do not have to know a word's history to have a lexical entry for it. Vague terms are supposed to have a general definition, but, as we saw for *coat*, sometimes you can make a general definition covering several uses of the word (e.g. 'a covering'), but other tests show the meanings to be more distinct. To give another example, I assumed for years that the word *ear* was a polyseme that could mean 'an organ for hearing' or 'a cob (of corn).' It seemed to me that cobs of corn came to be called *ears* (in North America at least) because they stick out from the stalk the same way that our ears stick out from our heads. But later I found out that (a) many people do not see a similarity between the two senses, and (b) the words for hearing organs and corncobs are not etymologically related. The historically different forms are better preserved in German (a relative of English), where they are *Ohr* and *Ähre*, respectively. On etymological grounds and in other people's minds, *ear* is a homonym. But is it right to say that it's necessarily a homonym in the lexicon of someone who sees them as related concepts?

These kinds of problems have led some to reject a firm distinction between homonymy, polysemy, and vagueness. David Tuggy (1993) has argued for treating these concepts as lying on a continuum – from maximal distinctness (homonymy) to maximal similarity, also known as **monosemy**, the state of having one meaning. Tuggy's ideas are situated in the Cognitive Linguistics framework, and involve relations between semantic structures, phonological forms, and generalized conceptual representations. This works similarly to the Conceptual Semantics approach to the lexicon that we saw in figure 4.1 in chapter 4, although the particulars of conceptual representation are different in Cognitive Linguistics and Conceptual Semantics. In order to get the gist of Tuggy's ideas, they're presented here in a less technical way than in his paper.

At one end of the meaning–variation continuum are cases like *bat*, which are truly ambiguous; *bat* can denote sticks or mammals and the senses do not overlap at all. In this case, we have two senses linked to one form, but any conceptual representation that could unite the two senses would have to be nearly empty because there is no common concept that covers the 'stick' and 'mammal' interpretations of *bat*. Perhaps it would indicate that it's a concept for some kinds of things that can move or be moved fast through the air. Meanwhile, these two uses of *bat* are known in the speech community as distinct senses; those senses are conventionalized. In the illustrations below, the bigger/bolder the type, the more **entrenched** – that is, well-learnt and easily activated in the mind – a concept or word is. The figure in (22) shows that the conceptual information related to two senses of *bat* is distant and indistinct, while the two senses are in bold to show that they are well entrenched as conventionally distinct uses of the word.

(22)

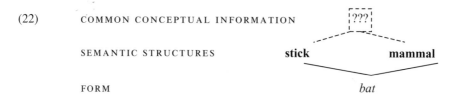

COMMON CONCEPTUAL INFORMATION	???
SEMANTIC STRUCTURES	**stick** **mammal**
FORM	*bat*

Further along the continuum are pairs of meanings that are designated by the same word form but have separate senses for which a common conceptual representation is available, like *coat*. In (23) we can see two separate senses (at the SEMANTIC STRUCTURES level) linked to a general, common notion, that of COVERING.

(23)   COMMON CONCEPTUAL INFORMATION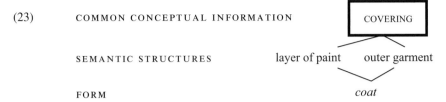

Vagueness involves two semantic structures that are not well entrenched as separate senses, and which have very strong, very close links to an elaborate shared concept, such as the case of *friend* in (24).

(24)   COMMON CONCEPTUAL INFORMATION

These three cases illustrate the beginning, middle, and end of the continuum, and we could add other examples that come between them, as shown in figure 5.2. All of these types of meaning variation are defined using the same types of structures and relations between them, but differ in the strengths of entrenchment and semantic relatedness found in those structures. For example, the interpretations of *book* as 'dictionary' or 'novel' are more distinct from one another than the 'female' and 'male' interpretations of *friend*, since there are cases in which *book* is used to just denote novels. For instance, if you are going to the beach and want to bring *a good book*, you are likely to mean the type of book with a story, not a dictionary (no matter how good that dictionary is!). Even more distinct are the two senses of *coat*, for which the separate senses are more conventionalized.

Since we do not expect that all speakers in all English-speaking communities have grasped every lexeme or concept in the same way, we could suppose that some items (like *ear*) might lie at different points in the continuum for different speakers. Thus, viewing polysemy as a continuum seems to be both consistent with the types of meaning variation that we see in language and with a mentalistic approach to meaning.

< conceptual distinctness   conceptual similarity >

< more entrenched   less entrenched >

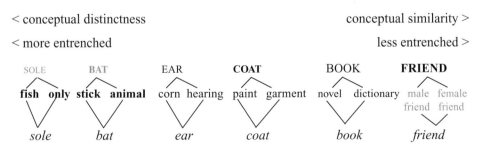

Figure 5.2 *Continuum of meaning variation*

5.3   Meaning variation and language change

Why is there so much meaning variation in language? Some of it serves particular purposes, and some of it is accidental. Vagueness exists because it is useful for us to have general ways of referring to things: the only way not to be vague would be to have a unique name for everything in the world, which would mean that we'd spend our whole lives learning our vocabulary and we would not be able to generalize about things by using words to refer to all members of the same category (since every word would denote a category of exactly one thing). So, most words (except for proper names) start out with some allowance for vagueness. Polysemy exists because it is fruitful to use old words in new ways, rather than having to learn new words all the time. We can usually extend words' meanings in predictable ways, using a number of processes that we'll discuss below, and thus people hearing an old word that is used in a new way will be able to appreciate the newly created meaning. Homonymy can develop through accident or through more severe processes in change of meaning. The following subsections consider the processes that give rise to homonymy and polysemy, starting with "co-incidental" sources of homonymy, and moving on to more regular processes of meaning extension.

5.3.1   Sources of "coincidental" homonymy

Homonymy arises in language mostly through coincidence or because the senses of a polyseme have become so separated from each other over time that we no longer perceive them as the same. One kind of coincidental homonymy arises from changes in the language that bring different words closer together in form. We have seen one example of this already: *ear*, whose body-part and grain (e.g. *ear of corn*) meanings have completely different historical roots and were originally pronounced differently. Similarly, the musical genre *pop* is a clipping from *popular music* and has nothing to do with the use of *pop* as an affectionate term for a father (from *papa*), or as the onomatopoetic verb for the action of bursting something like a balloon or a bubble. Each of these meanings of *pop* evolved in its own way and just happened to end up sounding and looking like one another.

The same situation holds when we borrow words from other languages that happen to be the same as existing words. For example, *yen* meaning 'yearning' (as in *I have a yen for fine whiskies*) already existed in English when *yen*, the currency of Japan, was borrowed into the language, so the two *yen*s are homonyms.

5.3.2   Processes of semantic change

We frequently assign new senses to old words. For instance, if someone were walking around putting cherries on people's heads, I could say to them *Cherry me next!* and we'd understand *cherry* to mean 'put a cherry on someone's head.' A semantic change occurs when a new use of an old word becomes con-ventionalized through repeated use (which is unlikely to happen for that sense of *cherry*, I must admit). If the word retains its old sense, then it becomes pol-ysemous. If the two senses later drift apart (for instance, if we start substituting gooseberries for the cherries, but keep saying *cherry*), then the lexeme may divide into two homonyms. Sometimes, the old sense is overshadowed by the new sense (or falls out of use for some other reason), in which case polysemy is just a stage in the transition from old meaning to new meaning. For example, *undertaker* originally meant anyone who undertakes some business for someone else, and this could include funeral preparations. Gradually, the broader sense of *undertaker* has been forgotten and it has become specialized to mean 'someone who undertakes funeral preparations for others.' Since the original sense has essentially died out, *undertaker* is not polysemous between the 'any job' and 'funeral' senses for most English speakers today. But the fact that so many words are polysemous shows that semantic changes often add meanings to the language without subtracting any.

Puzzle 5–3

To see how common it is for old words to gain new senses, have a look at a computer. How many of its parts and functions have names that used to (and probably still do) mean something else? How many have names that are neologisms (completely new words)? Are any of the neologisms homonyms or homophones of old words?

There are several ways in which an old word can develop a new sense, including: metonymy, metaphor, broadening/narrowing, conversion, and grammaticaliza-tion.

Metonymy is when a word is used to refer to something that is related to something else that the word can denote. For example, we might say that a farmer has *three hands* working for him. In this case, *hands* refers to laborers – i.e. people who use their hands – rather than to a body part. Similarly, we can refer to things or people by referring to the place where they are, as when we refer to a monarch as *the throne* or the American film industry as *Hollywood*. Another example involves using the same word to refer to plants and the food they produce, as can be seen in the two senses of *carrots* in (25):

(25) a.   Grover ate the **carrots**. (= 'edible root of the carrot plant')
     b.   Grover watered the **carrots**. (= 'carrot plant')

Metonymy can be used productively to create figurative language in a particular context. For example, on discovering a case of double-parking, a car owner might exclaim *Someone's blocked me in!* The *me* in this sentence means 'my car.' But if you look up *me* in a dictionary, you will not find the sense 'the speaker's car,' because that particular interpretation is absolutely dependent on the context.

Lexical change, resulting in polysemy in the lexicon, occurs when the new sense becomes conventionalized, as it has for *hand* 'laborer.'

Puzzle 5–4

We have seen that *hand* can be used to mean *person*. How many other body parts can refer to a whole person/body?

Like metonymy, **metaphor** is a means of using language figuratively, which can either be used in **nonce** (one-off) conditions, or can be conventionalized to create new cases of polysemy. Metaphor involves seeing similarities between different things and describing one as if it were the other. We can see an example of conventionalized metaphor in another sense of *hand*: as in *the hands of a clock*. Here the metaphor plays on the similarities between the hands on people and the pointers on a clock. Most of the polysemous computer terms that you came up with for Puzzle 5–3 are probably metaphorical. A computer mouse is so-called because it resembles a live mouse in terms of its shape and the way it "scurries." When we put files into a computer folder, we can see the similarity to putting papers into a cardboard folder in a filing cabinet.

Another way in which words can have different senses is if they are **autohyponyms** (see also §6.3.2): that is, if one of the word's senses is a more specific version of another of its senses. Historically speaking, this can happen through the **broadening** or **narrowing** of one of the word's senses. For example, the verb *drink* can mean 'consume liquid by mouth' or 'consume alcohol by mouth,' as in (26) and (27), respectively.

(26)   After surgery, Jen could only drink through a straw.

(27)   After his liver transplant, George swore never to drink again.

In this case, the 'consume alcohol' sense in (27) is a subcategory of the 'consume liquid' sense in (26) – the original 'liquid' meaning has been narrowed. An example of broadening is *Yankee*, which in its original meaning denotes specifically people from the northern United States (in contrast to those from the South), but now can also denote someone from any part of the US, in contrast to those from other countries.

Finally, words can also take on new senses by changing their grammatical category, for example from noun to verb, or, on a grander scale, from content word to function word. If a word keeps the same form (that is, it doesn't have a prefix or suffix and keeps the same pronunciation) when it changes from one category to another, then it has undergone a process known as **conversion** (or **zero derivation**). For instance, verbs expressing emotional or mental states can often be used as nouns for those states: *love, hope, fear*. In the noun-to-verb direction, all of the following names for liquids can also be verbs: *paint, oil, water, milk*. Have you noticed that one of these is not like the others? While the verbs *paint*, *oil*, and *water* all have senses relating to putting the liquid on/in something, the verb sense for *milk* involves taking the liquid out of something (an animal). In these cases, conversion from noun to verb has added some meaning, and we can see patterns in how lexical items in one category change when they are converted to other categories (see also chapter 7). Generally, conversions can happen from any lexical word class to another, though they tend to happen to morphologically simple words. For example, there is little point in making a verb out of the morphologically complex noun *denial* since there is already a morphologically simple verb *deny* to do the job.

You'll know from experience that conversion happens quite easily in English. For instance, recent technologies have spurred on noun-to-verb conversions like *to Google* 'to search for a word or phrase using the Google search engine,' *to friend* 'to select someone as your friend on a social networking site,' *to text* 'to send a text message.' Much rarer and slower are cases of **grammaticalization**, in which lexical content words change to grammatical function words or functional morphemes – yet this is how languages get most of their function words. For example, the modal verb *will*, which we use as a future tense marker, has come to modern English from the Old English lexical verb *willan*, which meant 'want (to do something).'

How did this happen? Well, if you want to do something, then you are probably talking about a future action. For example, if I say *I want to eat lunch*, I'm not eating lunch at the moment, but there is a good chance I will eat it in the near future. So the seeds of 'futureness' were already there in *willan*. The verb already appears before other verbs, so it is in the right position to be interpreted as an auxiliary verb. Over generations of learners, people paid less and less attention to the lexical 'want' aspect of the meaning and focused on the futureness of it – until the lexical meaning was mostly forgotten. This process is known as **semantic bleaching**, since the main force of the meaning has been washed away. The future marker *will* went a long way in its grammaticalization – losing all the grammatical markings of a lexical verb. Thus, as (28) shows, unlike the lexical verb *want* that *willan* was originally like, *will* does not appear with tense or agreement marking (the *-s* on *wants*) or an infinitive marker (*to*) on the following verb. And, again, unlike *want*, it cannot appear with a modal verb (in standard dialects of English).

(28)   *Ira wills to go home. (*vs.* Ira wants to go home.)

(29)   *Ira can will go home. (*vs.* Ira can want to go home.)

In other cases, we can see semi-grammaticalization – which may mean that we're still on the path to grammaticalizing a form. For instance, Romaine and Lange (1991) have suggested that the use of *like* to introduce reported speech, as in (30), is on its way to being grammaticalized as a 'quotative complementizer' – that is, a grammatical morpheme that links a main clause to a quotation.

(30)   Jody was like 'I can't believe it!'

Because it is still in the early stages of grammaticalization, the grammatical status of quotative *like* is hard to define (is it an adverb? a preposition? a complementizer?) and it still retains some of its comparative lexical meaning, in that we seem to be saying that Jody in (30) said something like *I can't believe it*, but didn't necessarily say it in those words or in the same manner as the reporter of the utterance has said it. But the prediction is that *like* will become much more regular in use and lose the association with comparison as it becomes more grammaticalized over the years. By the time that grammaticalization is finished, we should perceive the quotative *like* as a different word from the comparative preposition *like* in *days like this*. That is to say, it will become different enough from its original use that the relation between comparative *like* and quotative *like* will be a clear case of homonymy, rather than polysemy. For this reason too, we see the future marker *will* as a homonym of the 'document for expressing wishes in the event of one's death' *will*, although historically they come from the same verb.

In this section, we have seen a lot of ways in which words expand their uses and how they sometimes split off into being different words altogether. Now that we have described the range of phenomena that are related to meaning variation, let's look at how some semantic theories have tried to account for the fact that the relation between word form and word meaning is not one-to-one.

5.4   Approaches to polysemy

Theoretical approaches to polysemy are many, though different theorists often focus on different cases or limit their definitions of polysemy in particular ways. We can divide approaches to polysemy into two basic camps. The **monosemy position** holds that there is no need to represent multiple senses of lexemes in the mind. In this approach, each word is associated with a single, general semantic representation, which is elaborated as a more specific interpretation according to the context in which it occurs. The **polysemy position** holds that the different senses of a word must be separately represented in the mind. In the subsections below, we look at an example each of these types of approaches and their pros and cons.

5.4.1   A monosemy approach: GL

Generally speaking, monosemy approaches explain the relations between the senses of a polysemous word by stating that those senses are derived "on-line" from a single semantic representation of the word. This may be done in a number of ways, but we'll look at how it is done in Generative Lexicon theory (Pustejovsky 1995).

As its name suggests, Generative Lexicon theory holds that new senses can be "generated" from existing ones in the lexicon via a number of types of semantic transformations. As discussed in §4.3, GL represents lexical senses through a complex of structures, including argument structure and qualia, and these in turn build phrasal meanings. The lexical entry for a word gives specific information about what type of event or thing it describes. These entries may be **under-specified**, in that they leave out some information that needs to be filled in by context, or **overspecified**, that is, containing information that is relevant to different senses of the word, but not necessarily to all senses of the word. Pustejovsky (1995:62) says his approach "enable[s] us to conflate different word senses into a single *meta-entry*," and he calls these lexical "meta-entries" **lexical-conceptual paradigms** (lcps).

Overspecification: dot objects

Overspecification, provision of "too much" information in a lexical entry, is evident in the way that GL treats some polysemous nouns as simultaneously representing two types of things. These are called **dot-objects** because a dot is used to indicate the combination of these types, as can be seen in the top line of the Qualia Structure for *book* in (31). Here, the dot between **info** and **physobj** shows us that *book* represents a lexical-conceptual paradigm (lcp) that belongs both to the class of things that are physical objects and to the class of things that are information. In other words, a book can be considered to be a 'text' (the information communicated by the book) or a 'tome' (pages bound in a cover).

(31)

$$
\begin{bmatrix}
\textbf{book} \\[1em]
\text{ARGSTR} = \begin{bmatrix} \text{ARG1} = \textbf{x:info} \\ \text{ARG2} = \textbf{y:physobj} \end{bmatrix} \\[2em]
\text{QUALIA} = \begin{bmatrix} \textbf{info.physobj\_lcp} \\ \text{FORMAL} = \textbf{hold (y, x)} \\ \text{TELIC} = \textbf{read (e, w, x.y)} \\ \text{AGENT} = \textbf{write (e', v, x.y)} \end{bmatrix}
\end{bmatrix}
$$

(Pustejovsky 1995:101)

The Argument Structure (ARGSTR) for *book* shows that a book can take part in events either as information (**x**) or as a physical object (**y**). *Book*'s FORMAL quale shows the relation between those aspects: the physical object (**y**) holds the information (**x**). But when you read or write a book, both aspects are activated, as indicated by the dotted representation of **x.y** in the TELIC and AGENTIVE qualia. In such contexts, the sense incorporates both 'text' and 'tome' aspects of books. Because *book* belongs to the class of physical objects, we can use it with any verb that requires a physical object, as in (32). Similarly, with verbs that require an informational object, we'll understand *book* to denote 'text,' as in (33).

(32)   I kicked/threw/tore the book.

(33)   I agree/disagree with that book.

Semantic transformations: type coercion

The other main way to account for meaning variation in GL is through **semantic transformations**, through which the underspecified representation of one lexical item is elaborated through information in another item in the sentence. One type of semantic transformation is **type coercion**, in which context-particular senses of words arise through the interaction of semantic structures in phrases. Take, for example, (34) and the related sentences below:

(34)   Tallulah began the book.

(35)   Tallulah began reading the book.

(36)   Tallulah began writing the book.

(37)   Tallulah began burning the book.

Sentence (34) can usually be understood to mean the same thing as (35) or (36), but would not usually be used to mean (37). GL explains this by appealing to the information in the ARGSTR of *begin* and the FORMAL and TELIC QUALIA of *book*. The ARGSTR for *begin* in (38) tells us that beginning requires a person (x) and an event (e_2) – i.e. person x *begins* event e_2.

(38)

$$
\begin{bmatrix}
\textbf{\textit{begin}} \\[4pt]
\text{EVENT STR} \ = \ \begin{bmatrix} E_1 \ = \ e_1\text{:transition} \\ E_2 \ = \ e_2\text{:transition} \end{bmatrix} \\[10pt]
\text{ARGSTR} \quad = \ \begin{bmatrix} \text{ARG}1 \ = \ x\text{:human} \\ \text{ARG}2 \ = \ e_2 \end{bmatrix} \\[10pt]
\text{QUALIA} \quad = \ \begin{bmatrix} \text{FORMAL} \ = \ P(e_2, x) \\ \text{AGENTIVE} \ = \ \text{begin\_act}\,(e_1, x, e_2) \end{bmatrix}
\end{bmatrix}
$$

(adapted from Pustejovsky 1995:116)

This is straightforward for (35)–(37), since *Tallulah* describes a person and the verbs *reading*, *writing*, and *burning* describe events. But the object of *begin* in (34) describes a thing (*book*), not an event. Since *begin* requires an event, an event interpretation is **coerced** from *book*. This is only possible because event types (indicated by **e** and **é**) are included in the QUALIA for *book* (shown above in

(31)). Since the types of events specified for *book* are READING and WRITING (but not burning or eating), they are the ones that come to mind when we need to interpret *book* as an event.

Selective binding, another type of GL semantic transformation, is discussed in chapter 11, and Pustejovsky (1995) describes further types of semantic transformations.

Evaluating the GL approach

Monosemy approaches like this one are attractive because of their explanatory value and elegance. They are explanatory in that they show how two interpretations of a word are related and why the same word has been used to communicate these meanings. They are elegant because they allow for a simpler lexicon – instead of requiring that many senses of a word must be recorded in the mental lexicon, multiple interpretations are derived from a single semantic representation.

Despite their elegance, some monosemy approaches are criticized for downplaying the amount and range of polysemy found in natural language. Notice that the variant interpretations of *begin* and *book* (as a reading event or a writing event) in (34) are not what is usually counted as polysemy: dictionaries do not list specific senses of *begin*: ('begin to eat,' 'begin to read,' etc.). Instead, most dictionaries assume that these are cases of vagueness. GL's monosemy approach explains how such vague words are interpreted in context, and the notion of dot-objects helps explain some cases of polysemy (e.g. 'text' and 'tome' senses of *book*), but it is less clear that GL has anything to say about other cases that are traditionally considered to be polysemy, such as the senses of *coat* discussed in §5.2. For instance, because most cases of metaphorical meaning generation are irregular, GL must treat them as homonyms (with separate lexical entries), rather than as polysemes. This means that GL lumps together word forms with separate but related senses (e.g. *coat* = 'outer garment' and 'layer of paint') and word forms with separate and completely unrelated senses (*sole* = 'fish' and 'only') as "non-polysemous."

5.4.2   A polysemy approach: networks of senses

While monosemy approaches hold that multiple senses can be predictably derived from a single semantic representation, polysemy approaches hold that each different sense of a polyseme requires its own semantic representation. Unsurprisingly, then, while monosemy approaches tend to highlight sense variations that are part of regular patterns, polysemy approaches tend to highlight the more irregular cases – such as those created through metaphor.

An increasingly common way of approaching these irregular cases is to view concepts as complex mental representations that can be viewed from different perspectives or with different conceptual "filters" that allow focus onto just certain aspects of these complex mental representations. George Lakoff (1987) used the example of *mother*. In a most prototypical scenario, a mother is a woman who is related to another person by:

(a)   giving birth to them
(b)   contributing to their genetic material
(c)   nurturing and raising them
(d)   being their closest female ancestor
(e)   being married to their father

Each of these aspects of prototypical MOTHERHOOD can be used as the basis for other uses of the word *mother*. When referring to "non-prototypical" mothers, only some of these properties are relevant, such as (c) and possibly (e) for adoptive mothers, and (e) and possibly (c) for stepmothers. But we can also see how different aspects of MOTHERHOOD are relevant to other uses of the word *mother*, uses that we would call different senses of *mother* rather than non-prototypical instantiations of the core sense. For example, if we say that a woman *mothers* her boyfriend, it means she takes a nurturing role, focusing on (c). A *mother* in a syntactic tree is the node immediately above another node – i.e. its closest 'ancestor' (d), and a *mother lode* in a mine is the source that 'gives birth' to an ore (a). In this way, subsequent senses of *mother* are based on different aspects of motherhood, but these come about through convention, rather than being derived by rules. That is, we do not automatically use just any extension of the sense of *mother* based on (a) through (e), but the ones that have become established among a language's users. So, for example, while a car exhaust pipe could be said to 'give birth to' exhaust fumes, we could not call that a *mother* and expect others to understand us, since that sense has not been conventionalized in our community.

Lakoff called concepts like MOTHER **radial concepts**, since the other interpretations of *mother* "radiate" from the different aspects of the concept. This notion of "radiation" from key aspects of a concept is illustrated well in figure 5.3, part of the treatment of *crawl* by Fillmore and Atkins (2000), based in an approach called Frame Semantics. At the heart of the diagram is the core concept of crawling as 'moving while holding one's body close to the ground,' but there are several conditions in which crawling happens: by people or creatures, deliberately or due to injury. The link between being injured and crawling leads to associations between crawling and moving slowly and with effort – thus we extend *crawl* so that it has senses that indicate the slow movement of time or of traffic. While it does not show all twenty of the senses that Fillmore and Atkins found for *crawl*, figure 5.3 gives an idea of how a network of related senses might look.

Fillmore and Atkins' paper also provides a polysemy network for the French *ramper* 'crawl,' showing the ways in which its polysemy patterns differ from those of English *crawl*. While both words can be used for creatures teeming and for groveling, the French word is not used for the senses associated with slowness. They attribute this to different core concepts for *crawl* and *ramper*, with *ramper*

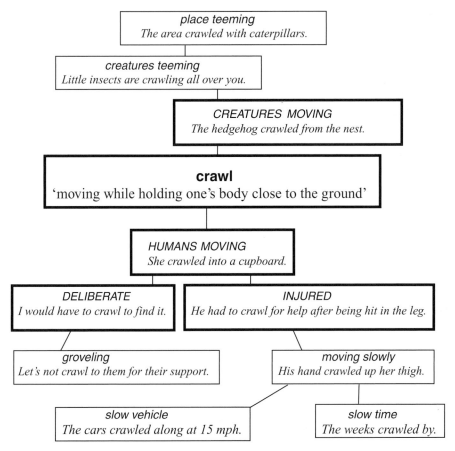

Figure 5.3 *Partial polysemy network for* crawl

focusing more on how the low body covers more space than an upright body, whereas *crawl* focuses more on the use of limbs to propel oneself – thus snakes *crawl* in English and *ramper* in French, yet babies *crawl* in English, but do not *ramper* in French (see Fillmore and Atkins 2000 for more details).

Evaluating the polysemy network approach

Fillmore and Atkins did their detailed study of *crawl* and *ramper* by first searching English and French corpora for uses of the words, then dividing these examples into groups that had the same or related senses, comparing these to dictionaries, and fashioning their network. One of their aims is to bridge the divide between theoretical linguistics and practical lexicography. While the monosemy approach discussed above sought to make generalizations across classes of words (such as how adjectives are interpreted differently with different nouns), the polysemy approach usually involves looking more deeply at individual lexemes and the full range of their senses.

Polysemy approaches like this one do not concentrate on predictable kinds of polysemy like those covered by the GL approach (e.g. the fact that *begin* is interpreted differently in *begin a book* and *begin lunch*). A network like the one in figure 5.3 can describe the polysemy of a word, but it cannot predict what new senses might be added some day. A thorough analysis of a word to identify its core sense and related senses may, however, allow us to gauge what new senses are unlikely. For instance, the differences between the core senses of English *crawl* and French *ramper* may lead us to predict that a computer mouse would be more likely to *ramper* than to *crawl*.

Critics might also question whether too many sense distinctions are made in this type of approach and whether the methods for distinguishing them are too subjective. For example, figure 5.3 shows both '[moving as a] slow vehicle' and 'moving slowly' senses of *crawl*, whereas another investigator might have considered these to be the same sense.

5.5   Summary and conclusion

We have seen in this chapter that polysemy is a central issue in lexical semantics, but that it can be tricky to define, since the interpretation of a linguistic form can vary due to vagueness (unspecific senses) or homonymy (coincidentally similar word forms) as well as polysemy. Because these three phenomena are not always clearly distinguishable, a continuum among them has been proposed. Theoretical approaches to polysemy fall into two schools of thought: (a) that the senses of a word can be derived by predictable processes from a single semantic representation (the monosemy position) or (b) that the senses of a word have separate, albeit connected, representations (the polysemy position). The proponents of these positions tend to focus on different types of polysemes, and so it is possible that these are really different phenomena, requiring different approaches.

5.6   Further reading

Ravin and Leacock's (2000) edited volume *Polysemy* contains a good introduction to the theoretical issues surrounding polysemy (chapter 1), as well as chapters on ambiguity tests and subtypes of polysemy by Alan Cruse (2000a) and the case study of *crawl*'s polysemy by Fillmore and Atkins. The basics of Cruse's discussion can also be found in his textbook *Meaning and Language* (2000b, chapter 6). As well as the Tuggy article discussed earlier, Geeraerts (1993) discusses the problems in positing a distinction between polysemy and vagueness. For a primer on the Frame Semantics approach, see Hamm (2009).

5.7   Answers to puzzles

5-1

Julia first understands *friend* to mean 'a person with whom one has a relationship of mutual affection,' but Jane indicates that this interpretation is not what she intended and emphasizes *friend* to show she wants Julia to understand a different interpretation of *friend*. When Julia understands this, she switches to talking about a man. However, this does not mean that *friend* has a female sense in the first instance and a male sense in the second. Instead, the other sense of *friend* (often pronounced with special emphasis) is 'person with whom one has a romantic/sexual relationship.' This sense can refer to a male or a female; it just happened to refer to a man in this dialogue because Julia is (apparently) in a heterosexual relationship.

5-2

Everyone will make up different examples for this puzzle. The key point is whether they sound "funny" because of the clash between the two senses of the words. Here are some examples:

a.   # I filed my nails and the papers.
b.   # One goat is high on the mountain and the other on cocaine.
c.   # The mouth of the Mississippi is bigger than mine.

5-3

There are many possible answers to this question, but here's a list to get you started. All of the following words had other senses before coming to have computer-oriented senses: *mouse, monitor, drive, disk, keyboard, port, window, program, buttons, web, file, folder, link, chat, mail, alias, menu, clipboard, bug, virus, worm.* New words to do with computers include: *software, hardware*, RAM, CD-ROM, *byte. Bit*, which is a blend of *binary digit*, is a homonym with *bit* meaning 'a small piece' – but you might be forgiven for thinking that it is a case of semantic change via polysemy since both meanings refer to small amounts (in the case of *binary digit*, it is a small amount of information in binary code). If we think about pronunciation only, RAM is a homophone of *ram*, and *byte* is a homophone of *bite*. If you're not sure about any of your answers, the etymology information in a good dictionary might help you make up your mind.

5-4

There are undoubtedly more examples than the following, but these can get you started:

a.   The university wants more **bums/bottoms** on seats.
b.   The teacher counted **heads** at the start of each class.
c.   What this gallery needs is a new **pair of eyes**.
d.   Get your sorry **ass/arse** in here.

5.8   Exercises

Adopt-a-word

A.   Use your word to illustrate the differences between (and tests for diagnosing) homonymy, polysemy, and vagueness (NB: Your word may not be a homonym, but you should still demonstrate that it is not). While using dictionaries might be helpful, note that they differ and that you should make your own conclusions about whether two interpretations of your word are different senses or not. Do your findings provide evidence for a continuum, like that described by Tuggy (§5.2.1)?

B.   Present a Fillmore–Atkin-style network diagram (see fig. 5.3) of the senses of your word. Start either with a collection of uses of your word from a corpus or with at least two dictionaries' treatments of your word. Make sure to show (a) the core concept for your word, (b) the relations between the senses, and (c) examples for each sense.

C.   Use the web or a corpus to find ten examples of your word's use. If there are hundreds of hits, use every tenth example. Using a standard desktop dictionary, determine which, if any, of the senses given by the dictionary go with each of the ten senses. Discuss whether dictionary coverage of your word shows its entire range of senses. If it does not, discuss whether this is appropriate to the dictionary's purpose/audience or not.

General exercises

1.   Are the following polysemes or homonyms? What kinds of evidence can be used to support your answer?

a.	*duck*	'an aquatic bird'	'to lower one's head'
b.	*pig*	'a farm animal with a curly tail'	'a glutton'
c.	*circle*	'a shape with all points equidistant from the center'	'a group of people' (e.g. *a reading circle*)
d.	*flyer*	'something that flies'	'a small handbill announcing an event'
e.	*drop*	'to let (something) fall'	'a portion of liquid' (e.g. *rain drop, eye drops*)

2. A **monosemy approach** to polysemy holds that a word's senses can all be generated from a single semantic representation. For example, we can make rules to describe the relations between the senses of *bottle* in the following examples:

a. I set the **bottle** on the table. [*bottle* = 'type of container']
b. I put a **bottle** in my drawing. [*bottle* = 'representation of a bottle']
c. I drank the whole **bottle**. [*bottle* = 'contents of a bottle']

If we start with sense (a), then two rules can be hypothesized to account for the new senses. These rules are **regular** in that they can apply to any word with a certain feature.

[physical object] → 'representation of physical object'
i.e. any word that has 'physical object' as part of its sense can be used to mean 'representation of that physical object,' as in (b).

[container] → 'contents of container'
i.e. any word that has 'container' as part of its sense can be used to mean 'contents of that container.'

We can test our rules by seeing whether indeed any word for a physical object (*cat*, *mountain*, *toenail*) can be used to mean 'a representation of x,' and whether any word for a container (*can*, *box*, *envelope*) can be used to mean 'the contents of x.'

Consider the following sentences (and their most culturally appropriate senses):

d. **Geography** is the study of the physical features of Earth.
e. **Geography** meets in this room on Thursdays.
f. You can't make much money in **geography**.
g. We have to consider the **geography** of the area that will be mined.

Discuss the following:

- What does *geography* mean in each of these sentences? Give a definition or paraphrase of its sense for each sentence.
- Develop rules (like those above) to predict how *geography* can have sense (d) but also senses (e) and (f). Make the rules as general as possible (i.e. applying to as large a class of words as possible), and give examples of other words in these patterns to demonstrate the generality of your rules.
- Is sense (g) related by regular polysemy to sense (d)?

6   Lexical and semantic relations

Key words: PARADIGMATIC, SYNTAGMATIC, SEMANTIC RELATION, LEXICAL RELATION, SYNONYM, CONTRAST, ANTONYM, COMPLEMENTARY, CONTRARY, CONVERSE, HYPONYM, HYPERONYM, MERONYM, HOLONYM, DICTIONARY APPROACH, THESAURUS APPROACH, SEMANTIC FIELD, LEXICAL BLOCKING

6.1   Overview

This chapter examines particular semantic relations among words. They are called **semantic relations** because they are relations between senses. Some cases of semantic relation can also be **lexical relations** in which it is not just the meanings that are related, but also other aspects of the lexemes, like morphological form or collocational patterns. After looking at the details of synonymy, hyponymy, antonymy, and other relations, we evaluate two approaches to the representation of semantic relations in the mental lexicon. In the first approach, the lexicon is theorized to be like a dictionary, which records senses but not necessarily relations among them. The second views the lexicon like a thesaurus, in which relations, but not meanings, are represented.

6.2   Paradigmatic relations: synonymy, antonymy, hyponymy

6.2.1   Paradigmatic vs. syntagmatic

Relations among words can be divided roughly into two types: paradigmatic and syntagmatic. **Syntagmatic relations** are relations between words that go together in syntactic phrases – like *ship's* and *captain* or *dogs* and *bark*. Notice that *syntagmatic* and *syntax* are from the same Greek roots, meaning 'touching together' – in other words, words in syntagmatic relations "touch" each other in phrases. Because they go together in phrases, syntagmatically related words often belong to different word classes – e.g. *dog* (noun) + *bark* (verb). Syntagmatic relations are studied more and more these days as corpus research highlights the ways in which words tend to occur with certain words rather than others. For instance, we can notice that the adjective *asleep* goes with certain modifiers to indicate 'absolute state of sleep,' as in *fast asleep* or *sound asleep*, and that it occasionally goes with some other general-purpose modifiers that indicate the same meaning, like *completely asleep*, but less with others, like *very asleep*. Our focus in this chapter is the more traditional area of study for lexical semantics: paradigmatic relations. We'll see some syntagmatic issues in the later chapters – including the issue of which modifiers go with which adjectives, in chapter 11.

Words in **paradigmatic relations** belong to the same word class and share some characteristics in common. The words in such relations can be said to form a **paradigm** – that is, a set of examples that show a pattern. One kind of paradigmatic relation is a morphological paradigm, such as the tense forms of a verb: *drink, drank, drunk*. Notice that the verbs in this paradigm have everything in common *except* their tense. We are interested in semantic paradigms, which involve word senses that share many semantic properties, but differ in some. So, for example, the set of basic color adjectives forms a paradigm whose members each refer to a different part of the color spectrum. Unlike syntagmatically related words, paradigmatically related words are usually substitutable for each other. For example, *red*, *white*, and any other member of the color paradigm can sensibly and grammatically occur in the same phrases, as in (1) and (2).

(1)   a red/white/green/blue house

(2)   a shade of red/white/green/blue

Lexical semanticists study paradigmatic relations because of their roles in logical relations among sentence meanings, such as entailment (see §2.2), and because of what they might tell us about how the mental lexicon is organized, as we'll see in §6.3. They are also interesting for their use in creating coherent discourse. Using related words allows us to describe the same things in different ways, thus providing varied information and avoiding repetition in discourse.

A few paradigmatic relations receive the most attention in lexical semantics. **Synonymy** is the relation of having (nearly) the same meaning. *Couch* and *sofa* are synonyms in many people's dialects. **Hyponymy** is the 'type-of' relation; for example, *house* is a hyponym of *building* because a house is a type of building. **Co-hyponymy** (sometimes called **lexical contrast**) involves a group of senses that make up a set, but which contrast with one another, for example *heart/club/spade/diamond*. That is, they are different varieties within a single type – in this case, playing card suits. **Antonymy** is a special case of contrast in which two words are opposites, for example *black/white*. We examine each of these relations in more depth in the following subsections.

While people often talk about *words* being synonyms or antonyms, it is more accurate to talk about *senses* or *lexical units* (form + sense-in-use – see §1.2.4) as being synonyms or antonyms, since a single word may have different synonyms or antonyms for different senses. For instance, when using the 'temperature' sense of *hot*, its opposite is *cold*, but when using the 'spicy' sense of *hot*, its opposite is *mild*. For this reason, semantic relations are sometimes called **sense relations**.

6.2.2   Synonymy

The term *synonym* comes from Greek roots *syn* 'alike' and *onym* 'name.' It refers to words that mean the same as each other, so the equals sign = is used to signal synonymy. Because it is rare for two words to have exactly the same meaning/use, discussions of synonymy frequently concern words that are not perfect synonyms, but that differ only slightly. The **substitutability test** is used to determine whether two words are synonyms. Words are substitutable if there is no change in the meaning of a sentence when one word is substituted for the other. So, for example, if the truth of (3) entails the truth of (4), and vice versa, then we have evidence that *person* and *human* are synonyms.

(3)   A person is standing beside me.

(4)   A human is standing beside me.

If we want to test whether *man* is a synonym for *person*, then we can compare (5) and (3).

(5)   A man is standing beside me.

In this case, since we can conclude that sometimes it would be true that a person is standing beside me at the same time when it is false that a man is standing beside me – since there things that can be referred to as *person* that cannot be called *man* – namely, women, girls, and boys. Hence *man* and *person* are not synonyms.

Absolute vs. sense synonyms

Words are said to be **absolute synonyms** if they are substitutable in any possible context with no changes in denotation or other aspects of meaning (including connotation – see §2.2.2). Using that criterion, it is easy to see that very few words are absolute synonyms. Take for example, *funny = peculiar* and *funny = comical*. Where *peculiar* is substitutable for *funny*, as in (6), *comical* probably is not substitutable and vice versa, as in (7).

(6)   My tummy feels a bit funny (= peculiar, ≠ comical) whenever I eat fish.

(7)   Anna told a hilariously funny (≠ peculiar, = comical) joke.

Funny has different synonyms in different contexts because it is polysemous, and its various senses match up semantically with different sets of words. Since they do not share all their senses, *funny* and *peculiar* are not absolute synonyms, and neither are *funny* and *comical*. Instead, they are **sense synonyms**, in that they each have one sense that means the same as one of the other word's senses.

> ### Puzzle 6–1
>
> For each of the following pairs, demonstrate that the two words are not absolute synonyms by giving a sentence in which they are not substitutable for each other. Describe why they are not substitutable (i.e. how their senses differ).
>
> a.   safe, secure
> b.   fake, false
> c.   big, large
> d.   (a tough one!) somebody, someone

The existence of large thesauruses proves that English has plenty of words that are very close in meaning. But if we look closely at those words, it is very rare to find pairs that are perfectly synonymous, even for just one of their senses. You may feel that *funny* and *comical* never mean exactly the same thing, so that *a funny joke* is a slightly different kind of joke than *a comical joke*. Roy Harris (1973:12–13) has gone so far as to claim that "If we believe there are instances where two expressions cannot be differentiated in respect of meaning, we must be deceiving ourselves." The rare candidates for perfect synonymy tend to be technical names for things like plants, animals, and chemicals. An example is *furze = gorse = whin*, which all name the same European evergreen plant. An American example is *groundhog = woodchuck*, which name the same animal. I leave it to you to decide whether you think, as Harris would, that I'm deceiving myself in claiming that these are perfectly synonymous.

Near-synonyms and variants

Far more common is for words' senses to overlap and be **near-synonyms**, like *fake ≈ false* in Puzzle 6–1. (We can use ≈ to signal near-synonymy.) Near-synonyms (in a particular sense) can often substitute for each other in some contexts, but not every context. An example is *obtain* and *acquire*, which pass the substitution test in (8), but fail it in (9). This is because *obtain* and *acquire* both have a sense that roughly means 'get,' but there are subtleties to those senses that are not shared by both words.

(8)   Ian **obtained/acquired** three diplomas.

(9) a.   Ian **obtained** permission to land. [?acquired]
   b.   Ian **acquired** a British accent. [#obtained]

So far, we have seen that so-called synonyms may differ from one another by being polysemous in different ways (i.e. sense synonyms that are not absolute synonyms) or by not having the exact same denotation (near-synonyms). Synonyms that are denotationally identical may still be different in non-denotational ways – for example, by belonging to different dialects, registers, or by having different connotations. So, we could say that the synonyms for *toilet facilities* are not strictly substitutable because the sentences in (10) would not be equally appropriate in all social contexts.

(10) a.   Where is the **john**?
   b.   Where is the **lavatory**?
   c.   Where is the **powder room**?

John, *lavatory*, and *powder room* are sense synonyms because they denote the same things, but because they differ in register and connotation, they are **variants** of one another. Synonyms can be variants with respect to any number of non-denotational properties, including connotation, register, dialect, and affect. The American sense of *bathroom* (which can refer to a room with a toilet but no bath) and British *loo* (which refers to a room with a toilet) are sense near-synonyms, but dialectal variants.

Why so many synonyms?

The moral of the synonym story is that it is very rare for two words to mean exactly the same thing. As Cruse (1986:270) has noted, "languages abhor absolute synonyms just as nature abhors a vacuum." English has many near-synonyms because it has readily borrowed words from other languages and because English productively makes new open-class words through the morphological processes of derivation and compounding (§1.3.4) and conversion (§5.3.2).

   In some cases, those new or borrowed words start out as perfect synonyms for existing words in the language, but over time one of two things generally happens. In some cases one of the synonyms "wins" and the other drops out of use. For example, the Greek-derived *Eucharist* began to replace the Old English *husl* toward the end of the Middle Ages, and now *husl* is obsolete. In other cases, the words' senses diverge. A famous example is what happened when Norman French words for certain livestock animals were borrowed into English in the Middle Ages. Before that point, English speakers had words for these animals and used them also to describe meat from those animals; so they ate *ox* or *sheep* or *pig flesh*. After the French words for livestock became available, English speakers came to use the French livestock words (which became anglicized as *beef, mutton, pork*) to refer to meat, while the native English words were retained for denoting the animals. Other animal words were not affected by French borrowings, either because the French word was not popularized in English (in the case of *lamb*) or because the word was added to the language later (in the case of *turkey*). Synonyms are also found in cases where one word is reserved for technical registers while the other sounds more folksy or poetic. For example, the Latinate *uterus* is a more "medical" sounding word than *womb*, which is more likely to be used in poetry.

   Languages react to synonyms in this way for a number of reasons. First, it is not economical or helpful to have many words for the same thing – it takes more effort to learn and remember two word forms when one is sufficient. When we go through the effort of having two words, we usually work under the assumption of a **principle of contrast** – that different linguistic forms are associated with different meanings. This means that if we come across a word that seems to mean the same thing as another word we already know, we expect it to have some difference – in denotation, connotation, or social meaning – from the other word. Clark and Clark (1979) give examples of when the common process of making nouns into verbs results in a new lexeme that contrasts with the extant verb, as for *to cook* and *to chef* in (11):

(11) a.   Phil cooked up a feast.
     b.   Phil chef'd up a feast.

To cook is an established verb, but if we read a new verb *to chef* that ostensibly denotes the same activity as *to cook*, then we presume it must mean something a little different than *cook*. For instance, one might interpret (11b) as connoting more professionalism or panache on Phil's part than (11a) does.

   In summary, while languages resist synonymy, they can nevertheless tolerate words that are very close in meaning. Having words that overlap in meaning can be seen as enriching, rather than duplicating, our vocabulary. While English is said to be particularly synonym-rich, this should not be taken to say it is more expressive than languages with fewer synonyms, since subtle differences in meaning can be conveyed as well through other syntactic, morphological, and paralinguistic (e.g. intonational, gestural) means.

6.2.3   Hyponymy and hyperonymy: inclusion relations

         Another type of paradigmatic relation involves meanings that contain, or are contained in, other meanings – or, to put it a different way, when the extension (§2.3.1) of one word is a subset of the extension of another. For example, the extension of *cheddar* is a subset of the extension of *cheese*; everything that is cheddar is also cheese, but everything that is cheese is not necessarily cheddar (since it could be gouda or mozzarella or feta instead). We could say then that cheddar is a type of cheese, and that the meaning 'cheese' is included in the meaning of *cheddar*.

Properties of inclusion relations

The inclusion relation is **asymmetrical**; cheddar is a type of cheese, but cheese is not a type of cheddar, so we need different names for the two directions in the relation: *cheddar* is a **hyponym** of *cheese*, and *cheese* is a **hyperonym** of *cheddar*. These terms come from the Greek-derived prefixes *hypo-* 'under' and *hyper-* 'over,' and this under/over imagery is useful in picturing hyponym paradigms as "family trees," as illustrated in figure 6.1, which shows the systematic classification, or **taxonomy**, of foods (with particular attention to cheese). Strictly speaking, we use the terms *hyponym* and *hyperonym* when speaking about the relations between words like *cheese* and *cheddar*. If we talk about cheese or cheddar itself, or the notion of CHEESE or CHEDDAR (rather than the words for

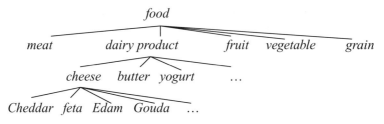

Figure 6.1 *A partial taxonomy of food, particularly* cheese

them), we refer to **superordinate** and **subordinate** categories. So, we can say that the word *cheese* is a hyperonym of the word *cheddar* and that the category CHEESE is superordinate to the category CHEDDAR. We can abbreviate this with < and >: *cheddar* < *cheese* and *cheese* > *cheddar*. The symbol always points toward the smaller category. Figure 6.1 shows that while one word may have several hyponyms, each hyponym has only one immediate (i.e. on the next level up) hyperonym.

As well as being asymmetrical, the inclusion relation is often said to be **transitive**, which is to say that if X < Y and Y < Z, then X < Z. For example, cheddar is a type of cheese and cheese is a type of food, therefore cheddar is a type of food too. But this is where defining hyponymy gets tricky, since not all 'type-of' relations are transitive, as (12) shows:

(12) a.   a specimen cup (as used for urine samples) is a type of cup
    b.   a cup is a type of drinking vessel
    c.   #!! a specimen cup is a type of drinking vessel

The intransitivity of *specimen cup* < *cup* < *drinking vessel* stems from the fact that the 'type-of' relations in (12a) and (12b) are not the same. The relation in (12a) involves proper inclusion; that is, the meaning *cup* is included in the meaning *specimen cup* – a cup is a container with a wide, round opening and a low profile that can hold liquids, and a specimen cup is a particular kind of low container with a wide/round opening. On the other hand, (12b) is not proper inclusion – the meaning of *cup* does not include the meaning of *drinking vessel* – instead a cup is an example of something that can be used as a drinking vessel. Cruse (1986) calls the proper-inclusion type of hyponymy **taxonymy** (since these are the relations found in classic taxonomies), while the case in (12b) can be called **functional hyponymy**, since we can say 'is used as' rather than 'is a type of' in describing the relation. Besides functional hyponymy, there are other types of hyponymy that many would not consider to be 'true' hyponymy. As Cruse (2000b) notes, all queens are women, but it's a bit funny to say *a queen is a type of woman* (but less funny to say *a queen is a type of monarch*). In other words, we'd probably not list *queen* in the same taxonomy in which we have the term *woman*, so *queen* < *woman* is not a taxonymic relation, while *queen* < *monarch* is. We can think of taxonyms as prototypical hyponyms, since they are reliably transitive and are easiest to describe in the terms 'X is a type of Y.'

Puzzle 6–2

The inclusion/taxonym relation is **asymmetrical** and **transitive**. Reconsider synonymy in light of these terms. Is synonymy symmetrical or asymmetrical? Transitive or intransitive? Is your answer the same for perfect synonyms and near-synonyms?

Folk vs. scientific taxonomies and the basic level

An important thing to notice about taxonomies is that the levels are not equally valuable to us on an everyday basis. *Dairy product* is somewhat artificial as a hyperonym for *cheese*. In everyday language we would probably say that *cheese* is a type of *food*, but in the language of supermarket managers, *dairy product* is a much-needed lexeme that allows for a contrast between the category that cheese belongs to and the one that potatoes belong to. The everyday kind of taxonomy that goes straight from *cheese* to *food* is called a **folk taxonomy**, while in more specialist contexts, we might need more elaborate taxonomies with more fine-grained levels of classification. For instance, in everyday situations, we are happy to say *a dog is a type of animal*, but a zoologist might need to specify *dog < canine < mammal < vertebrate < animal*. No matter how many levels a taxonomy has, though, the same principles generally apply.

Even among the smaller number of levels in folk taxonomy, one level is more salient – i.e. more readily used and noticed – than the others. Sticking with the *cheese* example, notice that if you make a sandwich out of cheddar, you are likely to call it a *cheese sandwich* rather than a *cheddar sandwich*. If you saw a picture of cheddar, you would probably say it was a *picture of cheese*. Even though you have more specific information about the nature of the cheese, you are likely to call it *cheese* rather than *cheddar* in many situations. We would not use more general names in these situations either; you would not say a *food sandwich* or a *dairy-product sandwich*. There is a level between too specific and too general that we generally attend to, called the **basic level**.

Rosch (1978) and others have noted that the basic level is special, both in linguistic and cognitive terms. In cognitive terms, the basic level is the level at which we notice and can easily differentiate between types of things. At the linguistic level, the names for basic level items tend to be more basic themselves – one morpheme rather than more – and are the terms we learn first. Some of the recognized properties of basic level items/terms are summarized in table 6.1.

Table 6.1 *Properties of the basic-level category* CHEESE *and the basic-level word* cheese

Typical properties of basic-level categories

Similarity of shape	food (superordinate): different shapes
	cheeses (basic level): similar shapes
	cheddars (subordinate): shapes that are indistinguishable from one another
Similarity of motor movements	food: meat, cheese, ice cream, nuts (etc.) are prepared and eaten with different motions
	cheeses: prepared and eaten with similar motions
	cheddars: prepared and eaten with identical motions

Typical properties of basic-level words

Most frequently used	*food*: used when referring to mixed collections of food (e.g. the contents of a grocery bag), but rarely used to refer to *cheese* specifically
	cheese: occurs about 5 times per million words in English
	cheddar: occurs less than 1 time per million words in English (Dahl 1979)
Most readily used	If shown a picture of some cheddar, most people say *it's cheese*, rather than *it's food* or *it's cheddar*.
Morphologically simple	superordinate: *dairy product* = 2 morphemes
	basic-level: *cheese* = 1
	subordinate: we often use compounds like *cheddar cheese* (2 morphemes) or *goat's cheese* (3 morphemes)
Earliest learned	Children learn to name *cheese* before hyperonyms *food* or *dairy product* or hyponyms *cheddar*, *feta*, etc.

Thus we can conclude that while we describe things at many different taxonomic levels, all levels are not created equal. The basic level is perceptually more salient, and therefore the most unmarked (i.e. morphologically simplest and most broadly used) level, linguistically speaking.

Hyponymy and word classes

So far, all of our examples of hyponymy have been nouns, and this is typical in discussions of hyponymy, raising the question of whether inclusion relations exist in other word classes. Certainly, it is more natural to use nouns in *X is a type of Y* statements, as shown in (13).

(13) a.   Cheddar is a type of cheese. [nouns]
     b.   ? To march is a type of to walk. [verbs]
     c.   ? Nauseated is a type of ill. [adjectives]

Cruse (1986) proposes that we test for hyponymy in verbs using the test sentence *Xing is a way of Ying* instead. We could extend this to adjectives by using the copular ("linking") verb *being*, as in (14b).

(14) a.   Marching is a way of walking.
    b.   Being nauseated is a way of being ill.

But while we can identify hyponym relations for verbs and adjectives, their taxonomies do not tend to have as many levels as noun taxonomies have. For example, it is hard to think of more verbs that could go on either end of the inclusion chain *marching* < *walking* < *moving* and even harder to think of what a hyperonym for *ill* could be. You might suggest that it would be something like *state of health*, but notice that *state of health* is a noun phrase, so not really in paradigmatic relation to *ill*. Lyons (1977) refers to relations like these, which cross word-class boundaries, as **quasi-hyponymy**. In chapter 10 we look at other types of inclusion relations for verbs.

Is hyponymy a lexical relation?

While inclusion relations are definitely relevant to the discussion of lexical semantics, it is not clear that such relations are specifically lexical in nature. This is to say that the relation between the words *cheese* and *cheddar* is a direct reflection of the relation between concepts (and the objects) CHEESE and CHEDDAR. The words are in a hyponym relation simply because the things that they denote are related by inclusion relations. Compare this to synonymy, for which denotative meaning is only part of the story – we noted that words are not "good" (i.e. fully substitutable) synonyms unless they match on issues like connotation, register, and dialect as well as denotative meaning. Hyponym relations are less sensitive to these non-denotational issues. It is true to say that *a kitty is a type of animal*, even though *kitty* and *animal* differ in register. We might prefer to say that *a cat is a type of animal*, just because it is odd to use a non-standard word in a pronouncement of *X being a type of Y*, but that does not change the fact that something called *kitty* is just as much an animal as something called *cat*. For this reason, it can be said that synonymy (and, as we shall see, antonymy) is both a **semantic** (i.e. denotational sense) **relation** and a **lexical** (word) **relation**, since it involves similarity on both denotational and non-denotational levels, but hyponymy is just a semantic relation.

6.2.4   Incompatibility, antonymy, and contrast

The relations discussed so far hold between words that denote overlapping categories. **Incompatibility** is the logical relation between words that cannot denote the same thing. So, for example, *flower* and *equation* are incompatible, as there are no flowers that are also equations – in fact, there is little that links flowers and equations. More interesting to us are cases of incompatibility that constitute semantic paradigms. Of these, the most discussed is **antonymy**, the

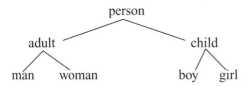

Figure 6.2 *Age/sex taxonomy for person categories*

relation of oppositeness, which holds between pairs of words, such as *black/white*, *old/young*, and *down/up*. (We use a slash "/" to signal incompatibility.) When the paradigm involves more than two words, it is called a **contrast set** or a set of **co-hyponyms** – that is, words that have the same hyperonym. We pay more attention here to antonymy, since it has particularly interesting properties.

Binarity

Antonymy is the only relation that is particularly **binary**– i.e. it holds between pairs of words. Any word sense can have more than one synonym (e.g. *furze = gorse = whin*) or hyponym (*cheese > {cheddar/gruyere/feta*, etc.}), but we tend to think of words as having only one antonym in any particular sense. In some cases, this is because there are only two co-hyponyms in a set, and so by default the contrast set is a pair. This is the case in the taxonomy in figure 6.2. In this case, *adult/child*, *man/woman*, and *boy/girl* can be considered to be antonym pairs because they are contrast sets of two. Pairs of antonyms can also arise through morphological derivation. English, for example, has several negating prefixes that can be used to create antonyms, such as **a**symmetrical, **in**frequent, **un**happy, **non**-partisan, and **dis**satisfied.

   In addition to these kinds of "natural" binarity, antonym pairs arise in cases in which a larger contrast set exists. For instance *black/white* belong to the larger set of achromatic colors *black/grey/white*, and *happy/sad* also contrast with *angry*, *afraid*, and *surprised*. Nevertheless, we oppose *black/white* and *happy/sad* as if there were no other possibilities. It seems that when people want to contrast things, they like to have just one other item to contrast it with. This raises the question of why we consider *black* the opposite of *white* instead of *grey*, and why *sad* is the opposite of *happy* rather than *angry*. You might answer that *black* is the opposite of *white* because it is more different from *white* than *grey* is, but that answer does not work so well for the *happy/sad/angry* problem since *sad* and *angry* are both very different from *happy*.

Minimal difference

The solution, on the contrary, is not how different the words are but how similar they are. For instance, *hot/cold* makes a better antonym pair than *hot/cool* because the senses of *hot* and *cold* are more similar to each other than the senses of *hot* and *cool* are. Antonymy is a relation between two lexemes that share all relevant properties except for one that causes them to be incompatible. This is to say that the meanings of antonyms are **minimally different** (Clark 1970). *Hot/cold* fits this definition better than *hot/cool*, since *hot* and *cold* have in common that they are both perceptions of temperature, and both are extremes on the temperature scale. They are different in that they are on opposite ends of the temperature scale. *Hot* and *cool* are both temperatures, but differ in both which side of the temperature scale they are on and whether or not they are extreme. As the basic componential analysis in (15) shows, *hot* and *cool* are less similar to each other than *hot* and *cold* are.

(15)

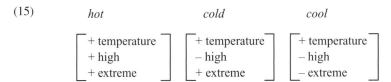

Similarly, *white* and *black* are antonyms because they are alike in that they denote extremes in the range of achromatic colors, but different in that they are at the opposite extremities of the color range, while *grey* is both a different color from *white* and *black* and not at an extreme point on the scale. And while *happy* contrasts with *sad* and *angry* and *surprised* and *afraid*, it seems to have the most in common with *sad*, since (among other reasons) *happy* and *sad* reflect states with reversed facial expressions (smile/frown) and postures (up/down). While these facial expressions and postures are different, since they are reversals of each other, they are similar (as opposed to expressions of anger and surprise, which are much more different expressions). In all these cases the principle of minimal difference allows for binary antonym pairs within a larger contrast set when two members within the set are perceived to be more similar to one another than to other members of the set.

Types of antonyms

There are several subtypes of antonym relation:

Contrary antonyms are those, like *short/tall* and *old/young*, in which the assertion of one entails the negation of the other, but the negation of one does not entail the assertion of the other, as illustrated in (16):

(16) a.   Gladys is tall. → Gladys is not short.
     b.   Gordon is not tall. ↛ Gordon is short.

Not tall does not entail *short* because *tall* and *short* do not describe all the heights that a thing or person could be. We can say that these contrary antonyms are **scalar** in that they describe the two extremes of a scale, as illustrated in figure 6.3. (A more sophisticated version of this scale is presented in the discussion of adjectives in chapter 11.) Each point on the line designates a height, which can be measured (e.g. 1 centimeter, 2 cm, 3 cm, . . .). The left and right extremes of the scale include *short* and *tall* heights, but the middle area includes height measurements that are neither tall nor short. So, *Gordon is not tall* does not entail

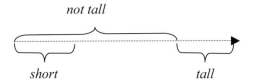

Figure 6.3 *Height scale (preliminary version)*

Gordon is short because he could have an unremarkable height instead. Thus *tall* and *short* constitute a contrary pair. Some authors (e.g. Lyons 1977, Cruse 1986) reserve the name *antonym* for precisely this type of scalar (or **gradable**) contrary relation.

Complementary (also called **contradictory**) antonyms are those for which the assertion of one entails the negation of the other and *vice versa*, as in (17).

(17) a.   That integer is even. → That integer is not odd.
    b.   That integer is not odd. → That integer is even.

In other words, the senses of complementary antonyms completely bisect some domain: every integer is either odd or even; there is no middle ground.

Not all adjectival antonyms fit so nicely into these categories. So-called **gradable complementaries**, like *dishonest/honest*, lie between complementarity and contrariety. They seem to contradict each other (*X is not honest* entails *X is dishonest*, and *vice versa*), but a middle ground seems to exist, since we can assert that some person is *neither honest nor dishonest*. Even classic examples of complementarity, like *dead/alive*, sometimes take on gradable qualities (e.g. *he's more dead than alive*).

Contrariety and complementarity are often discussed with reference to adjectives (see also chapter 11), although we can find contrary and complementary antonyms in other parts of speech. For example, *love/hate* (noun or verb) are contraries, whereas the verbs *stay/go* are in a complementary relation.

Converse antonyms describe the same relation or activity from different perspectives, and follow patterns like: if X is *p* to Y, then Y is *q* to X. Sometimes one needs to make adjustments to this test pattern in order to form a grammatical sentence, as the examples in (18) show. For example since Bill (X) is a parent (*p*) to Madeline (Y), Madeline (Y) is a child (*q*) of Bill's (X). In other words, Bill and Madeline have a relationship, and Bill's position in the relationship is *parent*, and Madeline's is *child*.

(18) a.   Bill is Madeline's **parent**. → Madeline is Bill's **child**.
    b.   John **gives to** Oxfam. → Oxfam **receives from** John.
    c.   Scotland is **above** England. → England is **below** Scotland.

Reversive opposites involve the undoing of some action: *tie/untie, construction/demolition*. Converse and reversive antonyms can be collected, along with other miscellaneous examples (e.g. *come/go*), in a general category of **directional** antonyms.

Some word pairs that are commonly considered opposites do not fit the above categories. For example, *learn/teach* seem to go together in a converse-like way, but they are not different perspectives on the same action, but rather two actions that typically co-occur. (They certainly do not always co-occur. *Lynne taught semantics to the students* does not entail that the students learned anything!) Other pairs of words that go together, such as *gin/tonic* can be argued to be minimally different (they are similar in being part of the same drink, but different in being alcoholic/non-alcoholic). However, many semanticists do not consider these to be proper antonyms since they cannot be described in terms of logical entailment relations like complementary, contrary, and converse relations can.

Some of these types of antonymy, including gradable contrariety and converseness, are necessarily binary relations, as they require either a scale with two ends or a relation with two perspectives. The notion of complementarity can be applied more generally in larger co-hyponym sets, though the test for complementarity has to be adapted to allow for more than one complementary possibility, as in (19):

(19) a. That ace is a club. → That ace is not a heart or a diamond or a spade.

b. That ace is not a club. → That ace is a heart or a diamond or a spade.

Puzzle 6–3

Determine whether the following antonym pairs are complementary, contrary, converse, or none of these. Briefly explain your answers.

a. *fast/slow*
b. *student/teacher*
c. *clean/dirty*
d. *female/male*
e. *feminine/masculine*

Is antonymy a lexical relation?

Finally, there is the question of whether antonymy, like hyponymy, is just a semantic relation or also a lexical relation, in which non-denotational properties of the words are relevant to the relation as well. Some opposite pairings do seem to be particularly lexical. If it were just the meanings that were relevant, then it should not make much difference whether *big* or *large* is the antonym of *little*. But ask anyone what the opposite of *little* is, and they will tell you it's *big*. This intuition is backed up by the fact that *big* and *little* occur together often in texts, but *large* and *little* do not (Muehleisen 1997). There are many similar examples; for instance, *dead/alive* seems "better" than *deceased/alive* and *ascend/descend* seems "better" than *rise/descend*. Since antonyms come in pairs, factors other than just meaning may come into play in determining the "best" antonym for a word, for instance morphological or phonological similarity (as for *ascend/descend*) and register (*deceased/alive*).

Because antonyms frequently co-occur in speech and writing, it is likely that we learn antonym pairs like *big/little* and *large/small*, and these get reinforced to the extent that we prefer them to other possible opposites like *large/little*. In this case, we are not just relying on our knowledge of the words' meanings to recognize their oppositeness; we are also relying on our knowledge of which words go together in language use. Some lexicologists use the term *opposite* to refer to the semantic relation and *antonym* specifically for opposites that are also lexically related. We are less likely to learn co-hyponym relations as lexical relations. Since whole large contrast sets do not co-occur in discourse as often as opposite pairs do, there is less opportunity to learn them as sets of related words. For instance, if I try to name the whole range of emotions, I get as far as *happy/sad/angry*, but then am less sure about which other items go on that list. (Which should I include: *afraid* or *frightened*? Is *surprised* in this contrast set?) However, some cases exist, like the playing card suits and scientific contrast sets, such as *solid/liquid/gas* and the prismatic colors, *red/orange/yellow/green/blue/indigo/violet*.

Further evidence that some opposites are also in a lexical antonym relationship comes from psycholinguistic experiments. Pairs like *high/low*, *happy/sad*, and *black/white* prime each other (§1.4.4), so that if you had just read *happy*, you would recognize the word *sad* much quicker than if you had not read *happy*. The same kind of test can show that a semantically opposite, but not lexically antonymous, word like *depressed* would not be recognized as fast as *sad* (Becker 1980). People are also quicker and more consistent in noticing the opposition between pairs like *happy/sad* than *happy/depressed* (Charles *et al.* 1994). This argues for a lexicological theory that represents the opposition of *happy/sad* in a more accessible way than *happy/depressed*, whose opposition we have to figure out on semantic grounds (see §6.3 below).

6.2.5   Other paradigmatic relations

Synonymy, hyponymy, and antonymy/contrast are the most important relations for semantic theories, but they are not the only paradigmatic semantic relations among words. We could name many more, like the relation between agents and the fields they work in (*teacher–education*, *actor–theatre*), organizations and their heads (*team–captain*, *club–president*, *committee–chair*), or the relations between animals and the sounds they make (*cow–moo*, *cat–meow*, *pig–oink*). Since these relations apply to relatively narrow ranges of vocabulary and have fewer logical implications, linguists have not bothered to give them *-onym* names.

An additional relation that has been named is the part–whole or 'has-a' relation, **meronymy**. Like inclusion, this is an asymmetrical relation, so we say that *finger* is a **meronym** of *hand* and *hand* is the **holonym** of *finger*. Also like hyponymy, meronymy does not rely on the lexical forms of the words – it is a direct reflex of the meanings of the words. Different subtypes of meronymy can be identified, such as **whole** > **segment** (*month* > *day*), **whole** > **functional component** (*car* > *engine*), **collection** > **member** (*pride* > *lion*), and **whole** > **substance** (*pipe* > *copper*). Meronymy is generally not thought to be as central to lexical/semantic organization as the other *-onym* relations. The relation between meronyms and holonyms is not as necessary as the relation between hyponyms and their hyperonyms. Many parts are optional (a wingless bird is still a bird) and the same part-names often apply to many different wholes – for instance, *handle* is always a part-name, but is not the part of any one particular kind of thing, since doors, jugs, suitcases, and hammers all have (very different) handles. Thus, while meronym relations can be helpful in defining words, they are not as widespread or as consistent as the other *'onym* relations.

6.2.6   Summary

Table 6.2 summarizes the facts about the relations discussed above.

Table 6.2 *Properties of paradigmatic relations*

	Synonym	Hyponym	Antonym	Co-hyponym	Meronym
semantic relation	similarity	inclusion	opposition	contrast	part/whole
binary	X	X	√	X	X
symmetrical	√	X	√	√	X
transitive	√	√ (taxonym)	not applicable	√	sometimes
lexical relation	√	X	often	sometimes	X

6.3   Two approaches to relations and the lexicon

Different schools of thought exist regarding the role of paradigmatic semantic relations in the mental lexicon. These can be classified according to whether the theory views the mental lexicon as more like a dictionary or more like a thesaurus. **Dictionary approaches** hold that the meanings of words are componentially represented in the mind – so these include the main approaches introduced in chapters 3 and 4 (e.g. Katz and Fodor 1963, Conceptual Semantics, Generative Lexicon theory). In this case, semantic relations do not need to be represented in the lexicon (i.e. nothing in the lexicon needs to say '*cold* is the antonym of *hot*') because those relations are derivable from the words' componential semantic representations. **Thesaurus approaches**, on the other hand, hold that semantic relations are represented in the lexicon. In this case, words (or senses) are linked to one another in order to indicate which words are synonyms, antonyms, and hyponyms of which other words. These mostly derive from the tradition of Structuralism that begins with Ferdinand de Saussure (1959/1915).

The most extreme thesaurus-style approaches hold that there are no definitions for words in the lexicon, as the meaning of a word can be derived from "the company it keeps" – i.e. which other words it is linked to. The following subsections exemplify these positions in turn, though it must be pointed out that many lexicologists take a middle ground, expecting that both definitional (dictionary) and relational (thesaurus) information is needed for a complete semantic representation of a lexeme.

6.3.1   Lexicon as dictionary

In chapter 3, we discussed the lexicon-as-dictionary metaphor in terms of how componential theories, like dictionaries, break down the meanings of lexemes into smaller parts. This means that the information needed for predicting synonym, hyponym, or antonym relations among words is available in their componential definitions. Thus most componential theorists take the view that the relations themselves do not need to be explicitly mentioned in the words' lexical entries. In other words, these theorists think that a representation like that in (20) is sufficient, so that the additional information in (21) is not necessary.

(20)   *man* [HUMAN, ADULT, MALE]

(21)   *man* ⌈ HUMAN, ADULT, MALE
             │ SEX ANTONYM = *woman*
             │ AGE ANTONYM = *boy*
             │ NEAR-SYNONYM = *gentleman, guy, chap, fellow*
             │ HYPONYM (MARITAL STATUS) = *bachelor*
             ⌊ HYPONYMS (JOB) = { *fireman, postman, handyman...* } ⌋

Approaches that do not include the relational information in (21) require another means of determining which lexemes are synonyms, antonyms, and hyponyms. This is done by specifying rules that determine these relations, such as those in (22):

(22) a.   X and Y are synonyms iff [i.e. 'if and only if'] they share all the same components
     b.   X and Y are antonyms (and/or co-hyponyms) iff only one of their components differs
     c.   X is the hyponym of Y iff it has all of the same components as Y, plus at least one more.

Using these rules, we can tell that *lady* (in the sense that denotes 'female adults' generally) is a synonym of *woman*, *man* is the opposite of *woman*, and *fireman* is a hyponym of *man*, as shown in figure 6.4.

Evaluating the dictionary approach

The dictionary approach is attractive because it explains why particular words are related to one another – that is, because they have semantic components in common. On the other hand, because it only concerns the words' semantic components, non-denotational properties (like the sound of a word or its social register) cannot contribute to these relations. So, according to the information

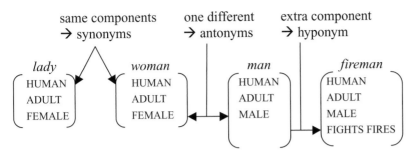

Figure 6.4 *Componential approach to semantic relations*

in figure 6.4, *lady* is as good an antonym for *man* as *woman* is. In other words, the classical componential theory only accounts for denotational semantic relations, and not for relations that involve other properties that words may have.

There have been attempts to extend the dictionary approach so that it considers non-denotational issues as well. For example, Murphy (2003) presents a pragmatic approach, in which words are related if, within a particular context, they share all relevant properties – including relevant non-denotational properties – except one. In the case of synonymy, the property that the words do not share is their form, and in the case of antonymy, it is typically an aspect of denotative meaning. The tricky part about this approach is deciding which properties are relevant or not within a context. (See Murphy 2003 for discussion.)

6.3.2   Lexicon as thesaurus

Theories that treat the lexicon as thesaurus-like hold that lexical entries (or sense subentries within them) are cross-referenced with or linked to other lexical entries (or sense subentries). Such models hold that the entry for *high* would somehow represent that its antonym is *low*. These models have their roots in Structuralist views of semantics (following on from Saussure and similar thinkers – e.g. Coseriu and Geckeler 1981), but have also been carried on in some computationally inspired approaches (e.g. Meaning-Text Theory, Mel'čuk 1996; WordNet, Fellbaum 1998b). Some proponents of thesaurus models aim to forgo componential sense representations altogether in favor of large networks of words that constrain one another's senses. In such models, because *high* and *low* are in the antonym relation, they are constrained to always denote the opposite ends of whatever scale they describe, and *high* will always refer to something different, but related, to *tall*, *long*, and *big*, since they are all types of SIZE.

Diagramming relations among words

One thesaurus-type approach is **Semantic Field Theory**, promoted by Adrienne Lehrer (1974). This approach can be illustrated by a **box diagram**, as in figure 6.5, in which each word cuts out some "semantic space" in a **semantic field** – an organization of related concepts.

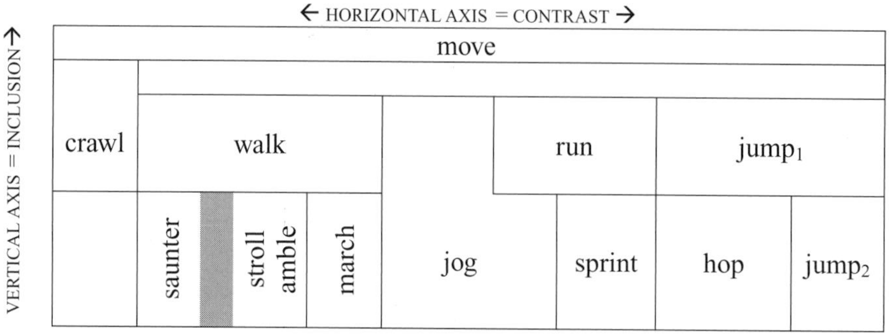

Figure 6.5 *Field representation for selected verbs of human locomotion*

Figure 6.5 gives a partial semantic field for English verbs of human locomotion, which shows all the relations that a box diagram can illustrate:

- The subscripted numerals on the two instances of *jump* indicate its polysemy. *Jump*₁ has a general sense 'to spring off the ground,' while *jump*₂ indicates springing and landing with both feet, as opposed to one foot, as for *hop*. *Jump*, then, is an **autohyponym**, a polysemous word that has a sense that is a hyponym of another of its senses.

- The horizontal axis represents contrast; if two lexemes on the same level are separated by a line, they contrast with each other and, transitively, with other words on that line. So, *crawl*, *walk*, *jog*, *run*, and *jump*₁ contrast as co-hyponyms of *move*. Note that some lexemes' boxes inhabit more than one level. *Jog*, for instance, is a member of two co-hyponym sets: *crawl/walk/jog/run/jump*₁ and *jog/sprint* (hyponyms of *run*). In other words, *jog* is sometimes used to contrast with *run* (as in *I don't run, I just jog*) and sometimes used to describe a kind of running (as in *When running, alternate jogging and sprinting for an extra good workout*).

- Viewing the vertical axis from the bottom up, we see hyponymy relations. So, *march* is a hyponym of *walk* and (transitively) of *move*. We've already seen that *jog* is a special case, as it has either *run* or *move* as its immediate hyperonym.

- Synonymy is indicated by two lexemes in the same box – as for *stroll* and *amble*. (They may not be perfect synonyms, but we can pretend that they are for the sake of this illustration.)

- Overlap in meaning (partial synonymy) is indicated where there is shading instead of a horizontal line between two terms, like *saunter* and *stroll–amble*. This means that some activities are definitely *sauntering* or *ambling* (but not both), but others (in the shaded area) could be called by either name.

- Blank areas in box diagrams show **lexical gaps**, which are potential senses that have not been lexicalized in a language. In this diagram, there is a box above *walk*, *jog*, *run*, and *jump* that contrasts with *crawl*. We can describe what that box symbolizes – the category of upright, bipedal locomotion – but there is no particular English lexeme that covers this meaning.

Box diagrams are also useful for comparing semantic fields across languages, in order to see differences in lexicalization.

Puzzle 6–4

Devise a box diagram for the following COLOR words.

red, *purple*, *yellow*, *blue*, *color*, *lavender*, *scarlet*, *orange*, *green*, *crimson*

To test your diagram:

- From the bottom up, ask yourself whether the lower words name 'types of' the above colors.
- Ask yourself whether all the color names on any horizontal level contrast with one another.

Alternatives to box diagrams include representing semantic relations as a network of senses with lines linking related senses (e.g. WordNet, Fellbaum 1998b) or by creating attribute–value matrices (see §3.2.1) in which lexical entries have features like ANTONYM and SYNONYM and the values specified for those features are other lexemes – as done in Meaning-Text Theory (MTT; Mel'čuk 1996). These are all fairly equivalent (e.g. the AVMs in MTT could be "translated" into a network diagram). The box diagram, however, gives a sense of the "semantic space" that the lexemes take up, so one can visualize certain uses of *walk* (e.g. to denote 'power walking') as closer to the *jog* boundary than other uses.

Evaluating the thesaurus approach

Proponents of thesaurus-style lexical models hold that the relations that one word has to others at least partly determines the word's sense. In other words, no meaning exists in a vacuum, instead meanings are created through relations. Box diagrams show these relations within the semantic field. Spaces are "carved out" for individual lexemes, and one can imagine the "tension" between words at their boundaries.

One type of evidence for the idea that lexical meaning depends on relations is the phenomenon known as **lexical blocking**, which can be exemplified by the meanings of *finger* and *thumb*, shown in the box diagram in figure 6.6. *Finger* can mean 'any digit of the hand', as in *I have ten fingers*. But that 'any digit' meaning is blocked when one refers to a single finger. So, if someone says *I broke my finger*, you would probably feel misled if you discovered that the finger in

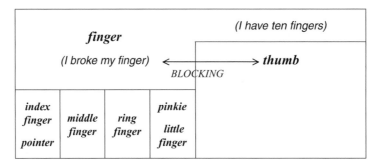

Figure 6.6 *Lexical blocking*

question was their thumb. In that case, you would have expected them to say *I broke my thumb*. The existence of *thumb* as a possible contrast term for *finger* **blocks** the interpretation of singular *finger* to mean 'thumb.' Thus we see that the semantic relations between *finger* and *thumb* affect how they are interpreted.

While thesaurus-style theorists have sometimes taken the extreme view that relations are all that is needed for meaning, no successful model of the lexicon has been able to rely on relations only and completely leave out any kind of definitional meaning. Figure 6.5 shows us that *walking* and *jumping* are different kinds of moving, but it does not tell us how to walk or jump. Similarly, if you looked at a box diagram of locomotion terms for a language you didn't know, you would be able to say which were the more general terms and which contrasted, but you probably would not be able to translate the words into English. This lack of definitional information has proved difficult for computational models that use thesaurus-style links among words. Most such models (like WordNet and MTT) include definitions as well as relations.

This raises the question: if thesaurus-style models require definitions, then why not just use a dictionary-style model, which has to have definitions anyway and which can account for relations by rules (as in (22) above)? The main argument in favor of representing semantic relations in the lexicon is that not all sense relations are completely predictable. In this case, their relations need to be represented in the lexicon, the repository of unpredictable facts about language. Recall the examples of antonymy like *big/little*, but not *large/little*, which seem to indicate that words' semantic properties are not sufficient to determine which of a range of synonyms will be its antonym. If that's the case and these relations are arbitrary to some degree, then they are facts about the language that must be recorded in the lexicon. Proponents of the dictionary view argue in reply that if you look closely enough, you can find semantic differences that predict, for example, that *big/little* is a better antonym pair than *large/little* because *big* and *little* are more *minimally* different than *large* and *little* (recall your solution to Puzzle 6–1c). But theorists with a thesaurus point-of-view might still reply that these words have developed slight variations in meaning precisely in order to accommodate the existing relations between them within their semantic field.

6.4   Summary and conclusion

This chapter introduced three major semantic relations – synonymy, hyponymy, and antonymy/contrast – their properties, subtypes, and problems in defining them. It also described and evaluated two approaches to the treatment of these relations. Dictionary-style accounts aim to predict relations on the basis of the words' semantic properties in the mental lexicon, while thesaurus-style accounts explicitly represent those relations in the lexicon. An accurate account of how the mental lexicon works is probably to be found somewhere between these extremes, since dictionary-style approaches cannot explain the effects of non-semantic properties (e.g. morphological form) on the "goodness" of these relations, and thesaurus-style approaches are not sufficient models of meaning on their own. We return to semantic relation issues when we examine inclusion relations for verbs in §10.6 and the connections between adjective meaning and antonym type in chapter 11.

6.5   Further reading

Textbooks by Lyons (1977, 1995) and Cruse (1986, 2000b) provide lots of detail and examples of the relations discussed here. Murphy (2003) includes discussion of the types and subtypes of relations, as well as extended discussion of history of the dictionary/thesaurus debate and of the importance of semantic relations in other fields, including philosophy, psychology, and computer science. Sources on the different thesaurus-style approaches are given in §6.3.2, but you can also explore WordNet on the web at http://wordnet.princeton.edu/.

6.6   Answers to puzzles

6–1

Your answers will vary, but here are some examples:

a.   *The car is safe/secure*. While both of these are acceptable sentences, they tend to mean different things. *The car is safe* means either that no harm will come to you if you drive it – or that the car is in a safe place (e.g. it won't be hit by a falling tree). *The car is secure* probably means that it is locked up and protected against thieves.

b.   *She was wearing fake/false teeth.* False teeth are dentures, used as a substitute for real teeth, but you might use fake teeth for a vampire costume.

c.   *A big/large movie star signed autographs.* A big star is very famous, but a large star is physically imposing.

---

d.   *I want to be a somebody/(#someone).* While these two words are usually substitutable, *somebody* (and not *someone*) has a noun use that means 'a significant person.'

6-2

Perfect sense synonymy is symmetrical and transitive. It is symmetrical since if *sofa = couch*, then *couch = sofa*, and transitive in that if *sleep = slumber* and *slumber = snooze*, then it should follow that *sleep = snooze*. However, because there are few perfect synonyms, there is often some "semantic slippage" among the near-synonyms that one can find in a thesaurus, which results in non-transitivity and sometimes even non-symmetry. It has been shown that if you look up a word in a thesaurus, then look up the synonyms of its synonyms (and so on), the synonym path between any word and its antonym is typically six steps or fewer, as is the case for *authentic/unauthentic* in *The New Collins Thesaurus* (reported in Church *et al.* 1994):

> *authentic → believable → probable → ostensible → pretended → spurious → unauthentic*

6-3

a.   contrary: things can have a 'medium' speed as well as being *fast* or *slow*.

b.   converse: if Max is Alice's teacher, then Alice is Max's student.

c.   contrary or complementary: sometimes *clean* is used to mean absolutely clean – in which case one speck of dirt renders something *dirty*. But when we are talking about, say, the state of someone's housekeeping, we often treat it as contrary – so that one could say that someone's house is neither clean nor dirty – it could be better or worse.

d.   usually assumed to be complementary: if someone told you that the university has 10,000 students, half of them female, you would assume that the other half is male. While states between maleness and femaleness are medically possible, we tend to ignore that possibility in our everyday use of the words.

e.   contrary: while *male* and *female* indicate a person's physiological sex, *feminine* and *masculine* describe behavior or appearance – and some people are neither feminine nor masculine in those respects.

6-4

A common mistake in this exercise is to put *orange* under or above *red* and *yellow*, since orange is 'made of' red and yellow. This 'made-of' relation may be relevant to paints that are orange and red, but not to the meaning of the words *orange* and *red*, which are in an overlapping, but contrasting, relation. The diagram should look something like figure 6.7.

All of the contrasting terms overlap, since color boundaries are very fuzzy – something turquoise, for instance, could be called either *green* or *blue*. Ideally, the diagram should be three-dimensional so that *purple* and *red* join up and overlap as well.

color						
red		orange	yellow	green	blue	purple
crimson	scarlet				lavender	

Figure 6.7 *Lexical field for color terminology*

6.7   Exercises

Adopt-a-word

A.   Explore the issue of synonymy by comparing your word to up to three synonyms found in a thesaurus. To what extent are the words really synonymous? Demonstrate using the substitutability test. Consider how synonymy is defined and, if the words are not absolutely synonymous, why the thesaurus proposed them as synonyms.

B.   Design a box diagram for a semantic field that your word (i.e. at least one of its senses) is in. Limit yourself to about twelve words, all in the same word class (e.g. noun, verb), if possible. Discuss the semantic relations within the field and critique the box diagram method. Are such diagrams more appropriate to some kinds of words than others?

General

1.   Show whether the following words are sense synonyms by demonstrating whether or not they are substitutable in all contexts.
         a. quick, fast
         b. sick, ill
         c. near, close

2.   Devise box diagrams that contain the words in the following lists. Briefly justify your decisions based on your own understandings of these words. Take into account whether any words are polysemous, but only consider senses that relate to the FURNITURE or BAKED GOOD fields.
         a. stool, barstool, chair, armchair, chaise longue, seat, sofa
         b. bun, roll, bread, cake, muffin, scone, bagel

3.   The following words have more than one antonym. For each, discuss whether this is because the word is polysemous. For instance, does the sense of *start* that is an antonym to *finish* differ from the sense of *start* that

is an antonym to *stop*? If the word has only one sense, then why do you think it has come to have two antonyms? A corpus or the Internet might help you to find examples to support your arguments.

a. start: finish, stop

b. good: bad, evil

c. sweet: sour, bitter

PART III

Word classes and semantic types

7 Ontological categories and word classes

Key words: WORD CLASS, ONTOLOGY, ONTOLOGICAL CATEGORY, SEMANTIC TYPE, TIME-STABILITY, DERIVATION

7.1 Overview

We are used to hearing descriptions like "a noun names a person, place, or thing" or "a verb is an action word." If you have already studied some linguistics, you've probably learnt that these semantic descriptions of word classes are insufficient, and instead categories like NOUN and VERB are best defined by their morphosyntactic properties – such as where they can occur in sentences and what suffixes they can take. After all, any English noun can head the subject of an English sentence, but not all such nouns denote persons, places, or things (e.g., *oblivion, unconventionality*), and all lexical verbs in English sentences agree with their subjects, but not all describe actions (e.g. *resemble, prefer*). Nevertheless, there may be something to the notion that nouns are more thing-like and verbs are more action-y. In this chapter we introduce ontological, or semantic, categories, which can be used to classify meaning types, and look at the degree to which these semantic types correspond to grammatical word classes. This includes looking at the question of what happens when we use different word classes to describe the same kind of thing. For example, does it mean something different to use an adjective rather than a noun, as in *Richard is optimistic* and *Richard is an optimist*?

7.2 Ontological categories and semantic types

Categories are groups of entities that have some properties in common. For example, STAPLER is the category of all machines that put staples into materials. It is not very useful, however, to approach semantics at such a specific level of categorization, and study, say, just the words that express the category STAPLER. After all, no linguistic rules apply only to words that refer to staplers. Instead, we start with more general semantic categories, the most general of which are called **ontological categories**. So, we can study staplers as instances of a more general category, such as PHYSICAL OBJECTS, or an even more general category, like THINGS, as opposed to other general categories like EVENT or PROPERTY.

Ontology is the philosophical field that attempts to organize everything that exists into a limited number of general categories. The field goes back at least as far as Aristotle's *Categories* in the 4th century BCE (translated as Aristotle 1941), and ontology continues to be a major endeavor of philosophers engaged in metaphysics (the study of being and knowledge). An **ontological system** (informally called **an ontology**) is a theory of what general categories there are and how they are structured with relation to one another. A complete ontological system would have categories for everything that exists – including abstract "things" like the property of being green or the state of owning a bicycle. As linguists, we are interested in ontology for specific reasons and in specific ways. Philosophers debate whether ontological categories exist in the world or in human minds. Since we're dealing with language, we are interested in investigating categories that affect linguistic structure and behavior. Thus we can view these categories as ways in which humans organize and lexicalize their experience of the world, and we can leave aside the philosophical question of whether these categories exist on their own, separate from human perception. These days, ontology is also a major area of concern in computer and information science, as a good set of categories is indispensable for development of artificial intelligence and for making information accessible in regular ways to users of the web, for example. Thus, computer scientists (and cognitive scientists more generally) have become major contributors to discussions of ontological categories.

The ontological systems devised by philosophers and cognitive scientists are the subject of much debate, and so if you read the works of different ontologists, you're likely to find that they propose different categories, different names for their categories, and different criteria for what counts as an ontological category. As an example of an ontological system, let's look at the system devised by Hoffman and Rosenkrantz (1997), in figure 7.1. We are interested in its structure here, so don't focus too much on the actual categories now. We can see a few general characteristics of ontological systems in this example. First, the system is hierarchically organized, with subcategories that are proper subsets of more general categories. There is no crossing of lines in this hierarchy – something that is a SUBSTANCE cannot also be an EVENT. Second, the categories are extremely general – right up to the level of the category ENTITIES, which includes everything that exists. The system does not include more specific categories, for example particular types of EVENTS or PROPERTIES. You may notice similarity between the structure of this ontological system and the taxonomies discussed in chapter 6 (see figure 6.1). The main difference between them is that the taxonomies can reveal relations between any lexicalized categories, i.e. categories that we have names for, while the ontology in figure 7.1 concentrates on the highest levels, for which we tend not to have everyday names. This is part of the reason that we often see different names for very similar ontological categories in different ontological systems – it is hard to find words that sound right to cover the top levels. But like the relations we studied in chapter 6, onto-logical categories stand in paradigmatic (see §6.2) relation to one another. This

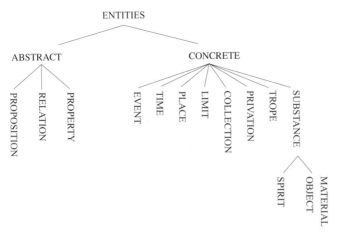

Figure 7.1 *Hoffman and Rosenkrantz's ontological system*

means that a substitution test can tell us whether two things belong to the same ontological category. If substituting one item for another in a statement results in a sensible statement (whether or not it still means the same thing), one could argue that they belong to the same category at some level. For example, in (1), it looks like *a chair* and *rice* belong to one category, but *plagiarism* and *boredom* are not in that category, since they don't seem to be the kinds of things that can be "owned."

(1) a.   Mary owns a chair.
    b.   Mary owns rice.
    c.   #Mary owns plagiarism.
    d.   #Mary owns boredom.

But if we look further we can see that *boredom* and *plagiarism* are substitutable for *chair* and *rice* in other contexts, as in (2):

(2) a.   Mary hates a chair.
    b.   Mary hates rice.
    c.   Mary hates plagiarism.
    d.   Mary hates boredom.

These substitutability facts lead us to believe that *a chair* and *rice* belong to a subcategory (SUBSTANCE in fig. 7.1) of a more general category that *plagiarism* and *boredom* also belong to (ENTITIES, in fig. 7.1's terminology).

Relating words to the ontological categories they designate helps us to classify words as **semantic types**, and thus to make generalizations about words belonging to those types. For instance, we have already seen that ontological category labels like EVENT and THING are used in Conceptual Semantics (§4.2), where they stand for semantic types. EVENT senses differ from THING senses in their internal structure and in how they interact with other senses. Once we have identified these types, we can ask questions like: What is the structure of an

Table 7.1 *Examples of ontological categories/semantic types*

Category/type	example expressions
THING	*hat, heart, Hildegard, jam, scissors, zebra*
SITUATION	
EVENT	*eat, perform, performance* [*We ate lunch.*]
STATE	*exist, resemble* [*Olaf is tall, Prudence resembles Napoleon.*]
PROPERTY	*happy, heavy, plaid, bored*
MANNER	*happily, heavily,* [*with gusto*]
PLACE	*here, there* [*in outer space*]
TIME	*yesterday, now* [*before I met you*]
DIRECTION	*backwards, up, into*
AMOUNT	*three, many, few, all*

EVENT sense? How does it differ from a THING sense? How are EVENTS realized in language? Does the semantic type of a word determine its morphological properties or its role in grammar?

Table 7.1 lists some common ontological categories/semantic types used in the semantic literature and some examples of expressions that denote members of those categories. Many of these categories can be illustrated with single words, although the same types can hold of phrases, as indicated by the examples in brackets. For SITUATION I've included the subcategories EVENT and STATE, and, although not included in this table, other categories have subcategories, some of which we explore in later chapters. We start our discussions of particular semantic types by asking: what is the relation between meaning and word class? In other words, does the ontological category associated with a word's sense determine whether it is a noun or a verb or something else?

The examples in table 7.1 demonstrate that while some of these categories seem closely linked with particular word classes, there is no simple match-up between any word class and a single ontological category. Closely linked are nouns and THINGS and adjectives and PROPERTIES. However, some nouns do not denote THINGS. Table 7.1 includes the SITUATION/EVENT noun *performance*, and we could add other nouns that refer to SITUATIONS, like *demolition* and *disappearance*. Lexical verbs only fall under SITUATION, although they are not the only ways of describing SITUATIONS.

If we look beyond the examples in table 7.1, the match-up between word classes and semantic categories becomes even less clear. Compare the adjectives *heavy* (3) and *corporate* (4):

(3) a.   It is a heavy tax.
   b.   The tax is heavy.

(4) a.   It is a corporate tax.
   b.   ??The tax is corporate.

While grammatically *corporate* is an adjective because it modifies nouns, it does not indicate a PROPERTY in the same way that *heavy* does. *Corporate* in (4) means 'for corporations,' and is more about a type of THING (corporations) that is associated with the tax than about a PROPERTY of the tax. Thus although adjectives frequently denote PROPERTIES, it is not clear that all adjectives denote PROPERTIES. Those that seem not to denote PROPERTIES tend not to occur in the post-verb position, as (4b) shows.

Finally, another reason to doubt a firm association between word class and ontological category is that different languages have different word classes, but no language lacks any of the general semantic types – after all, everyone everywhere needs to describe EVENTS, THINGS, PROPERTIES, and so on. The adjective category in particular is not universal. Some languages, like Mandarin Chinese and Yurok (spoken in North America), have no adjectives at all. In others, like Swahili and Hausa (both spoken in Africa), the adjective category is a closed class (see §1.3.2), so that only a handful of words are adjectives (Dixon 1982, McCawley 1992). In languages without a robust adjective category, PROPERTIES are described by nouns or verbs. For example, in Hausa, *She is intelligent* would translate literally as *She is with intelligence*, while in Mandarin, instead of saying *He is tall*, a stative verb meaning 'tall' is used – so it would be like saying in English *He talls*.

7.3 Word class prototypes

While there is no one-to-one correspondence between word classes and semantic types, some word classes tend to be associated with certain semantic types, and vice versa. This has led many linguists to view word classes as prototype-based categories, and we can see prototype effects for word classes, just as word meanings may involve prototype effects, as discussed in §3.4. For example, if you ask people to give examples of nouns, they will probably list words for concrete objects with clear spatial boundaries rather than words for ideas or events, and if you ask them to name verbs, they will probably give action words like *jump* or *eat*, rather than linking verbs like *is* or verbs for relations among things, like *resemble*. This suggests that PHYSICAL OBJECTS are more central to the NOUN category than EVENTS are and that ACTIONS are more central to the VERB category than STATES are, just as robins are more central to the BIRD category than ostriches are. What's more, nouns for PHYSICAL OBJECTS display more typical noun properties than nouns for EVENTS or PROPERTIES, just as robins have more typical BIRD properties – like flying and nesting in trees – than ostriches do. Table 7.2 shows some of the morphosyntactic properties associated with the noun classes, and the degree to which they are found in nouns of different semantic types. Similarly, verbs for ACTIONS that involve movement have more "verby" qualities than verbs for STATES, and

Table 7.2 *Prototypical properties of nouns*

A typical noun	PHYSICAL OBJECT	STATE/PROPERTY	EVENT
• can be preceded by a definite determiner, like *the* or *her*	*the boulder*, *their table*	*her purity*, *the greenness (of the grass)*	*her appearance*, *the recognition (of someone)*
• is not derived from another class	many are basic nouns: *chair, dog, rock* (some exceptions, like *stapler*)	many derived from adjectives: *greenness, purity* (some exceptions, like *beauty*)	mostly derived from verbs: *explosion, appearance, recognition*
• has a plural	*tables, boulders*	??*purities*, #*greennesses*	*explosions, appearances,* #*recognitions*
• can be possessive	*the table's legs*, *the boulder's size*	**the greenness's shade*	**the appearance's time*

adjectives for gradable PROPERTIES (properties that one can have more or less of) act more "adjectivey" than other types of adjectives, as we see in coming chapters.

So, while words in any word class can denote a range of categories, one category in each word class stands out as the most prototypical for that class. This is summarized in the following points (adapted from Bennett 2002):

•   The **central members of the NOUN category** designate types of PHYSICAL OBJECTS, and PHYSICAL OBJECTS are most typically designated by nouns.

    The most typical nouns designate types of objects that are also compact and clearly individual. Thus *rock* and *boulder* refer to more prototypical categories than *mountain* or *gravel* do.

•   The **central members of the VERB category** designate types of ACTIONS, and ACTIONS are most typically designated by verbs.

•   The **central members of the ADJECTIVE category** designate types of PROPERTIES, and PROPERTIES are most typically designated by adjectives.

These generalizations hold cross-linguistically – so when we translate word for a PHYSICAL OBJECT like *apple* into another language, we find that it is also a noun in the other language, and words for ACTIONS are most typically verbs cross-linguistically. In languages that have open-class adjectives, words for PROPERTIES are typically in the adjective class. In non-adjectival languages, in which PROPERTIES are described by nouns or verbs, the PROPERTY-describing nouns/verbs are not prototypical nouns/verbs.

Puzzle 7–1

Table 7.2 presented just a few examples of nouns in a few semantic categories and indicated whether these display typical "noun-like" properties. Test the following EXPERIENCE nouns using the criteria in table 7.2 in order to judge whether they seem to be "typical" nouns.

EXPERIENCES: *pain, pleasure, nausea, smell*

Consider the following questions:

*   Do all members of this category pass the same tests?
*   Are some items within the category closer to the prototype than others? Why might this be?
*   Do these words describe physical or mental experiences? Does that make any difference to their grammatical properties?

7.3.1   Word class prototypes and time-stability

Givón (1979) and others have associated the semantic qualities of word classes with how nouns, verbs, and adjectives relate to time – particularly, whether they represent ontological categories that are stable in time or not. Nouns have relatively time-stable meanings. You can be fairly sure that something that is called *a table* will still be a table (and not a goose or a song) from one moment to another. Verbs are not so time-stable – they tend to represent that which is temporary or changing. For example, if someone is singing, we do not expect that singing to last forever, nor do we expect that their singing will take the same form (e.g. the same note) at all 'singing' moments. Time-stability is not an all-or-nothing property – there is a continuum from very stable to very unstable, as can be seen in (5) (after Givón 1984:55). Noun and verb meanings are associated with the opposite ends of the time-stability continuum, and adjectives are somewhere in the middle. Along the continuum, particular nouns, verbs, or adjectives may be more or less time-stable than others.

(5)   time-stable   intermediate   rapid change

←——————————————————————————————→

NOUN   ADJECTIVE   VERB
boulder, child, purity . . . corporate, happy, visible . . . know, sing, kick

Relating this back to the prototype view, the category prototypically associated with nouns, PHYSICAL OBJECTS, is a particularly time-stable category, while the category associated with prototypical verbs, ACTIONS, is particularly time-unstable. Thus they are on opposite ends of the continuum.

The further from the ends or the center of this continuum a lexeme's sense is, the less prototypical of its word class it will be. As table 7.2 demonstrated, *purity*, which is closer to the ADJECTIVE part of the scale, is a less typical noun than *boulder*, which is at the "nouniest" end. Similarly, at the noun/adjective border, *corporate* is not a typical adjective, since it neither refers to a PROPERTY, nor does "adjectivey" things like being modifiable by *very* (*#It was a very corporate tax*). Being *corporate* is also typically more time-stable than being *happy*, for instance. A corporate tax stays a corporate tax, but, unfortunately, a happy person may soon be sad, and a tall person is only *tall* as long as she is in the company of mostly shorter people. On the verb end of the continuum, the action described by *kick* is very time-unstable, since it is both over quickly and ever-changing while it is going on. The beginning of kicking is different from the middle, which is different from the end. Compare this to the less prototypical verb *know*. When you know something, the knowledge just *is*, it does not change. (If it changed, we would call it *learning* or *forgetting* rather than *knowing*.) Thus, prototypical verb senses, which represent ACTIONS, are typically more time-unstable than less prototypical verb senses. Chapter 10 discusses some of the differences between EVENT/ACTION and STATE verbs and their effects.

7.3.2   Word class, derivation, and lexical semantics

The prototype/time-stability approach to word classes makes particular predictions about what happens when we use different word classes to describe the same situation. Consider the examples in (6).

(6) a.   Falstaff is drinking. [verb]
   b.   Falstaff is drunk. [adjective]
   c.   Falstaff is a drunk. [noun]

While the sentences in (6) all have to do with drinking and use a word that is obviously related to the verb *to drink*, the different word classes involved affect our perceptions of the time stability of the situations described. The first describes an ACTION that we assume will end at some point, the second a PROPERTY that Falstaff (probably temporarily) has, and the last a type of THING that Falstaff is – which is the most time-stable claim. If Falstaff got drunk only once in his

---

Puzzle 7–2

Compare the following pairs of sentences, and think about whether you are more or less likely to use one of the pair, or whether you would find one more polite than the other. Are the (i) sentences exact paraphrases of the (ii) sentences?

(a) i.   Lisa is Swedish.
   ii.   Lisa is a Swede.
(b) i.   Oscar is gay.
   ii.   Oscar is a gay.
(c) i.   Nan is blonde.
   ii.   Nan is a blonde.

Table 7.3 *Some examples of derivations/conversions that change word class*

	adjectives	nouns	verbs
deadjectival	–	*purity (pure + ity), happiness (happy + ness)*	*purify (pure + ify), finalize (final + ize)*
denominal	*nerdy (nerd + y), doglike (dog + like), statuesque (statue + esque)*	–	*grease* (conversion from a noun), *atomize (atom + ize)*
deverbal	*likeable (like + able), living (live + ing), respected (respect + ed)*	*abandonment (abandon + ment), construction (construct + ion), appearance (appear + ance), permit* (change of word stress from verb *permit*)	–

life, it would be appropriate to say (6a) or (6b) at that time, but it would be an exaggeration (and an insult) to say (6c) about him. In these cases, the different word classes are associated with different ontological categories: verb/ACTION ('drinking'), adjective/PROPERTY ('inebriated') and noun/THING ('someone who drinks too much').

Through derivation or conversion (recall §1.3.4 and §5.3), a word from one word class can be turned into a word in another class. For example, the verb *construct* becomes the noun *construction*, the noun *beauty* becomes the adjective *beautiful*, and the adjective *heavy* becomes the noun *heaviness*. In these cases, we use the terms **deverbal**, **denominal**, and **deadjectival** to signal the word class of the base word. For example, *construction* is a deverbal noun, a noun that is based on a verb. Table 7.3 gives some examples of the different types of derived forms. Not every derivational process changes word class – some make semantic changes only. For example, both *London* and *Londoner* are nouns, one describing a place and one a person.

Because of the apparent prototype-based link between word class and meaning, it stands to reason that if a word's class is changed through a derivational process, then its meaning will be affected. Derivational suffixes and processes vary, however, in what new semantic information they bring to a word. Compare, for example, the deverbal nouns *educator* and *education* in (7):

(7) a.   Kevin educates the children.
    b.   Kevin is the educator of the year.
    c.   The education of the children takes all of Kevin's time.

The base form *educate* describes an ACTION, while the derived noun *educator* describes a person (a THING) who does that ACTION. Thus, the *-or* suffix changes the ontological category of the word in a major way, from an EVENT type to a THING. As such, *educate* is a fairly typical verb, and *educator* a fairly typical noun. On the other hand, the noun *education*, as it is used in (7c), describes a type of EVENT. Although *educator* and *education* are both nouns, the THING described by *educator* is more time-stable than the EVENT described by *education*. If you point at the *education* described in (7c) at different times, you will be pointing at different stages of the activity, whereas pointing at the educator in (7b) always involves pointing at Kevin.

Another thing to notice about derivational suffixes is that some are apt to create polysemous words. This is the case for *education*, which can mean 'the process of educating' as in (7c) and (8a) or 'the end-product of education,' as in (8b). In (8b), then, *education* describes something more time-stable and THING-like than in (8a).

(8) a.   The education of the children takes all of Kevin's time.
    b.   Students leave this school with an education that is second to none.

Thus, while nouns generally represent concepts that are more THING-like than verb concepts are, one cannot simply look at the part of speech of a word in order to know its semantic type. Because of the prototype organization of word class categories, the relation between word class and semantic category is loose, and there is semantic variation within word classes.

7.4   Ontological categories and lexical semantics: some conclusions

Because we are interested in the relation between ontology and language, linguists focus on ontological category boundaries that have implications for language. For example, as the following chapters discuss, verbs that describe STATES behave differently in sentences from verbs that describe EVENTS, and nouns that describe SUBSTANCES have different semantic and grammatical properties from nouns that describe individual OBJECTS. The THING, SITUATION, and PROPERTY categories receive the most attention from here forward, as they are most associated with issues in noun, verb, and adjective meaning, respectively.

This chapter has discussed the usefulness of some of these ontological categories in explaining how words come to be members of different word classes. While the word classes NOUN, VERB, and ADJECTIVE are most reliably defined according to grammatical criteria, these grammatical categories are linked (via prototype structures) to particular ontological categories. Typical nouns describe INDIVIDUAL PHYSICAL OBJECTS, typical verbs describe PHYSICAL ACTIONS, and typical adjectives designate PROPERTIES. These prototypes can be described in terms of the time-stability of the things they denote. When similar meanings occur in different word classes, then, we tend to understand the noun version of the meaning as more thing-like, the adjective version as more property-like, and the verb version as more action-like – each of these more time-unstable than the last. In the coming chapters we concentrate separately on nouns, verbs, and adjectives and their associated ontological categories.

7.5   Further reading

On philosophical ontology, see the *Stanford Encyclopedia of Philosophy*'s article on Categories (Thomasson 2004) or the introductory chapters of Westerhoff (2005). John Sowa (2005) provides a good overview of ontology-making in computer science with a glossary of relevant terms. For some discussion of the application of ontology to linguistic theory, see William Frawley's *Linguistic Semantics* (1992). For more on viewing word classes in terms of time-stability, see Givón (1979). Paul Hopper and Sandra Thompson (1985) take a somewhat different view – instead of basing word classes on semantic properties of the words in question, they argue that word classes are based on the discourse uses to which those words are put. While following many of the claims made in this chapter, Ronald Langacker (1987) approaches the problem using the architecture of Cognitive Grammar. Rochelle Lieber (2004) provides an in-depth study of the semantic contributions of derivational suffixes, using a theoretical model that is close to Jackendoff's (§4.2).

7.6   Answers to puzzles

7–1

There is variation within the EXPERIENCE category as to whether the nouns have "prototypical" noun properties. All can occur with the definite determiner *the*. Most are natural in the plural (*pains, pleasures, smells*), but *nausea* is not (#*nauseas*). Note, however, that *pain* varies in pluralizability according to whether it describes physical pain (*Grandpa has many aches and pains*) or emotional pain (*Teasing and name-calling cause much pain* [*many pains] *to children*). This may reveal that we conceptualize mental pain and nausea as less like objects (i.e. the noun prototype) than we do for smells and physical pains. All can be possessive with a noun like *persistence* (*the pain's persistence, the nausea's persistence*, etc.). *Nausea* is not derived from another word class (the verb *to nauseate* is derived from it), but the other forms are all verbs as well as nouns.

7–2

Nouns typically indicate THINGS, and THINGS usually have many properties, whereas adjectives typically indicate a single PROPERTY. For instance *a Swede* indicates both 'Swedishness' and 'personhood.' We can tell this because we wouldn't say *My sofa is a Swede* (unless we're sitting on a person). *Swedish*, on the other hand, only indicates 'Swedishness,' and therefore can be used to describe Swedish weather or furniture, as well as Swedish people. In many contexts, it seems less polite to use a noun (*He's a gay*; *The gays want equal rights*) rather than an adjective (*He's gay* or *He's a gay person*; *Gay people want equal rights*). Identifying a person by a noun seems to indicate that they belong to a "type" and that there is only one dimension to their personality – that that noun describes them in full. This means that the noun may be seen as carrying with it any stereotypes that go with that property. For example, *Nan is blonde* may seem to just describe her hair color, whereas *Nan is a blonde* may be perceived as saying she fits the stereotype of blondes and is therefore empty-headed. The richness of noun descriptions as opposed to adjective ones is evident when we talk about "typical" Swedishness. If we say *Lisa is a typical Swede*, we are probably asserting that Lisa has many stereotypically Swedish properties (perhaps including being blonde, tall, quiet, and egalitarian). On the other hand, one is less likely to say *She's typically Swedish*, and if we do, we are less likely to interpret it as describing multiple aspects of Lisa. (See Wierzbicka 1986 for more on nouns versus adjectives.)

7.7   Exercises

Adopt-a-word

A.   If your word belongs to more than one word class,* discuss the relation between word class and ontological category with reference to your word. How does the meaning of the word differ in different word classes? To which ontological categories does it belong? (Note that due to polysemy, it may belong to more than one ontological category even within a word class.) Use the categories in table 7.1.

*If your word does not belong to more than one word class, you may do this project by adding derivational suffixes to your word to change its word class. Limit yourself to no more than three derived forms.

B.   Using a grammar of English or a grammatical dictionary (see §1.6 for suggestions), find the grammatical properties typical to your word's word class. Analyze whether your word has all of the properties of a typical member of its word class, and whether this reveals anything about the relation between word class and ontological category.

General

1.   Deverbal nouns are often polysemous between 'process' and 'product' senses, as demonstrated for *education* in (8) in §7.4. For each of the following deverbal nouns, demonstrate whether they have both 'process'

and 'product' senses by providing an example sentence for each sense. Make sure that the sentence sufficiently disambiguates the words, so that only the 'process' or the 'product' sense is sensible. To what degree do the two senses of the word fulfill the grammatical criteria for prototypical nouns?

a. composition
b. organization
c. flash (e.g. of light)
d. knowledge
e. arrival
f. disapproval

2.   Given the discussion in this chapter, we would expect that the most typical verbs are time-unstable and that they would easily occur in all morphological verb forms. Place the following verbs on a continuum from MOST TIME-STABLE to MOST TIME-UNSTABLE. Then test the verbs for whether or not they occur felicitously in the simple past form, i.e. *VERBed*, and the past progressive *was VERBing*. Discuss whether your analysis of these verbs is consistent with the prediction that the most time-unstable verbs will be the most morphologically typical verbs.

a. walk (as in *He walks to school*)
b. believe (as in *I believe that pigs fly*)
c. sound (as in *That sounds like a good idea*)
d. teethe (as in *The baby is teething*)
e. wrap (as in *She wraps presents*)
f. wait (as in *We'll wait until she arrives*)

8   Nouns and countability

Key words: COUNT, MASS, NON-COUNT NOUN, BOUNDED, INTERNAL STRUCTURE, INDIVIDUAL, AGGREGATE, GROUP, SUBSTANCE, LINGUISTIC RELATIVITY, CULTURAL RELATIVITY

8.1   Overview

If you tell people that you study lexical semantics or "the meaning of words," they are likely to assume that you spend your time thinking about things like "What does *love* mean?" or "What is a table, really?" While some lexical semanticists do think about questions like this, much lexical semantic work on nouns is instead focused on larger categories of nouns with particular morphosyntactic properties and patterns of polysemy. After discussing the types of issues that such nouns raise in the next section, this chapter looks at why it is that some nouns are **countable** and others are not. That is, some nouns, like *cucumber* or *bungalow*, can be preceded by numerals and made plural (*104 cucumbers, three bungalows*), and others are mass nouns and not usually made plural – for example *fog* (#*three fogs*) and *wheat* (#*twenty-seven wheats*). After discussing the issue of countability in general, we look at the Conceptual Semantics componential treatment of some countability categories and the polysemy of nouns in relation to those categories, then Chierchia's proposal that mass nouns are inherently plural. Lastly, we look at how languages may differ in their treatment of nouns for particular THINGS and ask whether these differences are arbitrary or culturally predictable, with particular attention to the Natural Semantic Metalanguage approach.

8.2   Thinking about nouns and things

In discussing theories of meaning and semantic phenomena in earlier chapters, most of the examples we used were nouns. This is not a coincidence. In many ways, nouns are the least complicated word class to use in illustrating semantic discussions, and they often feature in philosophical discussions of language and reference, since most noun senses are fairly self-contained and often refer to concrete things. Compare a noun like *apple* to a verb like *wear*. It is easy to imagine an apple in and of itself, but in order to imagine an instance of *wearing* we need to imagine other things too: something that is being worn and something that is doing the wearing. So, when illustrating lexical semantic theories or phenomena like polysemy and lexical relations, it is often easiest to use nouns as examples. At the same time, this self-contained property of nouns makes them less a priority to many linguistic semanticists because their effects on the meaning of the sentence as a whole are more limited than those of verbs.

Another reason why nouns are sometimes studied in less semantic detail than verbs is that it can be very difficult to distinguish where the discussion of a noun's sense stops and where discussion of its extension (the set of things it refers to; §2.3) begins. Recall from chapter 4 that most modern theories of linguistic semantics assume that meaning involves an interface between the linguistic and conceptual realms in the mind. A lexeme's formal properties – for instance, its pronunciation and inflection – belong to the linguistic realm. This form is mapped to some (set of) concept(s) in the conceptual realm. For example, the word form *pigeon* maps to a concept (we'll call it PIGEON) of a certain type of bird. We all have similar PIGEON concepts because we've all heard the word *pigeon* used to label the same kind of bird. To a certain degree, then, we linguists could say that *pigeon* means PIGEON, and then not investigate PIGEON any further, since the contents of the concept PIGEON are conceptual, rather than linguistic, in nature. In other words, the lines are fine between the linguistic question "What does *pigeon* mean?", the psychological question "How is our knowledge of pigeons organized?", and the philosophical/biological question "What is a pigeon?" For this reason, many theoretical linguists forgo deep discussions of the senses of specific nouns, like *pigeon* or *love* or *opinion*. A clear exception to this generalization – particularly for abstract nouns – is Wierzbicka and her Natural Semantic Metalanguage theory; see §4.4. The QUALIA in Pustejovsky's Generative Lexicon approach (see §4.3) give some information about the concepts associated with nouns, but these are typically used only to differentiate types of information that interact in building up compositional phrases (recall §1.2.2). Generative Lexicon practitioners, when faced with representing the meaning of *pigeon*, would represent that it denotes a type of bird, but probably would not get into the details that differentiate pigeons from other birds – because those details are unlikely to affect which verbs *pigeon* goes with or how adjectives that modify *pigeon* are to be interpreted.

What is of interest to most linguists is any aspect of noun (or verb or adjective) meaning that has an impact on how that word can be used in phrases and sentences – that is, what other words it can combine with, how its interpretation is affected by the larger phrase, what prefixes/suffixes it can take, and so forth. In the last chapter, we noted that the semantic category THING has a special relationship with the grammatically defined NOUN class. Now we want to look more deeply at this relationship and ask: are there subcategories within the THING category, and do they correspond with particular types of nouns? Or, to take the question from the other direction: can we find semantic motivations for the existence of different types of nouns?

8.2.1   Concrete and abstract

In this chapter, we concentrate on nouns for concrete entities and the relation between the types of entities that the nouns denote and their grammatical number (for instance, whether you can use the noun with *much* or make it plural). Some other semantic distinctions in nouns are worth mentioning briefly. One distinction is between **concrete** and **abstract** nouns – that is, ones that refer to tangible entities and those that refer to intangible things like emotions or mental states. We've already seen in chapter 7 that such nouns differ in the types of ontological categories their denotata belong to, and we also saw that non-concrete nouns do not always display all the grammatical properties that are usually associated with nouns, such as occurring in the plural or the possessive (table 7.2).

8.2.2   Common and proper

Another distinction within the noun category is between **proper names**, which designate particular TOKENS of a TYPE (recall §4.2.3), and **common nouns**, which name a TYPE. Generally, languages treat such nouns as grammatically distinct subclasses. If we want to use a common noun to refer to a particular TOKEN of its TYPE, we have to make it part of a noun phrase that includes a determiner (or other means of making a common noun particular) that points out an individual – for example, *the man* rather than just *man*. In English, proper names do not need the help of a determiner since they already point out individuals; thus we do not say things like *the Melanie* or *a London*. If we do combine proper names with determiners in English, it is because we are using the name to designate a TYPE instead of a TOKEN. In other words, proper names can be polysemous between a TOKEN-designating sense – *Melanie* as the name for my friend Melanie in (1) – or a TYPE-designating sense, as in (2), where it means 'the TYPE of person who is named *Melanie*.'

(1)   Melanie came to dinner.

(2)   She doesn't look like a Melanie.

8.2.3   Other noun subcategories

Other kinds of noun distinctions can be important in determining which adjectives or verbs the noun can combine with (recall our discussion of selectional restrictions in §3.3.2) and the patterns of polysemy that result from combining different types of nouns with different types of verbs or adjectives (recall our discussion of *finish lunch* versus *finish a novel* in §4.3 and §5.4.1). We'll see more of this when we discuss how we interpret adjectives – which depends upon the meaning of the noun that the adjective modifies – in chapter 11. At this point, we turn our attention to the issue of countability, an area of noun meaning that has received a fair amount of detailed attention.

8.3   Nouns and number: grammar and semantics

8.3.1   Count versus non-count

In English and many other languages, we can see a clear distinction between words that denote individual things that can be counted and words that denote stuff that is not individuated and counted. *Teapot* falls into the first category, called **count nouns**, and *mud* into the second, traditionally called **mass nouns**. While count nouns can be pluralized and preceded by numerals, as in (3a) and (3b), mass nouns are not pluralized and occur with non-counting **quantifiers** (determiners that indicate 'how much'), such as *much* instead of *many*, as in (4).

(3) a.   How many teapots does Shel own?
    b.   Shel owns fifty teapots.
    c.   #How much teapot does Shel own?

(4) a.   #How many muds are on the carpet?
    b.   #Danni tracked fifty muds onto the carpet.
    c.   How much mud is on the carpet?

In order to count the stuff denoted by mass nouns, we instead count units into which the stuff can be divided, such as containers or measurements, as in (5).

(5)   Danni tracked fifty kinds/clumps/ounces of mud into the house.

While this serves as a useful starting description of count versus mass nouns, the facts are a lot messier. First, as you may have already noticed, we can sometimes say things like *fifty muds*, as in (6):

(6)   Fifty muds were displayed at the science fair.

In this case *fifty muds* is interpreted as shorthand for *fifty kinds of mud*. Similarly, *teapot* acts as a mass noun in (7).

(7)   Shel got a lot of teapot for his money.

(8)   Shel got a lot of teapots for his money.

In (7), the singular, non-count use of *teapot* indicates that the teapot should be interpreted as if it is a substance rather than an individual thing, whereas in (8) the plural count noun *teapots* indicates many individual teapots. In (7), Shel got a single, particularly large teapot – that is, a lot of 'teapot substance,' rather than a lot of individual teapots.

The traditional count/mass dichotomy ignores a range of other types of (non-)countability. Wierzbicka (1985) lists fourteen types and Goddard (2009) lists a total of eighteen types just among concrete nouns. We won't go through all these types here, but the following three give a flavor of the range of types that exist:

- Singular words for classes of unlike things: *furniture*, *cutlery*

     Their hyponyms are countable (e.g. *tables*, *chairs*), but the group name is not (*a piece of furniture*/#*furnitures*). Some authors count these as mass nouns because they do not pluralize, but these intuitively seem to be a different kind of thing than mass nouns that refer to substances like *mud* or collections of tiny things of the same type, like *rice*.
- Plural names of 'dual' objects: *scissors*, *goggles*, *underpants*

     These are always plural – *a scissor* does not refer to half of a pair of scissors. In order to count these, we preface the noun with *pair of*, as in *a pair of goggles* or *three pairs of underpants*.
- Plural names for expanses of homogeneous matter, fixed to a certain place: *guts*, *woods*

     These are sometimes called *plural mass nouns*. But despite their plural marking, they cannot be counted, as shown by the oddness of: *I hate his guts* – #*all five of them* (McCawley 1975:320).

From this we can see that a simple count/mass distinction is just *too* simple; there are many types of nouns that are not countable. I'll use **non-count noun** to refer to any type of noun that is not countable (including *furniture* and *guts*) and reserve **mass noun** for those, like *rice* and *mud*, that are not plural and that refer to a SUBSTANCE – i.e. a mass of homogeneous matter.

8.3.2   The semantics of countability

So far we've seen that count, mass, and other types of non-count nouns are different subclasses of the grammatical word class NOUN. Our next question is whether these different subclasses of noun reflect different semantic (sub)types. We've already noted that the denotata of count nouns are perceived as individuals in a way that the denotata of mass nouns are not. In semantic terms, countable noun senses are **bounded**, while mass noun senses are **unbounded**. (Un)boundedness can be treated as a binary semantic feature, abbreviated as [±b].

An entity is **bounded** if and only if:

- it is **indivisible** – that is, it cannot be divided while retaining its identity, and
- it is **not additive** – that is, it cannot have more of the same type of entity added to it, while retaining its identity.

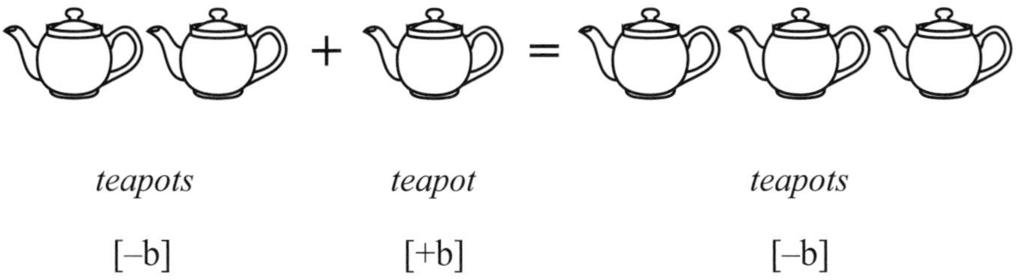

teapots   *teapot*   *teapots*

[−b]   [+b]   [−b]

Figure 8.1 *The unboundedness of plural* teapots

So, a teapot is indivisible because if you divide a teapot in half, it is no longer a teapot. It is non-additive because if you have a teapot, you cannot add more teapot to it while still having just one teapot. If we add another teapot, we end up with two individual teapots, rather than one massive teapot. Thus, *teapot* is [+b].

Mud, on the other hand, is not bounded: [−b]. If you have a handful of mud and drop half of it, the remaining stuff in your hand is still mud. Similarly, if someone adds more mud on top of your mud, you still have mud. Of course, if we get down to the molecular level, at some point dividing the stuff will not result in smaller portions of mud, but rather the component parts of mud (water, silicates, decomposed organic material). This level of divisibility is generally outside the realm of normal human ability or experience, since it would require special equipment and skills to divide mud in this way. Thus it does not affect how we conceptualize the countability of *mud* in our language.

While singular count nouns like *teapot* are bounded, their plural versions are not. If you have a collection of teapots and add one or more teapots to it, you would call both the original and the expanded collections *teapots*, as in figure 8.1. This raises two issues. First, we must account for the relation between [+b] count nouns and their [−b] plurals. We deal with that in the next section. Secondly, since both mass nouns and plural count nouns are [−b], we need a way to distinguish these two classes, since plural count nouns are still countable (*three teapots*) and mass nouns are not.

The semantic difference between plurals and mass nouns can be expressed in terms of another binary feature, ±**internal structure**, or ±**i**. This refers to whether the entity is made up of separate individuals or not. So, *teapots* is [+i], since we could pick an individual, bounded teapot out of a collection of teapots, but *mud* is [−i] because there are no bounded individuals within a collection of mud.

Four combinations of [±b] and [±i] feature specifications are possible, resulting in four possible types of MATERIAL ENTITY, as shown in (9):

(9)   [+b, −i] = individuals (a teapot, a mountain, a person)
             [+b, +i] = groups (a committee, a team, a set [of something])
             [−b, −i] = substances (mud, rice, water)
             [−b, +i] = aggregates (teapots, cattle, committees)

                                                  (Jackendoff 1991)

This summarizes the facts that we have already seen concerning INDIVIDUALS and SUBSTANCES, which are the prototypical semantic types for singular count and mass nouns, and the plurals of count nouns, included here in the broader category AGGREGATES. The AGGREGATE category also includes some inherently [+i] non-count nouns, like *cattle*, that do not have a singular counterpart in the INDIVIDUAL category.

The new category here is GROUP (you may also come across the term **collective noun**), which includes entities that are bounded and have internal structure. A good example of this is *band* (the musical type). The fact that we can discern individuals that make up a band indicates that *band* is [+i], like an AGGREGATE. But unlike an AGGREGATE, a GROUP functions as a bounded whole. If you see one member of a band on the street, you cannot truthfully say *I saw a band*. Even though there are individuals in the band, they are not of themselves 'band.'

Because GROUPS, like AGGREGATES, have internal structure [+i], it is not altogether surprising that they agree with plural verbs in many dialects, as in (10a). In these dialects, including Standard British English, the agreement on the verb can be more influenced by the [+i] feature than by the lack of morphological plural marking, which influences agreement in Standard American English, as in (10b).

(10) a.   The band were interviewed on the radio. [British English]
     b.   The band was interviewed on the radio. [American English]

We can conclude here that subject–verb agreement in American English depends more on the presence or absence of plural markers on the subject, while in British English it can be more influenced by the semantic properties of the subject – at least when the word refers to a group of people.

GROUP terms are countable, but because they are [+b], they involve a different kind of counting than [–b] AGGREGATES. When we put a numeral before the AGGREGATE term *teapots*, we understand the numeral as counting the individuals within the teapot collection, as in (11a). Example (11b) shows that this is true of aggregates even if they're not the plural forms of a singular INDIVIDUAL noun. Whether or not you consider *two cattle* to be grammatical, it has to be interpreted as counting individual animals, not groups. This is because one cannot count an unbounded entity, so we look inside that entity for something that can be counted.

(11) a.   two teapots = 'two individual teapots' ≠ 'two groups of teapots'
     b.   two cattle = 'two heads of cattle' ≠ 'two groups of cattle'

But when a GROUP term like *team* is made into an AGGREGATE through pluralization, its boundedness forces counting of the teams as wholes, rather than counting the members of the team, as in (12).

(12)   two teams = 'two collections of people' ≠ 'two people'

In order to count the internal structure of a GROUP in English, we name and count the parts of that group in a **partitive construction**, which expresses 'an amount of a part of a whole,' as in (13).

(13)   two members of our team

Puzzle 8–1

Determine whether or not the following are bounded and whether or not they have internal structure, in order to see which (if any) of the categories in (9) they belong to.

a.   lemonade
b.   forest
c.   furniture
d.   scissors

Are there any problems in determining the status of these? Do you think that these words' meanings fit properly into the categories in (9)? If not, why not?

8.4   Variation in countability: the Conceptual Semantics approach

The binary features [±b] and [±i] are components in Jackendoff's Conceptual Semantics (§4.2). Jackendoff (1991) also introduces means for creating new interpretations of nouns with different countability status than they usually have. This involves functional components, or **operators**, which are predicative components – that is, they take an argument made up of another semantic representation. So, for instance, there is an operator that operates on INDIVIDUAL meanings and makes them AGGREGATE plurals, and other operators can show the relations between the count and mass senses of a single lexeme.

8.4.1   Plurals: PL

Let's start with plurals. In order to show the regularity of the relation between singular INDIVIDUALS and plural AGGREGATES of those INDIVIDUALS, Jackendoff introduces the operator PL. PL takes as its argument a semantic description that has the specification [+b] – like the sense of *teapot* or *team* – in order to create a sense with the specifications [–b, +i] for *teapots* or *teams*. Thus the PL operator represents the function of the plural suffix *-s* and other markers of plurality. Figure 8.2 shows this in the abstract.

Another way of putting this would be "if you apply the PL plural function to bounded noun A, the resulting plural has the feature specifications [–b, +i]." The parentheses marked with subscript $_A$ in figure 8.2 contain the semantic

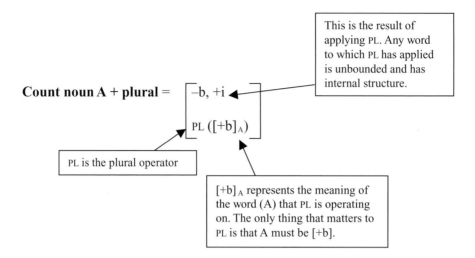

Count noun A + plural =

This is the result of applying PL. Any word to which PL has applied is unbounded and has internal structure.

PL is the plural operator

[+b]_A represents the meaning of the word (A) that PL is operating on. The only thing that matters to PL is that A must be [+b].

Figure 8.2 *The PL operation*

representation associated with the name for the individual items that make up that plural aggregate. (Most the details of the noun are left out in the examples here, since we're only concerned with [±b] and [±i] right now.) The sense of the plural noun (delimited by the outermost brackets) includes all that is found in the parentheses, except for the [–b, +i] specification in the outer brackets, which overrides the boundedness and internal structure properties of the singular noun. Examples (14) and (15) show how this works for *teapot* and *teapots*. In these examples, TEAPOT stands for our conceptual representation of 'teapothood.' The subscripted MAT label indicates that the meaning described within the brackets is of the ontological type MATERIAL ENTITY.

(14) $teapot = \begin{bmatrix} +b, -i \\ \text{TEAPOT} \\ _{MAT} \end{bmatrix}$

(15) $teapots = \begin{bmatrix} -b, +i \\ \text{PL} \begin{bmatrix} +b, -i \\ \text{TEAPOT} \\ _{MAT} \end{bmatrix} \\ _{MAT} \end{bmatrix}$

The representation of *teapots* in (15) shows the application of the PL operation in figure 8.2, to the semantic representation of *teapot* in (14). *Teapots* is, semantically speaking, *teapot* with the PL operator changing its boundedness.

Since PL requires only that the singular noun must be [+b], both [+b, –i] INDIVIDUAL terms and [+b, +i] GROUP terms can be made plural. But because the semantic representation of the singular word is available in the plural representation, we know that the plural *teams* refers to an AGGREGATE whose individual members are GROUPS, while *teapots* refers to an AGGREGATE of INDIVIDUALS. AGGREGATES and SUBSTANCES cannot be made plural, since they are not [+b]. This accounts for the usual oddness of mass noun plurals like *muds*.

8.4.2   The Universal Packager: COMP

In order to make sense of SUBSTANCE terms like *mud* when they occur with count-noun morphology (e.g. *two muds*), we must unusually interpret them as representing [+b] INDIVIDUALS. One way to do this is by invoking another operator, known as the **Universal Packager**, in which SUBSTANCE nouns are understood as being "packaged" into bounded portions. We can see this in (17), where we would typically interpret *tea* as meaning 'cup of tea,' as opposed to its unbounded use in (16).

(16)   Carol drank tea.   SUBSTANCE: [−b, −i]

(17)   Carol drank a tea.   INDIVIDUAL: [+b, −i]

The component representing the Universal Packager function is called COMP, for 'composed-of,' since *a tea* is an INDIVIDUAL that is composed of *tea*. This is shown in (18), which says that the COMP operator operates on a [−b] sense, resulting in a [+b, −i] sense.

(18)   **'packaged' reading** $= \begin{bmatrix} \text{+b, −i} \\ \text{COMP ([−b]}_A) \end{bmatrix}$

The representation in (20) shows the 'packaged' sense of *tea*. Note how it incorporates the SUBSTANCE sense of *tea* in (19) and the COMP structure shown in (18).

(19) $tea = \begin{bmatrix} \text{−b, −i} \\ \text{TEA} \\ {}_{MAT} \end{bmatrix}$

(20) $a\ tea = \begin{bmatrix} \text{+b, −i} \\ \\ \text{COMP} \begin{bmatrix} \text{−b, −i} \\ \text{TEA} \\ {}_{MAT} \end{bmatrix} \\ {}_{MAT} \end{bmatrix}$

This Universal Packager use of COMP thus gives a means for a regular polysemy (§5.2.2) between SUBSTANCE and INDIVIDUAL senses. Note that since the

$$teas = $$

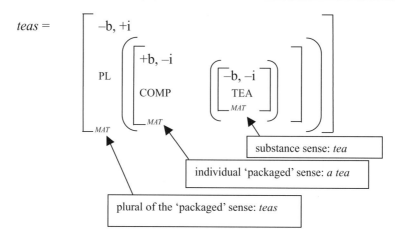

Figure 8.3 *Multiple operations on* tea

'packaged' SUBSTANCE noun results in an INDIVIDUAL sense, it can also be pluralized. So *teas* in (21) is represented as in figure 8.3, with three layers of [±b, ±i] specifications.

(21)   Carol drank 17 teas today.

8.4.3   Evaluating the CS approach

In this section, we've shown how two operators can be used to generate new meanings for nouns, demonstrating both how plural marking creates a new meaning based on an old one and how countable UNIT-OF-SUBSTANCE meanings can be derived for SUBSTANCE nouns. The CS approach can also be applied to other kinds of polysemy based on countability variations – for instance, 'type-of' meanings as in *The shop stocks 17 teas* and SUBSTANCE meanings derived from INDIVIDUAL meanings, as in *She has mango all over her face*. (These have been left for you to explore in the exercises at the end of the chapter.)

One of the most attractive things about Jackendoff's approach is that most of the components used here to account for count/mass differences and polysemy are also useful for representing other kinds of senses. We'll see ways to apply the [±b] feature to verb and adjective meanings in chapters 10 and 11. Goddard (2009), however, has criticized this approach as being far too broad and ignoring differences between different instances of these polysemy relations. We'll see aspects of his NSM approach in §8.6.

The operators PL and COMP are also useful for other kinds of expressions than those discussed here. For instance, COMP is used in the lexical semantic representation of words like *pile* or *stack*, since piles and stacks are necessarily composed of something, as in (22) and (23).

(22)   *pile* = $\begin{bmatrix} +\text{b}, -\text{i} \\ \text{PILE} \\ \text{COMP} ([-\text{b}])_{MAT} \end{bmatrix}$

(23)   *stack* = $\begin{bmatrix} +\text{b}, -\text{i} \\ \text{PILE} \\ \text{COMP} ([-\text{b}, +\text{i}])_{MAT} \end{bmatrix}$

Here we can see that while both stacks and piles are composed of other things, the types of things that they can be composed of differ in their boundedness and internal structure. That COMP has a [–b] argument for *pile* in (22) accounts for the facts in (24):

(24)   Yes: No:
            a pile of teapots [–b, +i]   #a pile of teapot [+b, –i]
            a pile of rice [–b, –i]   #a pile of committee [+b, +i]

But because a *stack* can only be composed of a [–b, +i] AGGREGATE, it is more limited in the types of things that a stack can include:

(25)   Yes: No:
            a stack of teapots [–b, +i]   #a stack of rice [–b, –i]
                                          #a stack of teapot [+b, –i]
                                          #a stack of committee [+b, +i]

Jackendoff (1991) only discusses a small range of countability types, so some questions remain unanswered. For example, *furniture* and other names for heterogeneous categories act like mass nouns in that they cannot be counted (#*three furnitures*) and they agree with singular verbs (*furniture is expensive*) – yet they seem to have clearer individuals within them than masses like *water* or *rice*. The test of divisibility works only so far for *furniture*: a sofa + a chair = *furniture*; subtract the sofa and the chair is still *furniture*, but break the chair in half, and one no longer has furniture. So, the level of internal structure seems to be different for *furniture* than for other non-count nouns like *water*. The approach in the next section addresses such differences.

Puzzle 8–2

Using the semantic type terminology in (9), how can you describe the difference between the two senses of *people* below?

a.   *People are strange.*
b.   *A people united can never be defeated.*

Is the relationship between these two senses a case of regular polysemy, like the polysemy created through COMP? To answer this, demonstrate whether other words have similar meaning patterns, concentrating on their [±b] and/or [±i] features.

8.5   Mass nouns as plurals

8.5.1   Chierchia's approach

Up to this point, we have treated mass nouns as words for SUB-STANCES and set aside other non-count nouns that describe things other than SUBSTANCES. Like much of the literature on count-versus-mass nouns, we have implicitly accepted that count nouns, which denote INDIVIDUALS, and mass nouns, which denote SUBSTANCES, are the two extremes of noun countability and thus have tried to account for those before accounting for the "in-between" or "difficult" cases. What would happen if instead we started with the difficult cases? This is the approach that Gennaro Chierchia (1998; following Gillon 1992) has taken. He argues that we can learn more about the semantics of "mass" nouns by starting with nouns like *furniture*, *clothing*, and *footwear* than by starting with "prototypical" mass nouns like *water* and *wheat*.

Nouns like *furniture* and *clothing* are singular and non-count, in that they agree with singular determiners and verbs, as shown in (26), and cannot be made plural, as in (27):

(26) a.   This furniture/clothing wears well.
      b.   *These furniture/clothing wear well.

(27)   *These furnitures/clothings wear well.

But they differ quite markedly from the SUBSTANCE mass nouns we've discussed already, in that they are general terms for heterogeneous categories of discrete things. For instance *furniture* can refer to chairs, tables, beds, and so forth, and *clothing* to shirts, skirts, trousers, and dresses. The SUBSTANCE mass nouns like *mud* and *wheat*, by contrast, seem not to be composed of individuals – mud is made up of mud, not of separate types of things with different individual category names.

Chierchia looks at mass-noun semantics from the starting perspective of the *furniture*-type nouns. One of the first things to notice is that many such nouns have plural counterparts that mean pretty much the same thing:

(28)   furniture   furnishings
        clothing   clothes
        change   coins
        footwear   shoes
        luggage   bags

The existence of plural semantic equivalents could be interpreted as a hint that mass nouns like *footwear* are semantically not too different from plural nouns like *shoes*. Furthermore, different languages make different decisions about which nouns are countable and which not. For instance, *hair* is a mass noun in English, but its equivalent in Italian, *capelli*, is a plural count noun. Chierchia takes this as a starting point for arguing that non-count nouns, whether *furniture* or *water*

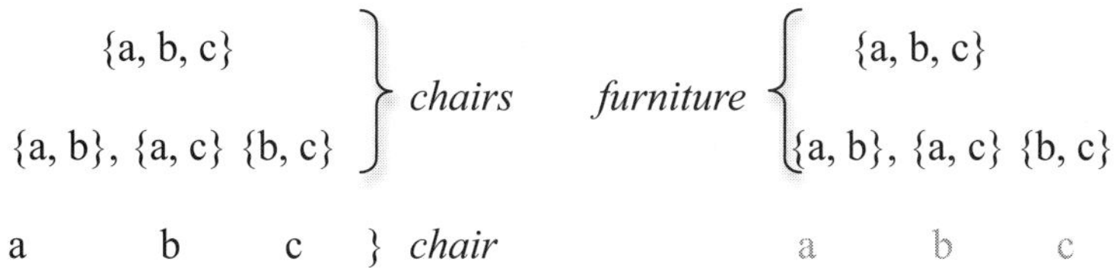

$$
\left.\begin{array}{c}
\{a, b, c\} \\[8pt]
\{a, b\}, \{a, c\} \ \{b, c\}
\end{array}\right\} chairs \quad furniture \left\{\begin{array}{c}
\{a, b, c\} \\[8pt]
\{a, b\}, \{a, c\} \ \{b, c\}
\end{array}\right.
$$

$$
\text{a} \qquad \text{b} \qquad \text{c} \ \} \ chair \qquad\qquad \text{a} \qquad \text{b} \qquad \text{c}
$$

Figure 8.4 *Pluralities and individuals*

or *rice*, do not refer to fundamentally different types of things than plural count nouns do. On this view, we do not say things like *furnitures* or *rices* simply because *furniture* and *rices* already refer to pluralities. To add an -*s* to a normal interpretation of *furniture* is thus redundant, just as it would be redundant to add a plural marker to other already-plural nouns (*cattles, *childrens).

However if words like *furniture* and *rice* are inherently plural words, then why aren't they countable? That is, we can count *two chairs*, so why not *two furniture*? The only way to count these is to use partitive constructions, like *a piece of furniture* or *a stick of furniture*, which define units into which *furniture* can be individuated. Chierchia's answer to the counting problem is that *chair* is associated with individual chairs and it undergoes the PL operation (as seen in §8.4.1) in order to make it plural, but *furniture*, not having undergone an INDIVIDUAL-to-AGGREGATE operation, applies equally well to INDIVIDU-ALS or sets of INDIVIDUALS. That is to say, the distinction between singular and plural is **neutralized** for *furniture*. But while the INDIVIDUAL-level structure is part of the semantic representation of a mass noun, it is not foregrounded in the way that INDIVIDUALS are foregrounded in cases in which a singular term has undergone pluralization, as illustrated in figure 8.4.

So, if we want to count *furniture*, no individual-level items have been already identified for it so the identity of the individuals to be counted is **vague**, whereas for *chairs*, we know exactly which individuals we're counting, as it says so right there in the word. You might think that in a case like *rice* it would be very clear what should be counted, and so Chierchia's approach would say that *two rices* should mean *two rice grains*. But Chierchia points out that it's not the case that the individuals in *rice* are necessarily the grains. A half-grain of *rice* could still be called *rice*, but we probably wouldn't say *the floor is covered with rice* if the rice had been ground down into powder. This tells us that while the individuals in *rice* could be smaller than whole grains of rice, they have to be bigger than the specks in rice powder. Since the border between being rice and being something else (powder) is indeterminate, we can't count *rice* unless we use a partitive construction in order to make the unit of counting clear.

8.5.2   Evaluating Chierchia's approach

We have not had the space here to look at all of the types of argument that Chierchia brings in favor of his proposal. Still, we've seen enough to appreciate that Chierchia proposes a solution that relies on the same countability features for two types of noun, countable plurals and non-count nouns. Instead of relying on an INTERNAL STRUCTURE feature in order to differentiate plurals like *chairs* and non-count nouns like *rice* and *furniture*, he says that the only difference between them is that *chairs* highlights the existence of individual chairs, while *rice* and *furniture* have plurality at their forefront, and it is hard to work backwards from that plurality to the countable individuals because their identity remains vague. That Chierchia can reduce the number of truly distinct countability categories while still accounting for a lot of the behaviors of these nouns is a positive thing, since it helps to explain how it is that we acquire these categories so easily.

Barner and Snedeker (2005) provide some experimental support that we understand non-count nouns as plurals, but they are less convinced when it comes to words that are flexible in whether they are understood as mass or count nouns. Take, for example, *string*. We can treat this as a count noun (*a string*, *two strings*) or a mass noun (*some string*). Chierchia treats all such instances as cases in which the Universal Packager plays a role. But note that the Universal Packager does not work equally well for all non-count nouns: we can have *a rice* (i.e. 'an order of rice') but not *a furniture*. Other approaches avoid this problem by assuming that the Packager only applies to substance nouns and that words for collections of objects, like *furniture*, have different semantic properties. Since Chierchia does not treat substances as a distinct category from other types of non-count nouns, it is less clear why *string* and *rice* can have mass and 'packaged' count interpretations, whereas *furniture* and *clothing* cannot.

In the next section, we move on to aspects of the NSM account, which addresses more types of countability while making claims about the relation between countability and conceptualization.

8.6   Cultural habits and countability: the NSM approach

In the last two sections, we have looked at ways to account for differences between count nouns and certain non-count nouns that refer to types of MATERIAL ENTITY. But there are still a number of mysteries relating to the countability/plurality status of various words. For instance, why are some heterogeneous [–b, +i] collections referred to by plural nouns (*vegetables*) and others by singular nouns (*fruit*)? Why can we hold a handful of *oats* but not *wheats? Why are we appropriately dressed in *a pair of trousers*, but doubly dressed in *a pair of bras*?

Comparing translational equivalents from different languages confuses the picture more. Strawberries and peas have the same general physical properties no matter where you are, but the English words for them are count nouns, and in Russian they're mass nouns. And why do the French speak of plural *informations*, while the English do not? Such facts have led some (e.g. Bloomfield 1933, Palmer 1971) to conclude that countability is to some extent arbitrary – one must learn which nouns are count nouns and which are not and store this information in the mental lexicon.

8.6.1   Wierzbicka: countability is semantically motivated

Wierzbicka (1985) departs from this view, arguing that if words differ in their countability, then it must be because we conceptualize their denotata differently. Take, for example, the differences between *oats* and *wheat*. Bloomfield (1933:266) claimed that because these are both words for 'particles of grain,' if the motivation for countability were semantic, then they should both have the same countability properties. But one is in the plural form and the other in the singular, so, he concludes, the distinction between count and non-count must be arbitrary – that is, there is no semantic reason for the difference. But Wierzbicka responds that there must be a semantic reason, since other variations in countability, for example between mass noun *tea* and countable noun *teas* as in (16) and (17), are meaningful. She holds that the difference between *oats* and *wheat* arises from differences in how we conceptualize the two grains.

In general, Wierzbicka says that we treat as countable anything whose individual units are big enough to be perceived as countable and interesting enough as individuals for us to want to count them. So, *oats* in this example comes under the category of things that could be counted, and *wheat* doesn't, since wheat grains are just that much smaller. However, English speakers do not really care about counting individual *oats*, either. After all, we rarely interact with a single oat, or even three or ten oats. This is consistent with the fact that *oats* does not act quite like a true plural count noun, such as *teapots*, in that we rarely use it in the singular and rarely use it with counting quantifiers. So, you probably would not say *many oats* or *four hundred oats* as in (29), but you also wouldn't use the mass quantifier *much*, which conflicts with the plural marking on *oats* in (30). Quantifiers that do not imply actual counting, like those in (31), sound best with *oats*.

(29)   ? The horse ate many/four hundred oats.

(30)   # The horse ate much oats.

(31)   The horse ate some/a lot of/plenty of oats.

Wierzbicka's study investigates the types of countability and pluralization behaviors seen in various types of nouns, and she concludes that at least fourteen different types of noun exist with respect to countability. The more individuable objects are, the more likely that their names will have all of the semantic and morphological properties of count nouns. The less individuable they are, the more likely that they will have the properties of mass nouns – but there are many other states in addition to these extremes.

8.6.2   NSM treatment

Wierzbicka (1985) used her Natural Semantic Metalanguage (NSM – see §4.4) to provide componential accounts of the different countability classes she identified, and Goddard (2009) develops a subset of these further. Take, for example, Goddard's NSM treatment for the class that includes *cheese* in (32), the one that includes *oats* (33), and the one that includes *teapot* (34):

(32)   singular names for homogeneous substances (*cheese, glass, paper*):

- something of one kind
- people can say what kind with the word *cheese* (*glass, paper*, etc.)
- people can't think about something of this kind like this:
  "this thing has many parts, someone can know how many"

(33)   aggregates of small, unnamed things (*oats, coffee grounds*):

- something of one kind
- people can say what kind with the word *oats* (*coffee grounds*, etc.)
- people can think about something of this kind like this:
  "this something is many small things
  there can be many of these small things in one small place
  people can do some things to one of these things with one finger"

(34)   countables (*cat, teapot, chair, dog*):

- something of one kind
- people can say what kind with the word *cat* (*teapot*, etc.)
- people can think about something of this kind in one of these ways:
  "this something is one thing of this kind"
  "this something is not one thing of this kind, it is more things of this kind"

Wierzbicka and Goddard hold that these explications represent subclasses of noun, each of which has its own behavior in terms of countability, pluralization (or singularization), the types of partitive expressions (e.g. *a flake of, a scoop of*) they can occur with, and so forth. Which of these subclasses a noun belongs to depends on how its denotata are conceptualized in the language community. Things that are thought of as individual are countable, things that are thought of as masses or groups are not, but these differ in whether they are pluralized or not (e.g. *wheat* versus *oats*), depending on whether they are conceptualized as something that cannot be counted or as things that are not worth counting, and so forth.

In an appendix to his 2009 article, Goddard sketches an approach to the regular polysemy patterns between mass and count nouns. He argues that more specific rules are needed than the general types of rule, like the Universal Packager, that Jackendoff uses. Goddard's examples focus on the converse of packaging, which is known in the literature as **grinding** – that is, using count nouns with mass interpretations, as in (35).

(35)   There's a lot of egg in this soup. (*vs.* There are a lot of eggs …)

In this case, we interpret *egg* as a kind of substance – an undistinguishable number of eggs outside their shells. This sense of *egg* (egg_2) is in a regular polysemy relation (§5.2.2) with the count sense, egg_1. For the derived egg_2 sense and similar food word senses, Goddard gives the following schema:

(36) egg_2 (*apple$_2$*, *tomato$_2$*, etc.):

- something of one kind that people can eat
- people can't think about something of this kind like this:
  "this thing has many parts, someone can know how many"
- before, it wasn't like this
- it is like this now because someone did some things to it before at this time it was part of something else of one kind
- people can say what kind with the word *egg* (*apple*, *tomato*, etc.)

Such words would usually have a count-noun interpretation as explicated in (34). The schema in (36) represents the differences between the count and mass interpretations of these words, but it applies to only a subset of count nouns – those to do with certain countable kinds of food.

Goddard gives a different schema (37) for deriving the sense of *cedar* that refers to wood (non-count) rather than trees (count). In other words, Goddard sees the 'grinding' process for trees as resulting in a different relation between the two senses of *cedar* from the relation that holds between the two senses of *egg*.

(37) $cedar_2$ (*pine$_2$*, *oak$_2$*, etc.):

- wood of one kind
- when people want there to be wood this kind somewhere, they do some things to trees of one kind
- people can say what kind with the word *cedar* (*pine*, *oak*)

Similarly, different schemas would be needed to show the relation between the count sense of *frog* and the non-count sense used in *there's frog all over the pavement* and so forth.

8.6.3   Cross-linguistic differences

Wierzbicka (1985) offers two types of explanation why nouns for the same things (like *pea* and *onion*) have different countability status in different languages. First, different languages/cultures set the boundaries for countability in different ways. For example, the size at which foods become "interesting enough" to be counted as INDIVIDUALS is larger in Russian than in English – so English counts peas and strawberries, while Russian *gorox* ('pea') and *klubnika* ('strawberry') are mass nouns in their base form.

Second, cultures may differ in how they interact with, and thus conceptualize, the denotata. For example, although people rarely bother to count it, in Italian *spaghetti* is a plural count noun (*1 spaghetto, 2 spaghetti*). In English *spaghetti* is treated as a mass noun. This is not just because English speakers do not know that *spaghetti* is a plural; we could very easily add our own plural marking to it to make it a count noun (*two spaghettis*), but we don't. It also is not because *spaghetti* is too small to be counted in English, since *noodle*, which denotes practically the same thing as spaghetti, is a count noun. Wierzbicka (in a lecture given in the early 1990s) pointed out that English speakers have a very different relationship to spaghetti than Italians. First, Italians are more connected to how spaghetti is made – historically it was made at home, where the individual strands would have to be handled. On the other hand, spaghetti generally entered English speakers' consciousness as something that gets poured out of a box into boiling water – with no need to handle individual pieces. Second, pasta is eaten differently in Italy and English-speaking countries. *Spaghetti* in English often refers to a whole dish, which is presented as a mass of pasta beneath an opaque tomato sauce. In Italy, pasta is traditionally a first course or side dish, where it may be eaten with just a bit of oil and garlic. In this case, the strands are more perceptible as individuals. Furthermore, some English speakers cut their spaghetti, destroying the integrity of the individual strings, whereas Italians instead wrap the strings around a fork or slurp them up without cutting them.

Puzzle 8–3

Compare the countability of *onion* and *garlic* in English. Can the differences between them be explained in terms of how we interact with these foods?

Wierzbicka's (1985) position is that the conceptualization of a thing determines whether the word for it is a count or non-count noun, and that conceptualization depends on how we perceive and interact with the thing – which may be influenced by our culture. On this thinking, *spaghetti* is a mass noun in English because when English speakers think about spaghetti, they think about a mass, rather than about individual strings, but it is a usually plural count noun in Italian because Italian speakers think of it as a bunch of individual strings. We can call this position **cultural relativity**. The contrary position would be that the countability of nouns is somewhat arbitrary, but that our conceptualization of objects is affected by our experience of whether the noun for it can be made plural or counted. In this case, *spaghetti* is a mass noun in English by accident (the people who borrowed it may not have realized it was a plural), and thus English speakers treat spaghetti strands as a mass. This position is known as **linguistic relativity**, the idea that language affects how we think and behave.

Judging the directionality of the connection between language and conceptualization is difficult. Let's take Wierzbicka's (1996) example of English *mouth* and Polish *usta*. Both words refer to the mouth, but the Polish word is always in the plural form, and Wierzbicka links this to the prominence of the lips in the Polish conceptualization of the mouth. Although there is another Polish word for 'lips,'

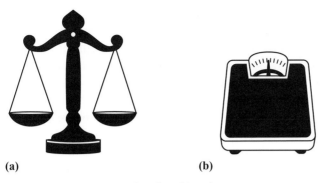

(a)   **(b)**

Figure 8.5 *Bipartite (a) and modern (b) scales*

one can also describe one's *usta* as being chapped or cracked or red with lipstick. In English, however, the singular count noun status of *mouth* focuses more on the cavity than on the lips – so we would not say we had *a chapped mouth* if our lips were chapped. The cultural-relativity way to think of this is that the Polish have a plural word because they think of the lips when they think of the mouth. But the linguistic relativity view, would instead suggest that the Polish think of the lips when they think of the mouth because *usta* is plural, and this draws attention to a visibly "plural" part of the mouth, the lips.

8.6.4   Evaluating the NSM approach

The NSM approach is very thorough in its taxonomy of different types of countable and non-countable noun, approaching each variation in noun behavior as marking out a completely separate subcategory of nouns. Such work calls our attention to a great number of fine points of noun use that need to be accounted for in a lexical semantic theory. However, this has raised the criticism that the "big picture" may be overlooked. For instance, we can raise the question of whether generalizations about count-to-mass regular polysemy relations have been missed in giving separate treatment of words for different types of substance (e.g. FOOD versus WOOD as discussed in §8.5.2). (See Jackendoff 2007 for related criticism.)

A criticism of the cultural relativity aspects of this account is that if count-ability is entirely based on how we interact with and conceptualize things, then changes in that interaction should as a matter of course bring about changes in the language – and it is not always clear that they do, or on what time scale they should be expected to change. The name for the weighing tool *scales* is a case in point. Historically, *scales* was plural because scales had two clear parts in which one thing was weighed against another, as in figure 8.5(a). Modern scales (figure 8.5(b)) do not involve balancing things in two plates.

American English has changed along with the scales, so that item (b) in figure 8.5 is usually called *a bathroom scale*. In Australian English, however,

it is still called (*a set of*) *scales* (Wierzbicka 1996). When Wierzbicka asked
Australians why the word is plural, they answered it was because there are lots
of little numbers on the contraption. This seems to be a case of the plural word
influencing the thinking about the singular thing. However, Wierzbicka notes that
Australian English has shifted from speaking of *a pair of scales* (for item (a)),
to *a set of scales* (for (b)), which indicates a way in which the language has
followed the cultural change to some degree. There is a level of bidirectionality
in the relation between language, culture, and conceptualization (as Wierzbicka
acknowledges), since language is a major tool in learning about things and in
passing on cultural practices from generation to generation.

8.7   Summary and conclusions

We have seen that the basic properties of countability and plurality
can be accounted for by the features of boundedness and internal structure. But
whether a noun is [+bounded] or [+internal structure] is a result of the ways in
which we conceptualize the denotatum, rather than what properties the denotatum
has in some absolute sense. This means that:

(a)   Thinking of the denotatum in a different way, for example thinking of
         onion as an ingredient or as a plant bulb, can change its countability
         status.
(b)   If different cultures interact with the denotatum in different ways, the
         two languages' nouns for that denotatum may have different gram-
         matical countability status.

Jackendoff's approach, which relies on binary features of boundedness and internal structure (§8.3.2–8.4), provides an efficient way of addressing issue (a),
though further development is needed to account for the full range of countability
types. Chierchia tries to reduce the singular/plural/mass/non-count distinctions to
the relationships between INDIVIDUALS and pluralities. Wierzbicka and Goddard more explicitly address issue (b). However, language and conceptualization
inform each other – thus the linguistic relativity and cultural relativity positions
discussed in §8.6.3 probably both have more than a grain of truth about them.

8.8   Further reading

For more on the approaches discussed in §8.3 through §8.6, see the
original sources cited in the chapter. John Lucy (1992) looks at the linguistic relativity implications of the count/non-count distinction in English versus Yucatec,
in which all nouns are basically non-count, and classifiers (a different word class)

are used in the counting of nouns. His 1996 overview of linguistic relativity gives a good introduction to the relevant concepts (Lucy 1996). Papafragou 2005 offers an overview of more recent studies of countability and linguistic relativity, with particular reference to language acquisition.

8.9   Answers to puzzles

8-1

(a)   *Lemonade* = [–b, –i] = SUBSTANCE. Note that, like other substances, it can only be *a lemonade* if we interpret it as denoting 'a glass of' or 'a kind of' lemonade.

(b)   *Forest* = [+b] because a forest has a boundary and thus is countable: *three forests*. You might think it's [+i] because a forest is made up of individual trees; however, forests are more than just collections of trees. They are particular areas of land with trees and other plants. This fits with the fact that we do not make partitive constructions using *tree* as the 'part' of the *forest*. So, #*three trees of a forest* sounds odd, while *three members of a team* sounds fine. Thus, *forest* is [–i], in the same way that *person* and *teapot* are [–i] – making *forest* an INDIVIDUAL.

(c)   *Furniture* is [–b], in that it is divisible and additive. So, if you have a chair and a bed in your room, you have *furniture*; if you destroy the bed, you still have *furniture*; and if you add a table, it's all still *furniture*. Its internal-structure status is more difficult to decide. *Furniture* denotes some number of individual [+b] pieces – in our example, a chair, a bed, and a table. This makes it seem like an AGGREGATE term, like *teapots* and *cattle*. However, it is different from the [+i] categories we've seen so far, since it typically denotes a heterogeneous collection, rather than a collection of like things. That is, while you could refer to three chairs as *some furniture*, you're more likely to use *three chairs* in that case, and to reserve *some furniture* for situations involving some chairs and some tables or beds, etc. *Furniture* does not act like a plural, like the [–b, +i] AGGREGATES do. For example, we say *The furniture is beautiful*, not **The furniture are beautiful*. This is not just because *furniture* has no plural suffix, as we can tell from the fact that *cattle* is a plural without a plural suffix, but still acts like an AGGREGATE: *The cattle are grumpy*, not #*The cattle is grumpy*. Thus, we must conclude that another semantic component is needed to mark items that have a heterogeneous internal structure, while reserving [+i] for meanings that involve homogeneous internal structure.

(d)   *Scissors* is an even more difficult case. It seems to be [+b], since pairs of scissors are neither divisible nor additive. However, we would expect for a [+b] item to be countable in a normal way, like *three teapots* and *five committees*, but as we've mentioned, #*three scissors* and #*a scissor(s)* are odd in most dialects. Does *scissors* have internal structure? Again, it's hard to tell. A pair of scissors is presumably *a pair* because we think of the two blades as being separate constituents of the pair. However, neither of these is *a scissor*. Neither can we use a partitive, as in #*a blade of scissors*. Again, it looks like more specific semantic components are needed in order to treat the words for 'pairwise' objects, like *scissors*, *underpants*, and *goggles*.

See Wierzbicka (1985) and Goddard (2009) for a Natural Semantic Metalanguage account of these and other types of countability.

8–2

In *People are strange, people* is an AGGREGATE term, which acts as the plural of *person*. In *A people united*... it is a GROUP term, which refers to some group of people – for example, an ethnic group or a citizenry – as a whole. They thus differ in that the AGGREGATE *people* is [–b], while *a people* is [+b]. This is not a case of regular polysemy, since when AGGREGATE terms are preceded by *a*, they are either ungrammatical (*a teapots) or interpreted as INDIVIDUALS [+b, –i]. Thus *a cattle*, while not to everyone's grammatical liking, must be interpreted as an individual bovine animal.

8–3

Onion is generally a count noun, and *garlic* generally a mass noun – one says *an onion* but not #*a garlic*, and *a head of garlic* but not *a head of onion* or *a bulb of onion*. *Onion* can be treated as a mass noun, however, in contexts like *This soup has too much onion*. (*Too many onions* is also possible, though it is interpreted slightly differently.)

While heads of garlic are usually smaller than onions, this is not the only reason for their difference – after all, there are small onions, like pearl onions and shallots, whose names are countable. Wierzbicka notes that both garlic and onions are used chopped up as an ingredient or flavoring for other foods. Since they're usually experienced chopped, their integrity as individuals is compromised. This is why both can be used as mass nouns (like other food words, when they're used as ingredients in other foods). But, Wierzbicka notes, whole onions are sometimes prepared and eaten too – for example, cocktail onions or some onions in stews. Heads of garlic are not eaten in this way because of the paper between the cloves.

8.10   Exercises

Adopt-a-word

If your word is a noun, explore its countability by (a) examining whether it can be made plural and counted (e.g. *three Xs*) or whether it can occur with non-count quantifiers (*how much X*), (b) analyzing it semantically – which of these uses is bounded and/or has internal structure? If it can be interpreted in more than one way (with respect to countability), describe the different meanings, how they relate to one another (can they be related by an operation like COMP?), and in what contexts you would use the various meanings.

1. In this chapter, we concentrated on nouns that refer to MATERIAL ENTITIES – THINGS and SUBSTANCES. The following nouns do not refer to physical things. Should they be classified as [+b] or [–b]? Or do they have both [+b] and [–b] senses? In what ways can non-physical things be bounded? Use linguistic evidence to support your claims.
   a. race (i.e. 'a contest of speed')
   b. race (i.e. 'a category of humans')
   c. admiration
   d. advice
   e. threat

2. The COMP treatment in §8.4.2 only accounts for the '17 cups of tea' interpretation of *17 teas*. Another possible interpretation is '17 different types of tea,' as in *That shop stocks 17 teas*. Develop a treatment of this type of polysemy ('x' versus 'type of x') by inventing an operator component called KIND-OF. Make sure to do all of the following:
   a. Determine what range of meanings this function can apply to (just substances or also other kinds of things?), describing them in componential (±b/±i) terms.
   b. Give the generic structure of such a 'type of' operation, in the style of the examples of other operations in figure 8.2 and (22).
   c. Give example(s) of how this structure applies to the type(s) of noun that the KIND-OF operation can apply to.

3. If one uses *watermelon* with mass-noun morphology – without a counting determiner and in singular form – it forces an interpretation in which *watermelon* is a SUBSTANCE, as in the following:

   There was a watermelon on Mel's car. (= one melon INDIVIDUAL)
   There was watermelon on Mel's car. (= melon-based SUBSTANCE)

   A function, sometimes called the **Universal Grinder** or GR, allows the interpretation of INDIVIDUALS as SUBSTANCES. Treating GR as the name for such an operator, develop a treatment of INDIVIDUAL-to-SUBSTANCE polysemy, using the instructions (a)–(c) in the previous question to guide your process.

9 Predication: verbs, EVENTS, and STATES

Key words: VERB, PREDICATE, ARGUMENT, ALTERNATION, CONFLATION, EVENT, STATE, MOTION VERB, FIGURE, GROUND, PATH, MANNER, CAUSATIVE, COPULA, RELATIONAL ADJECTIVE, RELATIONAL NOUN, PREPOSITION

9.1 Overview

Grammatically speaking, sentences (at least in English) are organized around a main verb, while semantically speaking the heart of a sentence[1] is its main **predicate**, which is often represented by a verb. Sentences represent SITUATIONS (either STATES or EVENTS), and so verbs can be expected to play a big part in the expression of SITUATIONS. But a verb itself usually does not express a complete SITUATION – so verbs interact semantically with other parts of the sentence, their **arguments**, in order to represent complete SITUATIONS. This chapter starts with a focus on verb meaning, since most verbs have predicative meanings and verbs are central to sentences. The next section discusses predication, followed by a section on differentiating STATES and EVENTS. We look at these distinctions and at the relationship between verbs and other participants in STATES/EVENTS through a detailed analysis of MOTION verbs, particularly with reference to Jackendoff's Conceptual Semantics model. At the end of this chapter we examine how other word classes can serve as semantic predicates too.

9.2 The semantics of verbs

Verbs can be semantically classified in three ways:
First, they can be classified according to **what type of situation they denote**. In this way, they can be classified generally by ontological category (see

---

[1] I refer here to the semantics of a *sentence*, while other texts might instead talk about the semantic **proposition** that a sentence represents. *Proposition* is a technical term for a meaning that can be true or false, as is the case for meanings of declarative sentences, like *Harold is angry* or *I love you*. I have preferred the term *sentence* here because *proposition* does not apply to the meanings of non-declarative sentences, such as questions.

chapter 7), such as EVENT or STATE, or more specifically by the semantic field (see §6.3.2) to which they belong – for example, verbs of MOTION, like *run* and *roll*, versus verbs of COGNITIVE ATTITUDE, like *know* and *believe*.

Second, we can group verbs according to **the types of argument structures** that they can have. This means looking at which other things and situations are needed to complete the verb meaning. For example, the situations described by *believe* and *report* both involve a conscious being and some proposition (that is believed or reported), as in *He believed/reported that aliens landed*. The SITUATIONS described by *crush* and *stroke*, on the other hand, both involve two things (whether conscious beings or not), one of which acts on the other, as in *The toddler crushed/stroked the flowers*. So, in this way we could say that *believe* and *report* belong to one category of verb while *stroke* and *crush* belong to another.

Finally, verbs can be categorized by **their interaction with time**, which affects which tense/aspect forms the verbs can take and what other temporal expressions they can go with. For instance, *recognize* and *arrive* describe actions that happen instantly, whereas *search* and *play* can go on for a long time. One can *search for hours* or *play for hours*, but one cannot #*recognize a friend for hours* or #*arrive at a conclusion for hours*. Thus in terms of their interaction with time, *recognize* and *arrive* belong to the same category – but note that if we were classifying them according to their argument structures or their semantic fields, they would belong to different categories. Since there are so many ways of classifying verbs, it almost goes without saying that there is a lot to keep in mind when analyzing verb meanings.

This chapter concentrates on the ontological categories represented by verbs and aspects of verbs' argument structures, while the next chapter focuses on the temporal issues. In both cases, we look at some particular verbal semantic fields and how they interact with these phenomena. We start in this section with the notions of predication and argument structure.

9.2.1   Predicates and arguments

In chapter 7, we noted that prototypical verbs describe ACTIONS, so let's start with a simple example of an ACTION verb, *pick*:

(1)   Fran picked flowers.

That sentence describes a SITUATION, and the type of SITUATION that it describes (an ACTION, which is a kind of EVENT) is determined by the verb. In that way, the verb is the semantic heart of the sentence, determining the SITUATION type. Grammatically speaking, the verb determines much of the structure of the sentence, for instance which other types of phrases need to be in the sentence – in this case, two noun phrases, a subject (*Fran*) and a direct object (*flowers*). That grammatical requirement is related to (but not the same as) the semantic requirements of the verb, in that the grammatically required phrases denote entities that are a part of the kind of SITUATION that the verb describes.

So, in a PICKING situation, there is more than just picking – there has to be something doing the picking and something that is being picked. We can think of verb meanings as having some "vacancies," or positions, that need to be filled in order to complete the description of the SITUATION. In discussing the meanings of verbs, we have to determine how much of the SITUATION description is communicated by the verb.

Let's start by discussing the types of semantic jobs that the elements of a sentence can do. We can make a distinction between the **referring expressions** in sentences, which refer to things, and **predicates**,[2] which tell what the referring expressions are doing, what they are or how they relate to one another. Noun phrases tend to be used as referring expressions, and verbs tend to be used as **predicators** (i.e. words that express predicates), although we have to be careful in making that equation, since *verb* and *noun phrase* are grammatical terms, and *referring expression* and *predicate* are semantic terms. So, we need to look at how a noun phrase is being used in a sentence to know whether it is a referring expression or not. For example in *It lives!*, *it* refers to something (perhaps Frankenstein's monster) that lives, whereas in *It is raining*, the "dummy" *it* does not refer to anything – so the form *it* doesn't tell us automatically what semantic job *it* does. In *Fran picked flowers*, *Fran* and *flowers* are referring expressions; they point out the things that are involved in the picking action. *Pick* is the predicator since it describes the situation that Fran and the flowers are in. We say that *pick* **predicates** a relation between *Fran* and *flowers*, and that *Fran* and *flowers* are **arguments** of the predicate *pick*. The usual way to show predication in a semantic representation is to put the predicate first, followed by its arguments, as in (2). (We have already seen this type of predicate–argument representation in the Conceptual Semantic representations in chapters 4 and 8.) Anything in parentheses is an argument of the predicate to the left of it.

(2)   pick (Fran, flowers)

9.2.2   Generalizing about situation types

So far, the grammatical requirements of the verb *pick* (in its sense 'pluck and collect') and its semantic requirements look quite similar; the verb requires two noun phrases to fill grammatical positions and there are two semantic arguments of the *pick* predicate – which we can call the PICKER and the PICKED. But the grammatical and semantic requirements are not quite the same thing. A sentence can be grammatical while being semantically **anomalous** as is demonstrated in (3).

(3)   #Pictures picked impishness.

---

[2] This is not the same as the use of the word *predicate* in traditional grammar, in which it means the same thing as *verb phrase*.

Sentence (3) has two noun phrases, as required for a sentence with *pick*, so it is grammatical. Nevertheless it is semantically odd because the apparent PICKER is inanimate (*pictures*) and the PICKED (*impishness*) is an abstract concept. This leads us to conclude that there are limits on the range of possible semantic categories that *pick*'s arguments might have, for example that the PICKER must be something that can move and the PICKED must be a physical entity that can be grasped. Here is where it is useful to be able to make general claims about verbs and the arguments they take. It is not just *pick* that requires two physical entities, including one that can move. We could say the same of *erase* and *lift*:

(4) a.   Elvis erased the picture.
    b.   #Flowers erased impishness.

(5) a.   Eliza lifted the stone.
    b.   #The stone lifted calm.

We can make two generalizations about *pick*, *erase*, and *lift* and verbs like them. First, they all involve PHYSICAL ACTIONS. That is, they are members of the same (very general) semantic category, which we can call PHYSICAL ACTION. Second, they all involve a THING that moves in order to affect another THING. Not all PHYSICAL ACTIONS involve two entities. For instance, *jog* and *wander* denote PHYSICAL ACTIONS, but the JOGGER does not affect anything – there is no JOGGED argument. By starting to categorize the verbs in this way, we can start to sketch semantic representations of them:

- *Pick*, *erase*, *lift*, and *jog* denote PHYSICAL ACTIONS.
- A PHYSICAL ACTION forms the basis of a SITUATION that must involve at least one MATERIAL THING, and that THING moves.
- Some PHYSICAL ACTION situations involve a second MATERIAL THING, which is acted upon by the moving THING.

We can use the type subscripting convention from Conceptual Semantics to represent these relations between the predicate represented by the verb and the arguments of that predicate. So, for instance, we might make a first attempt at a skeleton representation for *jog*-type verbs that looks like (6) and another for two-argument physical action verbs like *pick* and *erase*, which looks like (7). In (6), it says that the predicate is of the PHYSICAL ACTION (abbreviated as *PHYSACT*) type, that the predicate involves moving, and that there is a THING that the movement is predicated of – i.e. a MOVER. In (7), it says that there is a type of PHYSICAL-ACTION predicate that involves two arguments (which are THINGS), one of which affects the other.

(6) $[_{PHYSACT}$ MOVE $([THING])]$

(7) $[_{PHYSACT}$ AFFECT $([THING], [THING])]$

Now, the predicate elements MOVE and AFFECT that I have used here are not particular enough for any of the verbs we have discussed so far (we need to specify the type of movement for *jog* and the way in which things are affected for *pick* and *erase*, etc.) and they may not be the components that we want to stick with – §9.4 discusses some other useful predicate components. But they start us thinking about how verb meanings might be structured. What we can see so far is that part of what we need to say about a verb's meaning has to do with its arguments – the things that the verb says something about.

9.2.3   Arguments as verb components

The examples we have seen so far involve the verb's arguments being expressed by referring expressions in the sentence. In that case, the verb tells us how those referring expressions relate to the ACTION or other kind of SITUATION expressed by the verb. But arguments can also be part of the verb's meaning itself. In other words, some verbs come with some of their argument "vacancies" pre-filled. Consider *paint*, as in (8):

(8)   Whistler painted his kitchen floor.

Its meaning can be paraphrased as (9).

(9)   Whistler applied paint to his kitchen floor.

The paraphrase in (9) shows that *painted* is equivalent to *applied paint to*, and thus it makes explicit some of the elements that make up the meaning of *paint*: an ACTION, 'apply'; a THING, 'paint'; and a DIRECTION, 'to.' If (8) and (9) mean the same thing, then the fact that the referring expression *paint* is an argument in (9) indicates that there is also a semantic argument 'paint' in (8), even though the noun *paint* does not occur. Another bit of evidence that the verb *paint* carries an argument is the fact that it would be redundant to mention the substance *paint* if we have used the verb *paint*, as in (10):

(10)   ? Whistler painted his kitchen with paint.

So, a first step toward a representation of the meaning of the verb *paint* would be to represent it using the components that were expressed in the paraphrase, as in (11). Here, the main predicate represented by *paint* is APPLY, and its arguments include a THING that paints, a THING that is paint, and a complex argument 'TO (something).'

(11)   *paint* = [$_{PHYSACT}$ APPLY ([*THING*], [$_{THING}$ paint], [$_{PATH}$ TO ([*THING*])])]

The verbs *apply* and *paint* have in common that they express the movement of something to something by something else. But the meaning of *paint* is more complex than that of *apply* because it incorporates more information about the arguments, and the verb *paint* requires fewer other elements in the sentence. When a verb incorporates elements other than the predicate itself, we say it **conflates** those elements.

In addition to verbs like *paint*, which inherently represent a THING associated with the ACTION described, there are others that vary in how many of the semantic arguments must be expressed explicitly as grammatical arguments of the verb. For instance, sometimes verbs that usually take objects (that is, transitive verbs) are used without any object (intransitively). We see this in (12) and (13), where the (a) examples are transitive and the (b) examples are intransitive. In these particular cases, the intransitive versions are usually understood to paraphrase the (a) sentences here. Beth Levin, who has provided an extensive catalogue of verb-argument structures (Levin 1993), calls this the **unexpressed object alternation**.

(12) a.   I've eaten a meal already.
     b.   I've eaten already.

(13) a.   Jane drew a picture in her notebook.
     b.   Jane drew in her notebook.

These cases are a bit different from the conflation in *paint*. For *paint*, it was pretty obvious what the conflated argument was, since the verb has the same form as the substance whose application it describes: *paint*. In (12) and (13), the identities of the unspoken arguments are not obvious from the form of the verb. For example, (12b) says *I've eaten already*, not *I've mealed already*. Still, if someone uses intransitive *eat* to ask you *Have you eaten yet?*, it means 'Have you eaten breakfast/lunch/dinner yet?' (whichever is the most relevant meal for the time of day). So, if you had just eaten a breath mint or a slip of paper (because you are an international spy with evidence to destroy), you would not say *I've eaten already* even though, strictly speaking, you had just eaten something. Similarly, intransitive *draw*, as in (13b), is usually understood to mean 'draw a picture (or pictures),' and not just, say, 'draw a pencil line.' Thus something interesting is happening in these transitive/intransitive alternations that "adds something extra" to the interpretations of the verbs.

It is debated whether the identity of the unexpressed object is a lexical-semantic issue (part of the verb's meaning) or a pragmatic issue – that is, not part of the verb's meaning, but derivable from knowledge that we have about how the world works, and what kinds of objects are most relevant to these sentences. But while identifying the unspoken argument may be a pragmatic issue, whether or not a verb can drop an object is not just about pragmatics. For some of these types of alternations, semantic patterns can be discovered. For example, some verbs of 'caring for body parts' allow for unspoken arguments, as in (14). But none of the verbs to do with caring for the hair allow for the object to be left off, as (15) illustrates. In each of those cases, we need to add *her/his hair* to the sentence in order for it to be grammatical.

(14) a.   William shaved (his face) haphazardly.
     b.   Kira flosses (her teeth) nightly.
     c.   Joan washed (her hands) before coming to the table.

(15) a. 　*Rakesh combed after his shower.
　　　　　Rakesh combed his hair after his shower.
　　b.　　*Karen curled on her wedding day.
　　　　　Karen curled her hair on her wedding day.
　　c.　　*James parted a new way.
　　　　　James parted his hair a new way.

The only thing we comb is hair – so if the unexpressed object alternation just depended on the pragmatic issue of whether we could identify the missing object, then we would be expect to be able to say *Rakesh combed*, since it would be obvious what he had combed. And it would certainly be more obvious than what Joan washed or what William shaved in (14). Thus, verb-argument alternations are not just a matter of leaving off information that can be recovered from the context. The lexical entry for a verb must record which arguments must appear and which may be left off, and aspects of the semantics of the verb or its arguments may influence which arguments can be left off which verbs.

Puzzle 9–1

We said that in (12b) intransitive *eat* is interpreted as 'eat a meal.' Consider the following verbs that allow the unexpressed object alternation, and determine what their unspecified arguments are when the verbs are used intransitively. Can you find a pattern to what kinds of objects can be left unmentioned?

　　　drink, hum, iron, pack, read, vacuum

9.2.4　Summary

The points to take away from this section are:

* Sentence meanings are organized around a main predicating expression, which is usually a verb.
* Predicators tell us something about the referring expressions in the sentence: what they are doing, what they are or how they relate to one another.
* The nature of the predicate may determine what kinds of ENTITIES can fill its argument positions.
* The number of referring expressions required in a sentence is not necessarily the same as the number of arguments of the main predicate expressed by the verb.
* Some verbs have complex meanings that conflate some of their arguments.
* Some verbs can be involved in grammatical alternations, which can affect their interpretation.

Based on our observations so far, the semantic representation of a verb meaning should include:

- a SITUATION type (e.g. PHYSICAL ACTION, STATE, MENTAL EVENT);
- indication of how many and what kinds of ENTITIES need to be involved in such a SITUATION, and what roles they play;
- more particular information about what is being predicated of the ENTITIES – that is, what kind of EVENT or STATE they are participating in.

9.3   STATES and EVENTS

The ontological category associated with whole sentences is SITU-ATION, which might involve a number of THINGS, ACTIONS, PROPERTIES, a TIME, a PLACE, etc. The SITUATION category has two major subcategories: STATES and EVENTS. So, when we look at verb sense (as used in a sentence), a primary concern is whether it denotes a STATE or an EVENT. If it describes a STATE, it is called a **stative verb**, and if it describes an EVENT, it is a **dynamic verb**.

In chapter 7, we saw that different ontological categories have different temporal qualities. STATES and EVENTS can be distinguished by how they relate to time, with STATES being more constant across time, and EVENTS less so. Let's take the example of *stand*, which can describe a STATE, as in (16), and *stand up*, which describes an EVENT, as in (17).

(16)   The clock stands in the hall. [STATE]

(17)   The children stood up to greet the teacher. [EVENT]

Sentence (16) describes a SITUATION that is **static**, or unchanging. The clock is fixed to its spot in the hall. Sentence (17), on the other hand, describes a SITUATION that is **dynamic** – something is happening or changing. The children are going from a sitting position to a standing one. This is the essence of the difference between STATES and EVENTS, and therefore one test for whether a SITUATION is an EVENT is whether the sentence could be sensibly used as an answer to the question *What happened?* In (18), (a) is a strange answer to the question, since standing in a place doesn't really *happen*. But we can see that (b) is dynamic, since it is a reasonable answer to the question.

(18)   What happened?
        a. ??The clock stood in the hall.
        b. The children stood up.

There is much more to be said about the temporal aspects of stative and dynamic verbs – but we return to those issues in chapter 10. At this point, we are introducing the notions of STATE and EVENT so that we can look in more detail at the elements that make up verb meanings. We start doing this in the next section by looking at verbs of MOTION.

9.4   MOTION verbs

Verbs of MOTION have been the subject of a fair amount of semantic investigation. They make for a nice introduction to the componential analysis of verb meaning because they include a large number of fairly typical verbs and their meanings can be extended in various ways, allowing for further discussion of polysemy and metaphor. As we will see, it is also possible to conceptualize other types of EVENTS as if they were motions. Let's start by looking at what elements are necessary to a MOTION EVENT, then look at which of these elements are included within particular verb senses.

9.4.1   Components of a MOTION EVENT

MOTION verbs denote changes in location – that is, they are dynamic verbs that contribute to an EVENT description, as exemplified by the verbs in (19) through (21).

(19)   Sheryl **went** into town on foot.

(20)   Lance **cycled** across France.

(21)   Wilma **left**.

These can be compared with **LOCATION verbs**, which are stative verbs that locate something, but do not involve a change in location. (Note that most verbs are polysemous, and therefore they might have both stative and dynamic senses. Make sure to pay attention to the particular contexts in which they occur in order to identify the sense in use.)

(22)   The monument **stands** beside the fountain.

(23)   Switzerland **lies** north of Italy.

The MOTION verbs all involve something going somewhere, so we can represent the 'motion' component of the verbs as the predicate GO. The LOCATION verbs, on the other hand, involve no 'going' and so, following Jackendoff, we can treat those as having a stative predicate BE_{loc}, which stands for 'be located.'

Other than the issue of whether or not the SITUATION is an EVENT or a STATE, the MOTION and LOCATION have a lot in common. Both SITUATION types include the following elements:

•   **FIGURE** – the THING whose location is being discussed
•   **GROUND** (sometimes called **LANDMARK**) – the THING against which the LOCATION/MOTION of the FIGURE is judged

- **POSITION** – the (final) location of the FIGURE with respect to the GROUND
- **MANNER** – the way in which the FIGURE moves/is situated

In addition, MOTION EVENTS involve a PATH:

- **PATH** – the direction of the FIGURE's travel with respect to the GROUND

We can see how each of these elements is included in the MOTION sentence (19) and the LOCATION sentence (22) in table 9.1. In (19), each of the elements is presented as a separate expression in the sentence. Some are required (e.g. *Sheryl*), and some (e.g. *on foot*) could be left out without any grammatical consequences, and the only semantic consequence is that the sentence is less informative. In (22), FIGURE, GROUND, and PATH are separate expressions in the sentence, but the information on MANNER is conflated in the verb *stand*.

Putting this into a Conceptual Semantics (see §4.2) componential structure, GO or BE$_{loc}$ is the main predicative element, and these predicates take a THING (the FIGURE) as the first argument. LOCATIONS involve a PLACE as the second argument, while MOTION EVENTS have a PATH. PLACE is made up of another predicative element and one argument a THING (the GROUND), and likewise PATH involves a predicate and, as its argument, a PLACE. In other words:

(24) a. $[_{STATE}$ BE$_{loc}$ ([THING], [PLACE])]
i.e. one kind of STATE involves a THING located in a PLACE

b. $[_{EVENT}$ GO ([THING], [PATH])]
i.e. one kind of EVENT involves a THING going along a PATH

c. $[_{PATH}$ TO ([PLACE])]
i.e. one kind of PATH is TO a PLACE
(another type might be FROM a PLACE)

d. $[_{PLACE}$ AT ([THING])]
i.e. one kind of PLACE is AT a THING
(other types = IN, NEXT-TO, etc.)

Table 9.1 *Elements of a MOTION EVENT/LOCATION STATE*

	MOTION EVENT	LOCATION STATE
	(19) Sheryl went into town on foot.	(22) The monument stands beside the fountain.
	GO	BE$_{loc}$
FIGURE	Sheryl	the monument
GROUND	town	the fountain
PATH	to	–
POSITION	in	beside (at the side of)
MANNER	on foot (walking)	standing (upright)

We can follow Talmy (2000) in considering MANNER to be a **co-event** to the MOTION EVENT. In other words, Sheryl's *going on foot* in (19) involves a MOTION EVENT co-occurring with a 'being-on-foot' event. Since our attention is on the MOTION EVENT, we can abbreviate our treatment of MANNER, simply including it as an unanalyzed co-event to GO, as in (25), where (24b) is updated with the MANNER information. MANNER is optional (which is indicated here by the angle brackets), since not every MOTION EVENT description includes a MANNER. The details of sentence (19) are elaborated in (26) and as a tree in (27).

(25) $[_{EVENT}$ GO$<$+MANNER$>$ ($[THING]$, $[PATH]$)]

(26) $[_{EVENT}$ GO+on-foot ($[_{THING}$ Sheryl], $[_{PATH}$ TO ($[_{PLACE}$ IN ($[_{THING}$ town])])])]

(27)

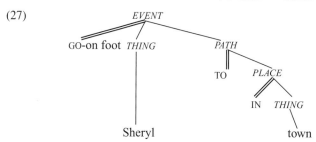

But enough about sentences – we're interested in verbs. What in (26) and (27) is the verb meaning, and what is the rest of the sentence? Since the verb is the element of the sentence that determines the SITUATION and the major argument requirements, the basic structure of (26) and (27) indicates the verb meaning. If we take out the parts of (27) that other elements in the sentence contribute, we are left with (28) as the representation of the MOTION sense of *go*.

(28)   *go* =

EVENT

GO   THING   PATH

= $[_{EVENT}$ GO ($[THING]$, $[PATH]$)]

This may seem a bit circular, since the predicate of *go* is just represented as GO. In this case, GO has been treated as a primitive component, which cannot be broken down further. Recall from §3.2 that semantic components may be presented in English for our convenience, but the components are not the words themselves and do not carry all the semantic baggage of English words. Furthermore, the meaning of *go* is not just the component GO – it is that component plus the rest of the information in (28), which includes identification of the SITUATION type and the argument structure that goes with GO. When we represent more complex MOTION verb meanings, we still use the primitive element GO. Let's take the example of *leave* in (20), *Wilma left*. Starting with the basic MOTION verb structure for *go* in (28), how do we differentiate the meaning of *go* from that of *leave*? The answer is to look for what elements of the MOTION EVENT have been conflated in *leave*. The FIGURE in *Wilma left* is *Wilma*, so that is not part of the verb meaning. Since there is nothing else in the sentence, the question is whether all of the elements (GROUND, PATH, POSITION) are in the verb or not. Remember, a test for whether something has been conflated can be whether it is redundant to mention it again. In the case of GROUND, (29) shows that it is not redundant to mention the place from which the leaver leaves. But it is redundant to say that the path was *from* the ground, as in (30). So it seems that PATH information is conflated in *leave*. Since *leave* says nothing about the means by which someone left, we can conclude that it does not conflate MANNER.

(29)   Wilma left a place.

(30)   *Wilma left from a place.

(31)   *leave* =

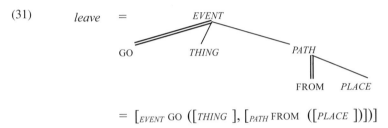

= $[_{EVENT}$ GO $([_{THING}$], $[_{PATH}$ FROM $([_{PLACE}$])])]

Puzzle 9–2

Try your hand at putting the following expressions into Conceptual-Semantic-style representations, using the models in (24) through (31) as inspiration. For each, give the representation in both the bracketed notation and a tree format.

a.   *The monument stands beside the fountain.* [= (22)]
b.   *Lance crossed France.*
c.   the LOCATION verb *stand*
d.   the MOTION verb *cross*

9.4.2   More about conflation

We have already seen some cases of conflation of elements in MOTION/LOCATION verbs. For example, *cycle* in (19) indicates MANNER ('by bicycle') as well as movement. *Leave* in (20) indicates the PATH, and so it can be paraphrased as 'go from.' MANNER and PATH are most frequently conflated in English MOTION verbs, but there are also some verbs that conflate the GROUND element, such as *derail* in (32), which also conflates the PATH.

(32)   The train derailed outside the city.

(33) $derail = [_{EVENT} \text{ GO } ([THING], [_{PATH} \text{ FROM } ([_{PLACE} \text{ ON } ([_{THING}\text{rail}])])])]$

Talmy (1985) observed that languages differ in their preferred patterns of conflation. For instance, in some North American languages including Atsugewi and Navajo, MOTION verbs conflate information about the FIGURE. One Atsugewi verb, *-lup-*, is for the movement of small, round, shiny things, and another, *-caq-*, is for slimy, lumpy things. Thus, in order to say 'the pebble moved' in Atsugewi, one must use a different verb than one would use in the equivalent of 'the toad moved.' Such FIGURE-conflating MOTION verbs are rare in other languages. In English, we can point to occasional examples like *swarm*, which only [+internal structure] FIGURES can do (recall §8.3.2), and *seep*, which is for the movement of liquids.

In some cases, it may be that the conflated information is not sufficient (either grammatically or to express everything that one wants to express). For instance, in the Atsugewi case above, only the shape-class of the FIGURE is indicated, so the precise identity of the FIGURE may be spelt out elsewhere in the sentence. Similarly, going back to our *paint* examples, it would be redundant to say (34), but not redundant to say (35), since the latter adds new information about the 'paint' argument that is carried by the verb.

(34)   ? Whistler painted paint on the kitchen floor.

(35)   Whistler painted a blue latex emulsion on the kitchen floor.

9.4.3   Another EVENT type: causation

Many verbs, including many MOTION verbs, indicate that something caused an EVENT or STATE to come about. Some MOTION verbs are inherently **causative**, including *raise*. So, in (36) an EVENT in which a flag moved was caused by Peter.

(36)   Peter raised the flag.
            [= 'Peter caused the flag to move upward']

Many other MOTION verbs are polysemous with both causative and non-causative meanings, such as *roll* in (37):

(37) a.   The ball rolled$_1$ down the hill. [not causative]
     b.   Sally rolled$_2$ the ball down the hill.
            [causative = 'Sally caused the ball to roll down the hill']

The causative sense of *roll$_2$* in (37b) takes one more argument (*Sally*) than the non-causative sense *roll$_1$* – so we can refer to a **causative alternation** in argument structure. Translating this into a componential representation, CAUSE is an EVENT-type predicative component that shows the relationship between two arguments: a THING that is the causer and another EVENT. Compare the representation of non-causative *roll₁* in (38) with the causative *roll₂* in (39). Example (40) shows how the full causative sentence (37b) is represented.

(38) $roll_1 = [_{EVENT} \text{GO+roll } ([THING], [PATH])]$

(39) $roll_2 = [_{EVENT} \text{CAUSE } ([THING], [_{EVENT} \text{GO+roll } ([THING], [PATH])])]$

(40) $[_{EVENT} \text{CAUSE } ([_{THING} \text{ Sally}], [_{EVENT} \text{GO+roll } ([_{THING} \text{ the ball}],$
          $[_{PATH} \text{TO } ([_{PLACE} \text{DOWN } ([_{THING} \text{ the hill}])])])])]$

Puzzle 9–3

None of the sentences below expresses a causative meaning, but some of the verbs involved may be polysemous, having a causative and a non-causative meaning. Determine which of these verbs are causative by adding an additional argument to each sentence. Based on these examples (and the case of *roll* above), form a hypothesis about which kinds of English verbs can have causative senses and which cannot.

Example:

*   *The bolt slid into place.*
*   Add an argument: *I slid the bolt into place.*
*   Does this mean 'I caused the bolt to slide into place'?
*   Yes: we can conclude that *slide* has non-causative and causative senses.

Now you try:

a.   Fred descended the staircase.
b.   The Boy Scout crossed the street.
c.   Magdalena waltzed into the room.
d.   Petals are falling from the flower.
e.   The note slipped out of the book.

9.4.4   Language typology and polysemy of MOTION verbs

Besides conflating different components of MOTION EVENT descriptions, languages can also vary in which pattern of conflation is **unmarked** – that is, which element is most "naturally" or "unremarkably" conflated in the language's MOTION verbs. The unmarked conflation pattern is the one that is most colloquial in usage, most frequently used, and most pervasive in the language's lexis.

In English, German, and Chinese, MANNER-conflation and MANNER/CAUSE conflation is unmarked. Verbs like *walk*, *roll*, and *run* are colloquial ways to express MOTION EVENTS, whereas PATH-conflating verbs like *enter*, *rise*, and *descend* are more rare, both in the number of examples in the English lexicon and in terms of frequency of use. So, while one could say sentences (41) or (42), (43) is the more "everyday" way of talking about such an event in English.

(41)   James entered the room.

(42)   James entered the room by walking.

(43)   James walked into the room.

Information that is conflated in the verb is perceived as being in the **background**, and information that is expressed by other sentence constituents seems **foregrounded**. Thus, while (42) and (43) report the same facts, you would probably reserve use of (42) for a situation in which it was particularly remarkable that James walked.

While English conflates MANNER, PATH-conflation is unmarked in Turkish and in the Romance languages, including French and Spanish. In fact, many of the PATH-conflating verbs in English, like *enter* and *descend*, came to us from French and Latin. Since it is not necessary to express the MANNER co-event in PATH-conflating languages, MANNER tends not to be mentioned as often. Compare, for example, the English original and Spanish translations of these passages in Lewis Carroll's *Alice's Adventures in Wonderland*:

(44) a.   . . . when suddenly a white rabbit with pink eyes **ran** close by her.
                                                           (Carroll 1865:2)

     b.   . . . cuando súbitamente **pasó corriendo** a su lado un Conejo Blanco de
           ojos rosados.   (Stilman 2003:17)
           '. . . when suddenly **passed running** at her side a White Rabbit with pink
           eyes.'

(45) a.   she **walked** on in the direction in which the March Hare was said to live.
                                                           (Carroll 1865:93)

     b.   ella **dirigió sus pasos** hacia el lugar donde, según se le había dicho, vivía
           La Liebre de Marzo.   (Stilman 2003:75)
           'she **directed her steps** toward the place where, according to what is said,
           lives the March Hare.'

While the English version in (44) uses the MANNER-conflating verb *run* with the preposition *by* giving the PATH information, the Spanish uses the PATH-conflating verb *pasar* 'to pass' and adds an adverbial *corriendo* 'running.' Both the PATH and MANNER information are mentioned, but the languages differ in which information belongs in the heart of the sentence, the verb. In (45), the literal translation of *dirigío sus pasos* 'directed her steps' or, more loosely, 'directed her path' sounds very unnatural in English, but it is the idiomatic way to say 'headed in a certain direction' in Spanish, again using a verb that has no MANNER information.

The unmarkedness of MANNER conflation in MOTION verbs has consequences for the polysemy of English verbs. Because MANNER is usually associated with MOTION, other verbs that encode an activity that could be associated with MOTION can be used to express a MOTION on a PATH, with the activity becoming the MANNER of MOTION. We can see this in (46)–(48). Notice that the (a) sentences make no claims about the subject moving anywhere; Whistler in (46) could be sitting in the middle of the room with a spray gun. But when a PATH description is added as in the (b) sentences, the verbs describe MOTION EVENTS. The NON-MOTION EVENT that is usually described by the verb is then understood as a co-event to the MOTION EVENT.

(46) a.   Whistler painted the room.
     b.   Whistler painted himself into a corner.

(47) a.   The train screeched.
     b.   The train screeched into the station.

(48) a.   The raft floated.
     b.   The raft floated down the river.

We understand the MOTION interpretation of the verb when there are other elements in the sentence that indicate a DIRECTION. So here we have another case of alternation – in this case between uses of verbs without a directional adverbial (i.e. an adverb or a prepositional phrase that indicates a DIRECTION

Puzzle 9–4

An alternation that is found for some MOTION + MANNER verbs is the **Locative Preposition Drop Alternation** (Levin 1993), in which the verb can either occur with a prepositional phrase indicating the PATH and GROUND, or the preposition can be omitted and the verb has a direct object indicating the GROUND. *Jump* has this alternation; you can express a 'jumping-over' EVENT either with or without *over*:

The athlete jumped over the hurdle.
The athlete jumped the hurdle.

Other MOTION EVENTS do not allow such an alternation:

The ball rolled along the road.
*The ball rolled the road.

First, determine which of the following sentences allow this alternation. Next, look at the sets of verbs that do and do not allow the alternation. Do their meanings have anything in common?

a.   Hilary climbed up the mountain.
b.   The boat drifted across the lake.
c.   John coiled the string around the spool.
d.   The crowd charged at the ticket booth.
e.   Earth revolves around the Sun.
f.   Nomads wander around the desert.

and possibly an endpoint for the movement) and verbs with them. And again the grammatical alternation is linked to a different semantic interpretation of the verb: the ACTIVITY sense versus a GO+[$_{MANNER}$ACTIVITY] sense.

9.4.5   Extending the LOCATION/MOTION structures

In chapters 3 and 4, we made the case that a strong componential approach to meaning should use components that can be recycled in a variety of meanings. The more useful a component is in describing a language's meanings, the better our justification for thinking that it is a basic building block of language, and the more different kinds of meanings that we can use that component in, the more explanatory the theory is. That is to say, it explains why we have the kinds of meanings we have by positing that there are primitive meanings that are just part of the way that humans think. While so far we have only considered components like GO and BE and semantic types like THING and PATH in the context of LOCATION and MOTION meanings, they can be extended to a range of other types of EVENTS and STATES (Jackendoff 1983, following Gruber 1965). Thus, it can be argued, the types of semantic structures discussed so far in this chapter are basic structures that can be applied broadly in language to different **conceptual fields** – that is, different types of situations that we can think about.

Let's start with the BE component, familiar from its BE$_{loc}$ location use. This BE can be the basis of many types of STATE, as illustrated in (49)–(51). Each of these applications of BE keeps the same basic structure of the locative BE, but varies in the types of arguments to be found in the PLACE. So BE$_{ident}$ indicates the STATE of having a PROPERTY, BE$_{poss}$ is the location of a THING in the possession of another THING, and BE$_{temp}$ is location in time. Their structures are the same as those used for location descriptions, except for the type of PLACE, which in these cases is a PROPERTY, a possessor THING, or a TIME.

(49)   HAVING A PROPERTY
Charles is giddy.
[$_{STATE}$ BE$_{ident}$ ([$_{THING}$ Charles], [$_{PLACE}$ AT ([$_{PROP}$ giddy])])]

(50)   POSSESSION
Hugh has a pencil collection.
[$_{STATE}$ BE$_{poss}$ ([$_{THING}$ pencil collection], [$_{PLACE}$ AT ([$_{THING}$ Hugh])])]

(51)   POSITION IN TIME
The seminar is at 5:00 pm.
[$_{STATE}$ BE$_{temp}$ ([$_{THING}$ the seminar], [$_{PLACE}$ AT ([$_{TIME}$ 5:00 pm])])]

Example (50) is the odd one out here, in that possession does not involve the verb *be* in English. However, in some other languages, possession is expressed with the 'be' verb. For example, in Latin *Est mihi liber* 'I have a book' is literally

'(There) is to me a book.' While English uses the form *have* for possession, the claim here is that underlyingly it involves the stative BE element.

The GO component can be extended in the same way, and it is telling that in English the word *go* can be used to express all of these types of EVENT.

(52) Charles went giddy.
$[_{EVENT}$ GO$_{ident}$ ([$_{THING}$ Charles], [$_{PATH}$ TO ([$_{PLACE}$ AT ([$_{PROP}$ giddy])])])]

(53) Hugh's pencil collection went to his heirs.
$[_{EVENT}$ GO$_{poss}$ ([$_{THING}$ Hugh's pencil collection], [$_{PATH}$ TO ([$_{PLACE}$ AT ([$_{THING}$ Hugh's heirs])])])]

(54) The seminar went from 2:00 to 5:00.
$[_{EVENT}$ GO$_{temp}$ ([$_{THING}$ the seminar], [$_{PATH}$ $\left\{ \begin{array}{l} \text{FROM ([}_{PLACE}\text{ AT ([}_{TIME}\text{ 2:00])])} \\ \text{TO ([}_{PLACE}\text{ AT ([}_{TIME}\text{ 5:00])])} \end{array} \right\}$])]

Just as for the LOCATIVE/MOTION conceptual field, the other GO components here can be included in the meanings of a wide range of other verbs. For instance, the temporal verb *last* can be represented using GO$_{temp}$.

(55) The seminar lasted until 5:00.
$[_{EVENT}$ GO$_{temp}$ ([$_{THING}$ the seminar], [$_{PATH}$ TO ([$_{PLACE}$ AT ([$_{TIME}$ 5:00])])])]

The meaning of *last* can be represented as 'going on a temporal path.' Bringing the CAUSE component into play, we can represent the temporal meaning of the prepositional verb *drag out* in (56).

(56) Professor Jones dragged out her lecture until 5:00.

(57) *drag out* = $[_{EVENT}$ cause ([$THING$], [$_{EVENT}$ GO$_{temp}$+with-effort ([$THING$], [$_{PATH}$ to ([$_{PLACE}$ at ([$_{TIME}$ 5:00])])])])]

Thus, a variety of verb meanings can be described by appealing to the similarities between literal motion and other kinds of EVENT and between literal location and other kinds of STATE. Table 9.2 summarizes the components and structures discussed above.

A final point to make about MOTION verbs is that they can also be used metaphorically to describe EVENTS that involve no locomotion, as the following show:

(58) A thought crossed my mind.

(59) The economy slid into recession.

MANNER-conflating languages tend to use MANNER verbs metaphorically more than PATH-conflating languages do (Özçalişkan 2004). But in general, the full range of MOTION verb types is available for metaphor, including causative verbs. For instance, in (60), the baby is not literally moved to another place. Instead *sleep* is treated as a PLACE where one can be moved to.

(60) Albert rocked the baby to sleep.

Table 9.2 *BE/GO predicates and their PLACE arguments across conceptual fields*

Conceptual field	STATE example	EVENT example	PLACE structure
Spatial location: BE/GO*loc*	*It is at/in/on the box.*	*It went to/into/onto the box.*	AT ([THING]) (or IN, ON, etc. instead of AT)
Temporal location: BE/GO*temp*	*The concert is at 8 o'clock.*	*The concert went past 8 o'clock.*	AT ([TIME])
Property ascription: BE/GO*ident*	*It is blue.*	*It went blue.*	AT ([PROPERTY])
Possession: BE/GO*poss*	*It is Jo's.*	*It went to Jo.*	AT ([THING])

Puzzle 9–5

Give bracketed Conceptual Semantics representations for sentence (60) and for the sense of the verb *rock* used in that sentence.

9.5   Non-verb predicates

So far, in considering predication in language, we have focused on verbs, since they most often represent the main predicators in sentences. But nouns, prepositions, and adjectives can be predicative too. In fact, we have already seen illustrations of predicate–argument structures represented by prepositional phrases. Recall sentence (19), re-presented with the PATH preposition highlighted in (61):

(61)   Sheryl went **into** town on foot.

Extracting the meaning of *into* from the analysis of the whole sentence (which was presented above in (26) and (27)), we get:

(62)   *into* $[_{PATH}$ TO $([_{PLACE}$ IN $([THING])])]$

This analysis shows *into* as consisting of a PATH predicate TO, which takes as its argument a PLACE. The PLACE, in turn, involves the predicate IN, which takes a

THING as its argument. Those predicate–argument relations can be expressed, as they were here, using a preposition, or, as we have also seen already (recall §4.2) through verbs like *enter*, which have complex predicate structures that conflate PATH information.

The rest of this section looks in turn at adjectives, nouns, and prepositions and the predicate–argument structures that they may present. This involves, in the next section, also considering whether every verb is a predicator.

9.5.1   Are adjectives predicates?

The Conceptual Semantic approach that we have concentrated on in this chapter treats stative sentences as involving the component BE, which looks just like the base form of the verb in English that we use to link a subject to a adjective, noun, or prepositional phrase. The English verb *to be* is called a **copular verb** or a **linking verb**, meaning that it links a subject to a predicate, and, in many formal semantic approaches, it is essentially ignored when determining the predicate-argument structure of a sentence. In other words, some approaches would treat sentence (63) as having the predicate–argument structure in (64), where *giddy* is a predicate that takes one argument, *Charles*.

(63)   Charles is giddy.

(64)   giddy (Charles)

Why would one want to leave out the *be*-verb (*is*) when describing the predicate-argument structure of (63)? There are a few reasons to be suspicious that this copular *be* adds anything to the basic predicate–argument structure of the sentence:

- First, note that not every language would put a verb in this sentence. As we noted in chapter 7, some languages (like Chinese) lexicalize properties like *giddy* or *tall* as verbs rather than adjectives. Similarly, for sentences with nouns on either side of the copula in English (like *Gertrude is a podiatrist*), other languages (like Arabic) would need no verb there or might use a pronoun to link the two nouns ('Gertrude she podiatrist'). If a verb does not need to be there in order to describe a complete STATE in other languages, we can question whether the verb is really making a semantic contribution in English.
- Furthermore, English requires that every sentence has a verb, so it could be argued that the only reason that we use the copula *be* is so that that grammatical rule is fulfilled in sentences in which there is no semantic requirement for a verb.
- Finally, many adjectives denote PROPERTIES, and PROPERTIES do not exist on their own. That is, there is no giddiness without things that are giddy; so a PROPERTY-denoting adjective occurs

with an expression that denotes something that is claimed to have that PROPERTY. We could thus interpret *giddy* as a predicate that requires an argument (in this case, *Charles*) in order to complete its meaning.

That is not how we have presented things in the Conceptual Semantics approach in the last section, however. Instead, there the PROPERTY is an argument deeper in the sentence structure, and it looks like the copular verb is represented as a predicate. That is a bit too simplistic a view of that approach, however, since the structure of a stative expression like *Charles is giddy* will include the BE predicate whether the language under analysis expresses it as *Charles is giddy*, *Charles giddy* or *Charles he giddy*. The BE component represents that the sentence as a whole represents a STATE, and in some languages that might map onto a verb that does the same job, and in other languages it might not. Jackendoff (1983) prefers this approach over the adjective-as-main-predicate treatment of (64), for which he sees two disadvantages. First, a semantic structure like *giddy(Charles)* bears little resemblance to the syntactic structure that is supposed to express it, at least for copular languages. Second, many adjectives cannot be interpreted without reference to their nouns. We come back to this in chapter 11, but for now note that an adjective like *good* relates to very different properties when it modifies different nouns:

(65)   That roller coaster is really good. (= 'exciting')

(66)   That nap was really good. (= 'restful')

If *good* is the predicate that runs the show, it is not terribly clear how the noun could have such a great effect on its meaning, rather than vice versa.

So, while some approaches hold that PROPERTY-describing adjectives like *giddy* or *good* are predicators, others do not. But all approaches must treat certain other adjectives as predicates because they express relations between at least two things. For example:

(67)   Nancy is fond of Paul.

(68)   Paul is proud of Nancy.

We can represent the meaning of *(be) proud (of)*, as (69), where 'proud' is a PROPERTY that takes a THING as an argument (as shown in bold) which can fit into a larger structure for describing the STATE of someone being proud of someone else, as in (69):

(69) $[_{STATE}\ \mathrm{BE}_{ident}\ ([THING],\ [_{PLACE}\ \mathrm{AT}\ ([_{PROP}\ \textbf{PROUD}\ ([\textbf{THING}])])])]$

This is to say that relational adjectives, like *fond* or *proud*, describe PROPER-TIES that take a THING argument, while non-relational adjectives do not take arguments in the Conceptual Semantic treatment.

9.5.2   Predicative nouns

If relational adjectives are predicates, then it stands to reason that relational nouns are predicates too. Which nouns are relational? The most obvious examples would be nouns for our family relations:

(70)   Linda is the mother of the bride.

Besides kin relations, we can use nouns to denote other types of relations:

(71)   Doj is the president of the Scrabble club.

(72)   Piglet is the runt of the litter.

In these cases, we have a type of THING (*mother, president, runt*) that takes another THING (*the bride, the Scrabble club, the litter*) as an argument. Just focusing on the argument structure of *president* (and leaving off the analysis of the rest of the sentence), we have:

(73)   [$_{THING}$ PRESIDENT ([$THING$])]

This represents that in order to be a president, one has to be president in relation to something else – that is, president *of* something. Similarly, one cannot be a mother without being someone's mother.

Deverbal nouns – that is, nouns that are morphologically derived from verbs (see §7.3.2) – can also take arguments. This should not be terrifically surprising, since the verbs that they are derived from also take arguments. Consider the relation between (74) and (75):

(74)   Stan recited a poem.

(75)   Stan's recitation of the poem

If *a poem* is an argument of *recited* in (74), it should also be an argument of the noun *recitation*, as in (75), since both examples describe an EVENT involving a recited THING. Notice, though, the contrast between the noun *recitation* in (76) and the gerund (i.e. the *-ing* form of the verb, used as a noun) *reciting* in (77):

(76) a.   The recitation of the poem was beautiful.
   b.   The recitation was beautiful.

(77) a.   The reciting of the poem was beautiful.
   b.   ? The reciting was beautiful.

While in both cases something is recited, the gerund is more natural with the overt expression of the 'recited THING' argument, while *recitation* is less so. This indicates that the gerund is more verb-like than the *-ation* form (since the verb also requires the argument) and a more direct expression of the EVENT than the *-ation* form, which puts the EVENT in a more THING-like package. (Recall §7.3.2.)

Of course, some deverbal noun senses do not denote EVENTS (§7.3.2), and in that case they will not reflect the argument structure of the EVENT verb from which they are derived. In the case of *decoration*, for example, the EVENT sense in (78) takes the argument *the office*, but in (79) *decoration* refers to a type of THING that requires no argument.

(78)   The decoration of the office took hours.

(79)   The decoration hangs on the wall.

9.5.3   Predication and prepositions

In chapter 1, we noted that prepositions are sometimes considered to be lexical (or content) words and sometimes grammatical (function) words, and so we have paid them less attention than the more robust lexical categories of noun, verb, and adjective. But they have sneaked into our discussions of verb meaning in this chapter, with respect to MOTION EVENTS and LOCATION STATES. These prepositions, like *into* and *beside* and *from*, have definite semantic content, and are represented as predicates that take a THING (or TIME or PROPERTY) argument.

But, as should be evident from the predicative noun and adjective examples above, not every preposition is contentful. In cases like *the president of the Scrabble club* and *proud of Nancy*, the *of* serves the purpose of sticking an argument after a predicate, but it adds no additional predicative meaning itself. So, in the semantic representation of *Paul is proud of Nancy* in (69), the *of* is nowhere to be seen, unlike *into* in *Sheryl went into town*, which, as we saw in (62), has a complex predicative structure that (when combined with a THING argument) expresses a PATH. Most prepositions can be represented as predicates (PATH or PLACE types) that take THING arguments. In this way, the semantic structure echoes the syntactic structure, as shown in (80), because grammatically a preposition is the head of a phrase that includes an object noun phrase.

(80)

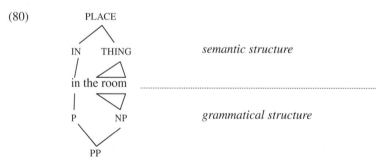

We have also seen (in §9.4.5) that the PATH and PLACE structures represented by prepositional phrases are used in a variety of conceptual fields. Note, for instance, that spatial prepositions like *in* (e.g. *in a room*) or *at* (e.g. *at the corner*) are also used in specifying TIMES (*in an hour*, *at noon*) and, in some cases, PROPERTIES (*you can get that dress in red*). But if you have studied another language, or if you have tried to teach English to anyone else, you will probably have found that the prepositions that seem to be each other's translations in the spatial realm often do not translate in the same way in other realms. For instance, an English speaker learning Swedish or a Swedish speaker learning English will have to learn that the Swedish preposition *till*, which translates as *to* for MOTION EVENTS, is also used for a range of other purposes that translate as other prepositions in English:

(81) a.   Edvin åkte **till** Stockholm.   = Edvin went **to** Stockholm.
   b.   Elin köpte en fisk **till** mig.   = Elin bought a fish **for** me.
   c.   Hon är rörmokare **till** yrket.   = She is a plumber **by** trade.
   d.   Vi stannade **till** igår.   = We stayed **until** yesterday.
   e.   Per är vän **till** mig.   = Per is a friend **of** mine.

It is in part this lack of predictability in prepositions' use that has caused them to traditionally be seen as a grammatical/collocational problem more than a semantic one, with our language teachers telling us that we'll just have to memorize which prepositions to use in which circumstances because there is no real system to it. In the past couple of decades, semanticists have started to question that received wisdom. Much of this work is in, or inspired by observations from, the Cognitive Linguistics school of thought (see §4.5.2) and deals in particular with the problem of prepositional polysemy – both within and beyond the spatial conceptual field. The strategies used to account for such polysemy include representing preposition meanings as complex networks of related senses or radical underspecification of prepositional meaning – that is, trying to find the essence of the preposition's meaning that predicts the ways in which it applies in different contexts.

9.6   Summary and conclusion

This chapter has introduced a number of key concepts related to verb meaning: predication, argument structure, argument alternation, and conflation. We have looked at two basic types of SITUATION, EVENT and STATE, and a componential analysis from Conceptual Semantics for representing a range of EVENTS and STATES. To do so, we started by looking at MOTION/LOCATION verbs – that is, verbs that describe spatial relations between things, as (a) they are fairly typical verbs in that they denote physical actions, and (b) they provide a good model for a range of other types of meanings. Analyses of such spatial verb meanings translate easily into analyses of other kinds of verb meanings (e.g. related to time or the having of properties), which indicates that notions of 'going' or 'being located' are fairly basic to our ways of thinking about EVENTS and STATES more generally. We have used two basic components, GO and CAUSE, to describe a range of EVENTS, and one basic component for STATES, BE. We have also seen how the notion of predication can apply to other word classes, besides verbs.

9.7   Further reading

Beth Levin's *English Verb Classes and Alternations* (1993) is an extremely useful reference for different verb types. Levin and Malka Rappaport Hovav's *Argument Realization* (2005) takes the issues raised by the existence of different verb classes and argument alternations further. Their chapter on "Three conceptualizations of events" offers a good comparison of approaches to verb semantics discussed in this and the next chapter. Further discussion of the Conceptual Semantics approach and the GO and BE components is available in Jackendoff (1983, 2002). Talmy (1985) describes cross-linguistic variation in the conflation patterns and use (including metaphorical use) of MOTION verbs to a much greater extent than attempted here. Jane Grimshaw (1999) provides a detailed analysis of the argument structures of deverbal nouns, introduced in §9.5.2. On the semantics of prepositions, some in-depth studies are: Taylor (1993), Tyler and Evans (2003) (a cognitivist approach to spatial prepositions in English), and Saint-Dizier (2006) (a collection of articles on prepositions from a number of languages).

9.8   Answers to puzzles

9–1

While some authors characterize the unexpressed object alternation as involving "prototypical" arguments, it is unclear that this characterization always works. In their intransitive forms:

drink = 'drink alcoholic drinks'
hum = 'hum a tune'
iron = 'iron fabric/clothes'
read = 'read books' (possibly particularly 'read novels')
vacuum = 'vacuum the carpet/floor'

In some cases, the unspoken object seems to be the only possible object – for instance, what else can you hum besides a tune? In other cases, it is the most usual object for the verb – while you can iron hair or vacuum the furniture, it is usually clothes and carpeted floors that we iron or vacuum. Arguably, in the case of *read*, book-reading is the prototypical kind of reading, but note that it is not the most usual – most people read more e-mails or food labels than books. But in the case of *drink*, it is hard to see why drinking alcohol would be considered the most prototypical kind of drinking – especially since not everyone does it. Because there is so much variation among verbs with the unspecified object alternation, there is a lot of variation in how to treat it semantically. Some might say that it involves a regular polysemy involving the conflation of a prototypical object, while others would say that the intransitive meaning needs to be represented in the mental lexicon with a specification of the object. We could also take the position that most cases involve a regular polysemy alternation, but some exceptions (like *drink*) require that the identity of the missing argument be specified in the lexicon.

9–2

a.   *The monument stands beside the fountain.*

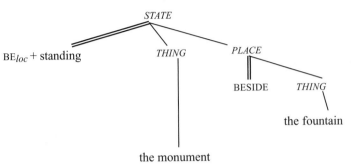

$[_{STATE}$ BE$_{loc}$+standing $([_{THING}$ the monument],
    $[_{PLACE}$ BESIDE $([_{THING}$ the fountain])])]

You might have chosen to represent *beside* as NEXT-TO or something similar, which is fine. Since we are not concerning ourselves now with the internal structure of the MANNER co-event, I have not broken it down into smaller parts here. It might be interesting for you to think about how that might be done, though.

b.   *Lance crossed France*

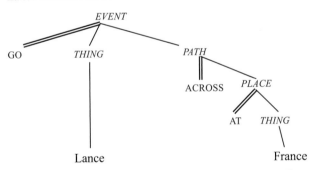

$[_{EVENT}$ GO $([_{THING}$ Lance], $[_{PATH}$ACROSS $([_{PLACE}$ AT $([_{THING}$ France])])])]

Here, I have used ACROSS as the PATH, since *cross* indicates the direction of Lance's movement with respect to France. AT is a generic PLACE predicate.

c.   the LOCATION verb *stand*

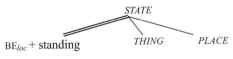

$[_{STATE}$ BE$_{loc}$ + standing $([_{THING}], [_{PLACE}])]$

d.   the MOTION verb *cross*

$$[_{EVENT} \text{ GO } ([THING], [_{PATH} \text{ ACROSS } ([PLACE])])]$$

9-3

a.   no: *Rose descended Fred the staircase.
b.   no: *The lady crossed the Boy Scout the street.
c.   yes: Humphrey waltzed Magdalena into the room.
d.   no: *The wind is falling petals from the flower.
e.   yes: Greta slipped the note out of the book.

All the 'yes' verbs here conflate MANNER, while the 'no' verbs conflate PATH, giving rise to the hypothesis that MANNER verbs can be made causative, but PATH ones cannot. This is generally a good hypothesis for English, but a few exceptions can be noted. Some MANNER verbs sound strange when made causative; for instance, while *I walked the dog downstairs* sounds fine, #*I sauntered the dog downstairs* doesn't. A few PATH-conflating verbs have acquired causative senses, but these are generally more restricted in their use. For instance, while *enter* means 'cause to move (into)' in *Gill entered the numbers into the database* or *Gill entered Harold in the competition*, the movement here is more figurative than literal – Gill doesn't pick up the numbers to put them in the database. The more literal 'locomotive' sense of *enter* is not made causative: *Gill entered the cake into the room.

9-4

Climb, charge, and *wander* have this alternation:

a.   Hilary climbed the mountain.
d.   The crowd charged the ticket booth.
f.   Nomads wander the desert.

One hypothesis could be that you can leave out the preposition if the usual PATH is clear from the verb, since climbing is usually 'up' and wandering is usually 'around.' But that hypothesis does not explain why *coil* (*John coiled the string the spool*) and *revolve* (*Earth revolves the Sun*) do not allow the alternation, since coiling and revolving are always 'around.' Instead, what *climb, charge,* and *wander* have in common (and *drift, coil, revolve* do not share) is that they typically describe movement by animate beings. (Note that it is the string, not John that moves around the spool in (c).) Not every MOTION+MANNER verb follows this alternation "rule," but it can be noted as a tendency.

9–5

Albert rocked the baby to sleep.

$$[_{EVENT} \; CAUSE \; ([_{THING} \; \text{Albert}], \; GO_{IDENT} + \text{rock} \; ([_{THING} \; \text{the baby}],$$
$$[_{PATH} \; TO \; ([_{PLACE} \; AT \; ([_{PROP} \; \text{sleeping}])])])]$$

rock [causative]

$$[_{EVENT} \; CAUSE \; ([THING], \; GO + \text{rock} \; ([THING], \; [PATH]))]$$

You might have kept GO as GO*ident*, which is fine, but note that the causative *rock* can be used for literal as well as metaphorical types of movement, so we might treat this as a vague sense that is compatible with any type of GO.

9.9   Exercises

Adopt-a-word

If your word is a verb, use your own intuitions and reference books (learner's dictionaries and/or Levin 1993) to determine the argument structure it is usually associated with, and any argument alternations that it has. Discuss the extent to which the verb's semantics and its grammatical behavior (in terms of argument structure and alternation) are intertwined and whether there is a general pattern of alternation for verbs in its semantic field.

General

1.   Recall the use of the verb *paint* in example (8):

Whistler painted his kitchen floor.

In (11), the following description of this sense of the verb *paint* was given:

$$paint = [_{EVENT} \; APPLY \; ([THING], \; [_{THING} \; \text{paint}], \; [_{PATH} \; TO \; ([THING])])]$$

Rewrite this semantic representation without APPLY, but instead with Conceptual Semantics predicative components discussed in this chapter (i.e. BE, GO, and/or CAUSE).

2.   Assume that DEAD is a PROPERTY that a THING can have. Given this assumption, devise Conceptual-Semantics-style representations for the verbs in the following sentences. For each, give both the representation for the entire sentence and for the verb alone.
      a. The tulips died.
      b. Gordon killed the tulips.

3.   In this chapter, we saw that MOTION EVENTS involve certain elements
          and that MOTION verbs can conflate some of those elements, such as
          PATH (as in *enter*) or MANNER (as in *walk*). Now let's consider
          STRIKING EVENTS and verbs of striking, as in the following sentence:

          The girl struck the ball hard with her bat.

          STRIKING EVENTS like this one involve a number of elements besides
          the striking action itself:
          • a STRIKER (*the girl*)
          • a STRUCK object (*the ball*)
          • an INSTRUMENT of striking (*her bat*)
          • a MANNER (*hard*)
          Given this, answer the following questions:
          (a) The following verbs all conflate one of these elements. Which one?
              For each of these, identify the hidden argument.

              kick, slap, punch, elbow

          (b) For each of the following, determine if it conflates the same type of
              element (i.e. STRIKER, STRUCK, INSTRUMENT or MANNER) as
              the examples in (a) did, if it conflates a different element or if it
              conflates nothing. Do any of these conflate more than one element?

              head-butt, poke, wallop, hit, spank

10   Verbs and time

Key words: AKTIONSART, ASPECT, STATIC, DYNAMIC, DURATIVE, PUNCTUAL, TELIC, ATELIC, VENDLER CLASS, ACTIVITY, ACCOMPLISHMENT, ACHIEVEMENT

10.1   Overview

As we saw in chapter 7, typical verbs denote change – that is, the SITUATIONS they describe are not time-stable. The last chapter concentrated on predication and the conflation of arguments into verb meanings, but it also discussed two types of SITUATION that differ in their relationship to time: STATES and EVENTS. Stative verbs describe SITUATIONS that involve little or no change, while dynamic verbs describe EVENTS in which changes, including physical actions or changes of STATE, happen. This chapter delves further into the relationship of verbs with time, exploring the differences between STATES and EVENTS and among various kinds of EVENT. We are particularly interested here in **lexical aspect**, also known as **Aktionsart**.

The next section defines *lexical aspect* and contrasts it to other related terms. Section 10.3 looks at various ways in which verb senses can differ in their relation to time. In §10.4, most of the elements from §10.3 are organized into aspectual types – the Vendler classes. Section 10.5 relates the notion of telicity to the notion of boundedness (introduced in chapter 8) and asks whether telicity can be considered to be a lexical matter or not. In 10.6, we revisit semantic relations, last discussed in chapter 6, to ask what types of logical entailment relations exist among verbs and how those relate to time.

10.2   Tense, aspect, and Aktionsart

Language is very sensitive to matters of time. When we talk about SITUATIONS, our sentences represent both when the SITUATION happened (or happens or will happen), and how it progressed (or progresses or will progress) through time. Much of the information about time, in many languages, is grammaticalized and expressed through inflectional morphology, usually attached to verbs – for example, *yawn*, *yawned*, *yawning*. But verbs themselves, regardless of whether they have been inflected, carry quite a bit of information about time in themselves. Consider, for example, the difference between *know* and *realize* in (1) and (2).

(1)   I **knew** why I liked semantics.

(2)   I **realized** why I liked semantics.

Both verbs relate to having some knowledge, but *realize* involves a change in knowledge that happens in an instant, while *know* indicates an unchanging situation that can go on and on. Categorizing verb senses according to their relationships to time can help us to identify particular classes of meaning, and these types of meaning have repercussions when the verb is used in a sentence – since the temporal properties of the verb sense affect the other kinds of temporal information in the sentence.

Before we go any further, we should define some terminology. **Tense** is the grammatical marking of the *when* of a situation – past, present, or future. Tense information may be found in verbal inflections, but it is not part of the verb meaning itself. For example, there are no lexical (content) verbs that refer only to the past. While there are verb forms like *flew* that express past tense without the *-ed* suffix that usually indicates past in English, such verbs are always past tense forms of lexical verbs – that is, they can be considered to be variants on the same lexeme.

Aspect is *how* the situation relates to time, rather than *when*. For example, an action could happen in a prolonged way or a repetitive way; we could describe the onset of the action or its continuation; and the action could happen in a flash or very slowly. English has many ways of marking aspect in sentences, including those in (3)–(6):

(3)   *Through functional morphology* [auxiliary verbs and verbal inflection]:
            The children **are** play**ing** tag. [progressive – on-going event]
            The children **have** play**ed** tag. [perfect – completed event]

(4)   *Repetition of the verb*:
            The bell **rang and rang**. [repetition]

(5)   *Verb particles*:
            They ate **up** the cake. [completion]

(6)   *Certain "helping" verbs*:
            Arthur **kept** talking. [continuation]
            Enid **used to** jog. [habitual]
            Ida **stopped** eating her lunch. [non-continuation]
            Oliver **finished** eating his lunch. [completion]
            Ulla **started** making dinner. [onset]

This chapter is about the "in-built" aspectual properties of verbs themselves. Thus, we are less concerned about describing grammatical aspect, as marked by functional morphology and grammatical structures, and more interested in looking at **lexical aspect**. Lexical aspect is sometimes called by the German term **Aktionsart**, meaning 'type of action' (plural: **Aktionsarten**), because studying lexical aspect involves sorting verb senses into different categories based on how the SITUATION described by the verb unfolds in time. In order to detect the aspectual properties of verbs and to sort them into Aktionsart categories, we often use diagnostic tests involving grammatical and other means of expressing aspect. For instance, if a verb is never used in the progressive, or if putting it into the progressive changes its meaning in a different way from other verbs in the progressive, then that tells us that there is something about that verb's relation to time that prevents its normal interpretation in the progressive.

A caveat here is that the aspectual qualities of a verb itself can be intertwined with the verb's interactions with its arguments. As we saw in the last chapter, argument structure is an inherent part of verb meaning, yet the arguments are usually separate expressions from the verb. Those arguments themselves may contribute or entail particular aspectual information. To start, we concentrate on verbs that differ in their aspectual properties, but toward the end of the chapter we look at how arguments can change the picture.

10.3   Aktionsart categories

Verb meanings can be categorized into classes in terms of various temporal properties they might have. The following subsections introduce some of the main distinctions.

10.3.1   Static and dynamic

In chapter 7, we saw that ontological categories differ in their temporal qualities, and chapter 9 introduced the two major subcategories of SITUATION: STATES and EVENTS. In this section, we look in more detail at the properties of STATES and EVENTS and how to tell them apart. STATES are more constant across time, and EVENTS less so. Let's take the example of *know*, which describes a STATE, and *learn*, which describes an EVENT:

(7)   Jack knew Swedish. [STATIC]

(8)   Jack learned Swedish. [DYNAMIC]

Sentence (7) describes a situation that was relatively unchanging, or **static** (also called *stative*). Example (8), on the other hand, describes a **dynamic** situation – something happened or changed – that is, Jack went from not knowing Swedish to knowing Swedish. This is the essence of the difference between STATES and EVENTS. Thus, as we saw in chapter 9, one test for whether a SITUATION is a STATE or an EVENT is whether the sentence could be sensibly used as an answer

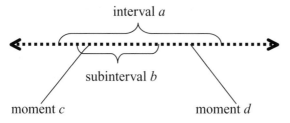

Figure 10.1 *Divisions of time*

to the question *What happened?* In (9), (9a) is a strange answer to the question, since *knowing* doesn't really *happen*. But we can see that *learn* is dynamic, since (9b) is a reasonable answer to the question.

(9)   What happened?
         a. ??Jack knew Swedish.
         b. Jack learned Swedish.

Before looking at other tests for distinguishing STATES and EVENTS, let's look in more depth at how to define *static* and *dynamic*, following work by semanticists David Dowty (1979) and Emmon Bach (1986). They propose that time is divided into **moments**, which are the smallest discernable units of time, and **intervals**, which are made up of some number of contiguous moments. Intervals can also be broken down into **subintervals**, contiguous groups of moments within an interval. A STATE **saturates** its time interval – in other words, the SITUATION holds equally at all moments within the relevant interval. An EVENT, on the other hand, only saturates a subinterval of the interval – not every moment within the interval. This can be visualized using the timeline in figure 10.1. Each black or white space on the line is a moment. Interval *a* is a stretch of time in which a SITUATION might take place. Subinterval *b* is a time within that interval.

In (10) and (11), the relevant interval is 'when Jack was young,' which we can visualize as interval *a* in figure 10.1.

(10)   Jack knew Swedish when he was young.

(11)   Jack learned Swedish when he was young.

Because (10) describes a STATE, if we were to look at any moment in interval *a*, such as moment *c*, we would find that he knew Swedish then. But the EVENT in (11) is different. If we looked at what Jack was doing at any particular moment on this timeline, we would not necessarily find that what he was doing at that moment would be recognizable as 'learning Swedish.' We don't expect that 'learning Swedish' was happening at every moment of Jack's youth, but rather that some subinterval of it (e.g. his school days) involved some learning of Swedish. We also expect that *learning Swedish* took different forms at different times – e.g. sometimes Jack memorized vocabulary and sometimes he practiced pronunciation. If we say that Jack *knew Swedish*, we don't expect that at some moments he knew verbs and at others he knew sentence structure. We imagine *knowing Swedish* as a fairly uniform situation. While STATES are time-sensitive to the extent that they are not necessarily permanent, their distribution through time is nevertheless more even and unchanging than is the case for EVENTS.

As ever, we must remember that words are polysemous and that context can affect how we interpret the meaning of a word. So, a particular verb form may be associated with both static and dynamic meanings, depending on which sense is used or how the context affects the interpretation. Using the *What happened?* test on different sentences with the verb *stand* illustrates this:

(12)   What happened?
          a. #The clock stood in the hall.
          b. Jill stood when the teacher arrived.

According to the *What happened?* test, (12a) looks to be static – *stand* here means something like 'is located in an upright position.' Sentence (12b), on the other hand, uses a different sense of *stand*, one that involves movement to an upright position, and that sense is dynamic. Those examples show that two senses of the same word may differ in their aspectual type. Still there are some cases that are less clear. For example, the answer in (13) is stranger than (12b), but not as clearly static as (12a) is.

(13)   *What happened?*
          ?Jill stood (still) under an umbrella.

The difference between a person standing still under an umbrella and a clock standing in a room is that we expect that people stand themselves in particular positions, since we know that people are **volitional** beings – that is, they have free will to do things. Arguably, then, we have three interpretations of *stand*: to be located in a standing position (12a), to hold oneself in a standing position (13), and to move to a standing position (12b), and these have different levels of stativity. In other words, there seems to be a continuum from static to dynamic, which is affected by pragmatic issues like whether we know that the STATE was achieved volitionally or not.

In order to get a clearer idea of whether a particular verb sense represents an EVENT or a STATE, other tests can help us. The more tests that say that a SITUATION is static, the further it is toward the static end of the static–dynamic continuum.

One test is whether a sentence that uses that particular sense of the verb can be rephrased in **pseudocleft** form. In other words, can you change a sentence in the form *X VERBED Y* to *What X did was VERB Y*? Because the *do* verb in the cleft indicates an EVENT rather than a STATE, EVENTS are more natural in pseudocleft form:

(14)   #What Jack did was know Swedish. [STATE]

(15)   What Jack did was learn Swedish. [EVENT]

Another test that works well for English is whether the verb can be used in the **progressive** (*be V-ing*) form. The progressive form indicates that the SITUATION is in progress – that it started but, at the time we're talking about, it has not yet ended. This makes us perceive the SITUATIONS described by progressive statements as temporary and changing, which conflicts with the longer lasting and unchanging nature of STATES. Thus, static verbs are often strange in the progressive, as shown in (16), while the progressive dynamic verb in (17) is perfectly normal.

(16)   #Jack is knowing Swedish.

(17)   Jack is learning Swedish.

Finally, another test that relates to volitionality is whether the verb can be used in the **imperative** (command) form. Since STATES are not volitional, it does not make much sense to command someone to be in one. So, if you wanted Jack to know Swedish, you would tell him to take action toward getting to that STATE, as in (18), rather than telling him to be in that STATE, as in (19).

(18)   Learn Swedish, Jack!

(19)   ?? Know Swedish, Jack!

Puzzle 10–1

While *know* and *learn* provide clear examples of static and dynamic verbs, we have noted that the distinction between static and dynamic senses is sometimes not so clear, as shown for the 'hold oneself in an upright position' sense of *stand* and the *What happened?* test. Try the other tests with the three *stand* sentences below and fill out the rest of the table using the following symbols. Be very careful not to inadvertently change the sense of the verb when making your judgments.

√ = passes the test   ? = odd, but not impossible   **X** = fails the test
!! = the sense of the verb has changed in the test conditions.

Sentence	Test *What happened?*	Pseudocleft	Progressive	Imperative
The clock stood in the hall.	X			
Jill stood under an umbrella.	?/!!			
Jill stood when the teacher arrived.	√			

10.3.2   Punctual and durative

E VENTS can be divided into those that happen in an instant and those that develop through time. (S TATES are all relatively time-stable and thus cannot be divided in this way.) E VENTS that happen in a moment are said to be **punctual** (or sometimes *punctive*), while longer ones (involving intervals) are **durative**. While one can usually tell punctual from durative predicates just by thinking about the E VENTS they describe, we can also use some linguistic tests to support those intuitions. Durative predicates, like *search*, go well with the progressive in English, but punctual ones, like *find*, do not.

(20)   I am searching for my keys. [DURATIVE]

(21)   #I am finding my keys. [PUNCTUAL]

The progressive indicates the on-going nature of an E VENT. Since punctual E VENTS take place in a moment, rather than an interval (i.e. a series of moments), they cannot really be 'on-going.' Not all punctual verbs sound as strange in the progressive as *find* in (21) does, but still we can tell that they are punctual because they are not interpreted in the same way as durative verbs in those contexts. For example, *to flash* involves a momentary burst of light, so it is punctual, but it seems fine in the progressive, as in (22).

(22)   The light is flashing.

But compare the interpretation of *flash* in (22) to that of *search* (20). Sentence (20) describes one SEARCHING EVENT. In (22), we understand that multiple FLASHING EVENTS have occurred. In other words, in order to reconcile the punctual nature of the verb meaning and the understanding that progressives indicate intervals, an **iterative** (i.e. indicating repetition) interpretation is construed within the context. We get such interpretations with punctual verbs that denote perceivable actions that are repeatable, like *flash*, *beep* or *punch*, but less so with mental punctives, like *realize* or *recognize*, which, like *find* in (21), are just plain odd in the progressive. (Notice, however, that we can get an iterative interpretation for the mental punctives if we use the *keep X-ing* construction – for example, *I kept noticing the clock.*)

Since *punctual* and *durative* refer to length in time, we could view them as gradable properties along a continuum, not just a binary distinction. For instance, the length of a moment in which one can recognize someone is probably shorter than the length of time it takes for a light to flash. Nevertheless, there does seem to be a perceptual distinction between E VENTS that happen so quickly that we perceive them as being instantaneous and those that go on for more extended periods of time. The distinctions between those two types are played out in the linguistic contexts in which the verbs describing those E VENTS occur.

10.3.3   Telic and atelic

The term **telic** is derived from the Greek *telos* 'end,' and refers to EVENTS that can be followed through to a state of completion. Having a 'state of completion' has a couple of consequences: if an EVENT described by a telic verb is stopped partway through, then the telic verb can no longer be used to describe it. So, *slam* is telic because (23) would not be true if Esme had started to slam a door, but, say, a gust of wind kept it from closing all the way.

(23)   Esme slammed the door. [TELIC]

If Esme did succeed in slamming the door, then in order to slam the door some more, she would have to undo the outcome of the previous action (by opening the door) and then slam the door again. She could not continue to do the same slam once she had slammed the door. However, note that it is not only at the moment when the door slams that we would say that she is *slamming* the door. Telicity does not necessarily involve punctuality. Carol Tenny (1987) describes this in terms of a 'measuring out' of the action on the door. If a high-speed camera were to photograph Esme's action, there would be many moments in which we would see Esme's interaction with and force on the door – the door would change position in each photo. But at some point, the door would be closed, and it is that moment that determines the completion of the EVENT, even though it is not the entire EVENT.

Atelic verbs, on the other hand, describe SITUATIONS that could go on without a conclusion. For (24), if Esme started pushing the door, and then got distracted and stopped pushing, it would still be true that she had pushed the door.

(24)   Esme pushed the door. [ATELIC]

Starting the action of pushing is thus the same as doing the action, whereas starting to slam is not the same as slamming.

You might say, "Well, there is a natural conclusion to pushing the door: the door moves. So, *push* must be telic." But there's a problem with that reasoning; 'movement' is not part of the meaning of *push*, nor part of the meaning of (24). The reason you might think that *push* involves movement is because you know why people usually push doors. In that case, you would be relying on pragmatic reasoning rather than relying on the semantics of *push*. Since we can have pushing without moving, as in (25), we can see that the *push* action could occur without a 'moving' outcome.

(25)   Esme pushed the door, but she couldn't move it.

Another test for telicity is whether the sentence still makes sense with an *in* time phrase or a *for* time phrase. Telic EVENTS make sense with *in*, but atelic EVENTS need *for* instead:

(26)   Esme slammed the door in an instant/#for an instant. [telic]

(27)   Esme pushed the door for an hour/#in an hour. [atelic]

Puzzle 10–2

Determine whether the sentences represent telic E V E N T S or not.

a.   Nadine spotted Jay.
b.   Nadine watched Jay.
c.   Jay dropped his hat.
d.   The hat fell.

10.3.4   Inchoative

Verbs whose meanings involve 'beginning' or 'becoming' are referred to as **inchoative**, from the Latin for 'begin.' Inchoative verbs describe a change of S T A T E or a beginning of having a S T A T E. For example, *blacken* means 'become black' and *open* denotes the change from being closed to not being closed.

Inchoatives are a type of E V E N T. In Conceptual Semantics, they can be represented using the predicative component I N C H (like G O and C A U S E, discussed in chapter 9). This I N C H predicate takes a S T A T E as its argument, as in (28).

(28) $[_{EVENT}\text{ INCH }([STATE])]$

In (29) we see how this is spelt out for the meaning of *blacken* – it says that *blacken* denotes an inchoative E V E N T in which something starts to be black.

(29) $blacken = [_{EVENT}\text{ INCH }([_{STATE}\text{ BE}_{ident}([THING], [_{PLACE}\text{ AT }([_{PROP}\text{ black}])])])]$

Break is another inchoative verb, which, in the sense used in (30), describes the change from the S T A T E of being whole to the S T A T E of being in pieces.

(30)   The glass broke.
          $break = [_{EVENT}\text{ INCH }([_{STATE}\text{ BE}_{ident}([THING], [_{PLACE}\text{ AT }([_{PROP}\text{ broken}])])])]$

Break belongs to a class of verbs for which we can see polysemy between the inchoative sense and a causative sense (recall §9.4.3) that incorporates the inchoative, as in (31).

(31)   Ian broke the glass.
          $break = [_{EVENT}\text{ CAUSE }([THING], [_{EVENT}\text{ INCH }([_{STATE}\text{ BE}_{ident}([THING],$
          $[_{PLACE}\text{ AT }([_{PROP}\text{ broken}])])])])]$

Puzzle 10–3

Determine whether each of the following change-of-S T A T E verbs has an additional causative sense by devising example sentences that use the inchoative and causative senses of each verb:

   close, darken, dry, pale

Table 10.1 *Vendler classes*

SITUATION TYPES *examples*	Static – dynamic	Punctual – durative	Telic – atelic
STATE			
Dee **liked** Dom.	static	(durative)	n/a
Dom **resembled** Dee.			
ACTIVITY			
Dee **danced**.	dynamic	durative	atelic
Dom **considered** the problem.			
ACCOMPLISHMENT			
Dee **emigrated**.	dynamic	durative	telic
The flower **bloomed**.			
ACHIEVEMENT			
Dee **arrived**.	dynamic	punctual	telic
Dom **fainted**.			

10.4   Vendler classes

The philosopher Zeno Vendler (1957) described types of verbs based on their inherent aspectual differences, and these classes can be broken down componentially according to the three dichotomies we've seen so far. These are shown in table 10.1. His classification remains one of the most popular in describing SITUATION types.

Table 10.1 shows the breakdown of the Vendler classes STATE, ACTIVITY, ACCOMPLISHMENT, and ACHIEVEMENT using the binary distinctions static/dynamic, punctual/durative, and telic/atelic. Note that if a verb sense describes a static SITUATION, then the other two dichotomies (punctuality and telicity) do not really apply to it, since those are properties of dynamic SITUATIONS. Nevertheless, static SITUATIONS are sometimes labeled 'durative' because they tend to hold for long periods of time.

Since Vendler, other classifications have been proposed, but many still make reference to Vendler's classes. Bernard Comrie (1976) added a **SEMELFACTIVE** category, which includes atelic, punctual events, such as in a non-iterative reading of (32).

(32)   The computer beeped.

Among other authors, it is not unusual to see STATES, EVENTS, and ACTIVITIES (or some variations on those terms) as the main SITUATION types, with ACHIEVEMENTS and ACCOMPLISHMENTS being subtypes of EVENT. In other words, some authors reserve the term *EVENT* for telic situations.

While Vendler initially thought of his categories as categories of verb meaning, they are more properly types of SITUATION – and it takes more than a verb to describe a SITUATION. In particular, a single verb sense can occur in sentences about both telic and atelic SITUATIONS. For example, (33) describes a telic ACCOMPLISHMENT – once three apples are consumed, the SITUATION is complete. On the other hand, (34) is atelic, since the apple-eating ACTIVITY could go on indefinitely.

(33)   I'll eat three apples.

(34)   I'll eat apples.

Clearly, it is the specification of a quantity of apples in (33) that makes the SITUATION telic, so we could think of *eat* as a verb that is dynamic and durative but unspecified for telicity. In other words, its meaning is consistent with describing ACTIVITIES or ACCOMPLISHMENTS. The question arises: is telicity only a property of whole verb phrases, rather than of lexical verbs? We consider this question further in the next section.

10.5   Boundedness and telicity

One of the criteria by which the telicity of a verb can be diagnosed is the possibility of the action being interrupted, yet still describable by that verb (§10.3.2). So *scream* is atelic because if you start to scream then stop, it is still true that you have screamed. This criterion probably sounded a little familiar, since it is much like the criterion by which we decided whether or not a noun was bounded or not in §8.3. Recall that *mud* was [–bounded] because if you had some mud and dropped half, you would still have some mud. So just as screaming for half as long as expected is still screaming, having half as much mud as you expected is still having mud. This similarity has been exploited by theorists who apply the concept of boundedness to both nouns and verbs. The difference, however, is that boundedness in verbs is heavily dependent on non-lexical contributions to meaning, including tense and the verb's arguments.

It would be tempting to think of boundedness in verbs as being the same as telicity, since telic EVENTS are 'bounded' by their natural end-points. However, the term *bounded* is used to refer to any (durative) situation that comes to an end. Once tense is added into the mix any SITUATION can be bounded – since anything described in the simple past tense is understood to have ended already. So *I screamed* is bounded (because it refers to a SITUATION that ended), but not telic (because the screaming could have gone on, even though it didn't).

While the tense of the verb can affect its boundedness, it does not affect its telicity. What does affect telicity are the verb's arguments – and their boundedness. As was shown in (33), the addition of arguments can create a telic situation – but this depends on the boundedness of the arguments. Only bounded arguments force telic interpretations. So EATING APPLES in (34) is atelic, but EATING

THREE APPLES in (33) is telic because the *three* has put a boundary on the apple-eating EVENT.

Because telicity is so dependent on clausal elements besides the verb, it could be debated whether it is represented in verb meaning at all. In order to explore that debate, let's start by comparing *watch* and *eat*. Examples (35) and (36) provide a minimal pair, in that the only element that differs in the two sentences is the verb.

(35)   I watched a fish. [ATELIC – ACTIVITY]

(36)   I ate a fish. [TELIC – ACCOMPLISHMENT]

Since the sentence with *watch* is atelic and the sentence with *eat* is telic, it seems we must conclude that the verb is responsible for the (a)telicity of the sentence in these cases, and that *watch* is by its nature atelic. However, that easy conclusion is complicated by the fact that telic SITUATIONS can also be described with *watch*:

(37)   I watched a film. [TELIC – ACCOMPLISHMENT]

The key to whether each of these SITUATIONS is telic or not is in the second argument – the verb's object. In the atelic *watch* example (35) and the telic *eat* example (36), the arguments look identical. Go a little deeper, however, and the arguments do not seem so similar. When one eats a fish, one eats its physical body. When one watches a fish, it is more than the physical body of the fish that is relevant – one watches a fish doing something, even if all it is doing is existing. That is, when one watches, one watches not a THING, but a SITUATION. If the SITUATION that is watched is telic (e.g. the playing of a film), then so is the watching SITUATION. If the watched SITUATION is not telic (e.g. the existence of a fish), then neither is the watching SITUATION. So, we cannot conclude that *watch* itself is telic or atelic, but we can conclude that the semantics of *watch* tell us that it has a SITUATION argument, and that the watching activity is **co-extensive** with (i.e. happens at the same time as) the argument's SITUATION. In other words, if there is information about telicity in *watch*'s lexical entry, it is indirectly represented through its argument structure.

Many verbs are like this – their telicity is directly influenced by the boundedness or telicity of their arguments, and so we must conclude that those verbs themselves are unspecified for telicity. But some verbs do seem to be inherently telic or atelic. Intransitive verbs don't have object arguments that would force particular telicity interpretations in the same way as the *eat* and *watch* examples above. In the case of *foam*, (38) below, we can see that even with a bounded subject, the situation can be read as atelic:

(38)   After the chemical spill, the pond$_{[+b]}$ foamed {for a month/#in a month}.

In the same context, *die* is understood as telic:

(39)   After the chemical spill, those trees$_{[+b]}$ died {in a month/#for a month}.

In (39), *those trees* is bounded (since we have identified a particular, finite set of trees), so we could wonder whether making an unbounded entity the subject of *die* would make 'dying' atelic. But, at least as far as my idiolect goes – the result seems a bit odd, as shown in (40):

(40)   ??After the chemical spill, trees$_{[-b]}$ died for a month.

If (40) is interpretable, then it must be interpreted as involving many dying EVENTS, rather than one. We can observe this for certain other verbs, like *notice*, *discover*, and *find*, which are telic in their 'discovery' senses. For any of these verbs, their telicity status can be reversed if just the right other elements are present in the sentence. For instance, one could get an atelic interpretation of *the grass died* in (41) if it is understood to be iterative – in which case some grass dies, then some new grass grows and then dies, and on and on indefinitely.

(41)   After the chemical spill, the grass died for a month. [ITERATIVE]

The iterative interpretation is even clearer when we use the CONTINUOUS marker *kept Xing*, as in (42) and (43).

(42)   After the chemical spill, the grass kept dying.

(43)   I kept noticing her accent.

The fact that any verb can be used to describe both telic and atelic situations has led some (e.g. Verkuyl 1993, Ramchand 1997) to conclude that it doesn't make sense to talk about lexical verbs in terms of telicity or Vendler classes. Instead, they reason, telicity is a property of entire clauses, with any arguments,

---

Puzzle 10–4

A frequent type of noun-to-verb conversion creates a verb meaning 'to put NOUN on [something].' So, *to saddle* is 'to put a saddle on [something]' and *to paint* is 'to put paint on [something].' Yet these verbs differ in their telicity, even when they occur with similar types of objects – singular, bounded things in the following examples. *Saddle* is only interpreted as telic, whereas *paint* could be interpreted as either telic or atelic, as the *for/in* test shows:

> *Kerstin saddled the horse {in a minute/#for a minute}.*
> *Martin painted the bench {in an hour/for an hour}.*

Investigate the following verbs (given here with example objects), determining whether they fall into the same telicity class as *saddle* or as *paint*. Then try to find a semantic reason for their differences.

shoe (the horse)	*water (the garden)*	*oil (the machine)*
butter (the toast)	*cap (the bottle)*	*blindfold (the contestant)*
(wall)paper (the hall)	*shutter (the window)*	*sugar (the doughnut)*

aspectual marking, and adverbial modification taken into account. Others argue that telicity should be represented lexically. Olsen (1997) holds that some verbs are [+telic] – that the iterative interpretations of telic verbs in contexts like (42) and (43) do not cancel out the fact that the verbs denote an EVENT type with a natural completion point. Instead, the fact that iteration is the only way to make the EVENT atelic is considered to be evidence that the verb is [+telic] – since the iterative interpretation retains the 'completion' aspect – it just repeats it.

10.6   Semantic relations among verbs

Chapter 6 reviewed a number of semantic relations among words, which were mostly illustrated with nouns and adjectives. Relations among verbs have a dimension not covered in chapter 6: the possibility of relation in time. Christiane Fellbaum (e.g. 1998a) and her colleagues in the WordNet lexical database project have developed the taxonomy of entailment relations among verbs presented in figure 10.2. Because verb meanings denote SITUATIONS that happen through time, two verb senses can be related to each other in terms of whether they describe SITUATIONS that happen at the same time, whether one SITUATION is within the other's time interval, or whether one precedes or follows the other. The first dichotomy in figure 10.2 divides those relations on the basis of whether **temporal inclusion** (i.e. occurring in the same time interval) forces an entailment relation between the two verbs or not. The temporally inclusive relations are troponymy and proper inclusion.

Troponymy is also referred to as hyponymy among verbs (see, for example, the semantic field treatment of verbs of MOTION in figure 6.5 in chapter 6). The term comes from the Greek *tropos* meaning 'manner,' and it refers to relations in which one verb expresses a specific MANNER (see chapter 9) in which the other verb's ACTION (or other SITUATION type) could be done. Like hyponymy

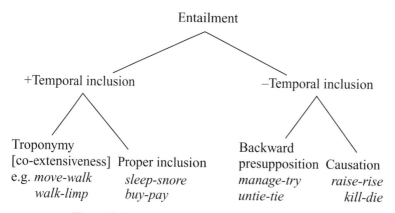

Figure 10.2 *Entailment relations among verbs (after Fellbaum 1998a)*

(§6.2.2), troponymy is an asymmetrical relation – *walk* is a troponym of *move*, but *move* is not a troponym of *walk*. Instead, we can use the term *hyperonym* (as in §6.2.2) to refer to the relation between a broader sense (*move*) and a narrower one (*walk*). Verbs in the troponymy relation are entirely co-extensive – that is, any time a MANNER-specifying verb like *fry* is used, its hyperonym *cook* could also describe the SITUATION. Every moment within a FRYING event can also be described as *cooking*. It's the same for *walk* and *move* in (44), where → stands for 'entails.'

(44)   Troponymy:
         Morgan walks → *Morgan moves*
         WALKING inhabits the same time interval as MOVING
                   → WALKING is temporally included within MOVING

The other temporal inclusion relation among verbs is **proper temporal inclusion** (also known as ***non-troponymic inclusion***). In this case, the EVENT described by one verb happens within a subinterval of the other verb's EVENT. For instance, *paying* describes a SUB-EVENT of a *buying* EVENT and *snoring* is a SUB-EVENT of a *sleeping* EVENT, as in (45).

(45)   Proper inclusion:
         Leonard snores → *Leonard sleeps*
         SNORING inhabits a subinterval of a SLEEPING interval
                   → SNORING is temporally included within SLEEPING

Here the terminology does not distinguish between necessary SUBEVENTS and merely possible ones. 'Paying' is a necessary part of 'buying,' but while 'snoring' EVENTS are always contained within 'sleeping' EVENTS, not every 'sleeping' EVENT contains a 'snoring' EVENT.

   The other two relations in figure 10.2 are temporally related, but the entailed EVENT does not temporally include the entailing EVENT. In **backward presupposition**, in order for one verb's sense to be true, the EVENT described by the other verb must have already happened. For instance, if someone *manages* to do something, then one must have *tried* to do it. If you *untie* something, someone must have *tied* it earlier. In this case, one EVENT must precede the other, but the earlier EVENT does not necessarily result in the later EVENT. Just because one *tries* doesn't mean they will *manage* to do something, and if something is *tied*, it doesn't force a later 'untying' EVENT.

(46)   Backward presupposition:
         Bea managed to do it → *Bea tried to do it.*
           ● MANAGING is preceded by TRYING – not temporally included

   Causation involves a necessary relation between a causative verb (see §9.4.3) and the verb describing the EVENT that is caused. If someone *kills* something, then the something necessarily *dies*, and if someone *raises* an object, the object *rises*.

(47)   Causation:
          a. *Paul killed the tulips.* → *The tulips died.*
          b. *Ellen raised the flag.* → *The flag rose.*

It is tempting to think of the causative EVENT as being earlier than the 'caused'
EVENT, since we say that if someone kills something it *follows* that the thing
dies. But to *follow* in a causal sense is not the same as to *follow* temporally.
Ellen's *raising the flag* and the flag's *rising* happen at more or less the same time,
and we cannot say that *Paul killed the tulips* until the tulips have died. That the
temporal relation is different from backward presupposition is evident from the
fact that the entailment relation can be expressed with the temporal conjunction
and then in the backward presupposition cases in (48), but not in the causation
cases in (49).

(48)   Backward presupposition:
          a. Bea tried to finish her homework, and then she managed to finish her homework.
          b. Warren tied his laces, and then he untied his laces.

(49)   Causation:
          a. #Paul killed the tulips, and then they died.
          b. #Ellen raised the flag, and then it rose.

The causation cases act more like the temporal inclusion cases in this way,
since they too are strange with *and then*, as shown in (50) and (51).

(50)   Troponymy:
          #John limped and then he walked.

(51)   Proper inclusion:
          #Amy bought the peaches and then she paid for them.

The only possible way to interpret these sentences (if they are interpretable at
all) is to ignore the temporal inclusion relation between the verbs and interpret
the two clauses as describing entirely separate EVENTS. For instance, (50) only
makes sense if we ignore the possibility that *limp* and *walk* can refer to the same
EVENT and instead construe *walk* as meaning 'walk without a limp.'

If 'caused' EVENTS occur within the same time intervals as their related
causative EVENTS, why has Fellbaum classified them as temporally non-
inclusive? The difference is that temporal inclusion in the cases of troponymy
and proper inclusion causes the entailment relation between the verbs. *Snoring* entails *sleeping* because SNORING always happens within the time when
SLEEPING happens. But it is not temporal co-extension that determines the
entailment relation between *killing* and *dying*. Note that if one of these EVENTS
is 'shorter' in time than the other and is included in the other's time interval, it must be the 'dying' EVENT that is the shorter, included one. Still, the
'shorter' EVENT described by *dying* does not entail the 'longer' *killing* EVENT
that surrounds it. Instead, it is *killing* that entails *dying*: the entailment relation
arises because the meaning of *die* is included in the meaning of *kill*: 'cause
to die.'

Causation also differs from the other relations in figure 10.2 in that it involves verbs with different argument structures (recall chapter 9), as shown in (52)–(53).

(52)   Troponymy: *Morgan walks* → *Morgan moves*
        Proper inclusion: *Leonard snores* → *Leonard sleeps*
        Backward presupposition:
        Bea managed to do it → *Bea tried to do it.*

(53)   Causation:
        a. *Paul killed the tulips.* → *The tulips died.*
        b. *Ellen raised the flag.* → *The flag rose.*

All of the examples in (52) involve the same argument structures – the 'doer' of the action in the entailing sentence is the same person as the 'doer' in the entailed sentence. In (53), in contrast, the 'doer' of the causing action is not an argument of the entailed verb. For instance, in (53a), *Paul* is not to be found in the *die* sentence, although he was a key element of the *kill* sentence. So, while causation is a semantic relation among verbs, it is the odd one out in figure 10.2, since the relation between the verbs is not determined by their temporal relation.

10.7   Summary and conclusion

In comparison to other parts of speech, verb meanings are particularly temporally complex, describing various levels of dynamism and various lengths of time, and with more or less attention to the beginnings and conclusions of SITUATIONS. Each of these dimensions of time-complexity has linguistic repercussions, as we saw in the various tests for telling whether a verb sense is dynamic or stative, durative or punctual, telic or atelic, and inchoative or not. Still, lexical aspect is but one contributor to the overall aspectual character of a clause, particularly when it comes to telicity. For many verb senses, telicity seems to be unspecified, allowing for different telicity properties to arise with different arguments or other aspectual markers.

The temporal complexity of verb meanings affects the types of semantic relations that verbs enter into. Unlike noun and adjective meanings, verb senses are typically related by temporal relations – for instance, occurring in contiguous or subsequent time intervals.

10.8   Further reading

Several scholarly sources on aspect are cited in this chapter. Bernard Comrie's *Aspect* (1976) remains a valuable textbook for the description of aspect, particularly grammatical aspect. William Frawley's *Linguistic Semantics* (1992) has a thorough discussion of STATE and EVENT types, including the tests discussed here, though he prefers a different classification system from Vendler's. On categorizing semantic relations among verbs, see Fellbaum 1998a.

10.9   Answers to puzzles

10–1

Some of the tests can be tricky to interpret, so see the footnotes beneath the table for clarification.

Sentence	Test Pseudocleft	Progressive	Imperative
The clock stood in the hall.	**X** #What the clock did was stand in the hall.	√ The clock was standing in the hall.[a]	!! Stand in the hall, clock![b]
Jill stood under an umbrella.	?/!! What Jill did was stand under an umbrella.[b]	√ Jill was standing under an umbrella.	X/!! Stand under an umbrella, Jill![b]
Jill stood when the teacher arrived.	√ What Jill did was stand when the teacher arrived.	!! Jill was standing when the teacher arrived.[c]	√ Stand when the teacher arrives, Jill!

[a] Note that making the *clock* sentence progressive gives the impression that the clock is only temporarily in the hall. The non-progressive version seems more permanent.

[b] These sentences may be misleading, since if they sound fine, it is probably because you have reinterpreted them as having the 'move to standing position' rather than the 'be standing in a place' or 'hold oneself standing' meanings that were evident in the original versions. Remember, a verb sense only passes the test if it remains the same sense in the text sentence. The 'hold oneself standing' senses might be possible in these clauses, but one is much more likely to interpret *stand* in those sentences as 'move to standing position.'

[c] Note that putting this sentence in the progressive forces us to interpret the verb differently. Now it sounds like Jill was already standing when the teacher arrived. In order to clearly get the 'move to upright position' sense of *stand* in this case, one may have to make the action more explicit, as in *Jill was in the process of standing (up) when the teacher arrived.*

10–2

a.   *Spot*: telic – spotting is completed once Nadine has gained sight of Jay.

b.   *Watch*: atelic – there is no natural conclusion to watching and it is interruptible.

c.   *Drop*: telic – the action is completed when the hat is released.

d. *Fall*: atelic – though we know that falls are usually broken by the ground, there is nothing in the meaning of *fall* itself that makes it telic. If the hat did not fall all the way to the ground, it would still have fallen, and if it fell down a bottomless pit, it would fall indefinitely.

10–3

Only *pale* does not have a causative sense:

INCHOATIVE	CAUSATIVE
The door **closed**.	I **closed** the door.
The sky **darkened**.	I **darkened** the page with ink.
My hair **dried**.	I **dried** my hair.
She **paled** at the thought of mice.	*I **paled** my face with powder.

10–4

If you've given up on this one, **don't look at the answers yet!** Have another look at the verbs, keeping this hint in mind: remember from chapter 9 that arguments can be conflated in the verb.

You should find that the verbs fall into the following two categories:

***saddle* type** (*in/#for a time*)	***paint*-type** (*in/for a time*)
shoe (the horse)	*water (the garden)*
cap (the bottle)	*oil (the machine)*
blindfold (the contestant)	*butter (the toast)*
shutter (the window)	*sugar (the doughnut)*
	(wall)paper (the hall)

As observed by Heidi Harley (1999), the key to the two classes is the type of noun from which the verb was derived. The verbs that derive from nouns for [–bounded] substances can be telic or atelic, while those that derive from [+bounded] count nouns are telic only. In each of these cases, the denominal verb conflates one of its own arguments (the THING that is being put – recall our discussion of *paint* in chapter 9), and it is the boundedness of that internal argument that determines the telicity of the verb.

10.10   Exercises

Adopt-a-word

A.   If your word is a verb, explore its aspectual qualities, using the diagnostic tests described in this chapter to determine its properties. Starting with a single sense of your verb, consider:

- Is it static or dynamic? Punctual or durative?
- Is its telicity affected by the nature of its arguments?
- Is it inchoative?

If your verb has more than one sense, discuss whether its senses differ in their aspectual properties. For example, does it have both static and dynamic senses?

General

1. All of the following verbs, in the senses found in these example sentences, can be considered stative, since they refer to fairly static situations. Nevertheless, some of them sound better in the progressive than others. Test each in the progressive, classifying them into two categories according to whether they sound good or odd. Examine the verbs in each of these categories and determine whether they have any semantic characteristics in common. Can you offer any hypotheses as to why the two groups differ in their interpretation in the progressive?
    i. The room **smells** awful.
    ii. Phil **lives** in England.
    iii. The portrait **hangs** in the National Gallery.
    iv. The soup **tastes** great.
    v. That **sounds** like Harriet.
    vi. My suitcase **sits** in the attic.

2. Classify the verb senses in each of the following song titles according to their Vendler classes. Point out any ambiguities or difficulties of interpretation and discuss whether the interpretation of telicity is due to the verb itself or some other element in the sentence.
    i. (You gotta) **Fight** for your right to party.
    ii. Nothing **compares** to you.
    iii. **Fly** me to the moon.
    iv. **Shake** your booty.
    v. Smoke **gets** in your eyes.
    vi. **Unbreak** my heart.

3. The verb *eat* seems to be unspecified for telicity.
    - As an intransitive verb, it can be interpreted as telic or atelic – passing both the *in* and *for* tests:

      I ate for an hour. [ATELIC]
      I ate in an hour. [TELIC]

    - Its telicity is determined by the boundedness of its argument.

      I ate rice. [ATELIC]
      I ate a bowl of rice. [TELIC]

Test the verb *drink* to see whether it follows the same pattern. Explain any differences between *eat* and *drink*. (It might help to review chapter 9.)

4.   Using the terminology and tests presented in §10.6, describe the semantic relations between the following pairs of verbs. Consider whether there are entailment relations in both directions (i.e. *a* entails *b* AND *b* entails *a*).
   a. *show–see*
   b. *sleep–nap*
   c. *whisper–speak*
   d. *golf–swing*
   e. *have–hold*

11   Adjectives and properties

Key words: SELECTIONAL BINDING, GRADABLE/NON-GRADABLE, SCALE, SCALAR/NON-SCALAR, ABSOLUTE/RELATIVE, DIMENSION, INTENSIFIER, POSITIVE/EQUATIVE/COMPARATIVE/SUPERLATIVE, STANDARD OF COMPARISON, NEUTRAL RANGE, OPEN/CLOSED SCALE, NEUTRALIZATION

11.1   Overview

As discussed in chapter 7, adjectives typically denote PROPERTIES, many of which are gradable. In this chapter, we examine types of gradable and non-gradable adjectives and go into some detail about the use of dimensional scales (introduced in §6.2.4) to represent adjective meaning. We'll see how such scales can help to clarify aspects of the interpretation of gradable adjectives (e.g. why a *deep ocean* is deeper than a *deep bowl*) and the neutralization of some adjectives in some contexts (i.e. why we can say a child is *six years old* without committing ourselves to the proposition that the child is old). Before exploring these issues, we look at another source of variability in adjective meaning – why, for example, a *good knife* is sharp, but a *good chair* is not.

11.2   Adjectives and the nouns they modify

11.2.1   Selective binding

What adjectives can denote is notoriously fluid, since their interpretation is tied up with the interpretation of the nouns that they modify. This is because typical adjectives denote PROPERTIES, and PROPERTIES are properties *of something*. Adjective meanings can vary with respect to the nouns they modify in two ways. First, many adjectives describe measurements of some sort, that is, the degree to which something has a particular property. But the measurement values that an adjective can indicate depend on the nature of the thing being measured. For example, *tall* does not indicate a particular set of heights, since, for instance, a tall person falls into a different range of heights than a tall building does. *Tall* has the same sense in each case – meaning something like 'of great height.' But what counts as 'great' varies according to the type of thing being measured. We come back to this issue in §11.4.

The other way in which adjective and noun meanings interact is that PROPER-TIES may apply in different ways to different kinds of THINGS. In this case, we would paraphrase the meaning of the adjective differently according to the type of noun it modifies. For example, *a fast runner* is someone who can run quickly, but *a fast game* is a game that finishes soon after it starts (Pustejovsky 1993). And *long* can have spatial or temporal interpretations:

(1)   a long snake = 'a snake that has a large measurement from head to tip-of-tail'

(2)   a long DVD = 'a DVD that takes a significant amount of time to play'

While many dictionaries would represent these as separate senses, another option would be to propose that *long* has one sense, which indicates 'a great extent,' and that the differences in interpreting *long* in (1) and (2) come from *long*'s interaction with the nouns and the kinds of extents that the nouns can have. This is the approach taken in Pustejovsky's Generative Lexicon approach (GL; see §4.3).

Pustejovsky (1995) proposes that these interactions come about because an adjective's lexical entry specifies which of a noun's QUALIA roles (or *quales*) it can modify. In GL, this is called **selective binding** as the adjective "selects" which QUALIA role(s) it "binds" to. Recall from §4.3.1 that QUALIA features give information about what a word's denotatum is made of, what it is for, where it comes from and how it differs from other items of the same type. In (1) and (2), *long* modifies the FORMAL and TELIC quales, respectively. The *snake* in (1) is judged to be *long* with respect to the FORMAL quale, that is, the physical form of the snake. DVDs, on the other hand, all have the same spatial dimensions (otherwise, they wouldn't fit into a DVD player), so we wouldn't have much reason to say that any particular DVD takes up a *long* amount of space. In this case we look for another way in which a *long DVD* can be long, and that is respect to its TELIC role – that is, its function. The function of a DVD is to be played and watched, and playing and watching are activities that happen over time. So a DVD is *long* if it takes a relatively large amount of time to play and watch.

Since the lexical entry for *long* says that it can modify the FORMAL and TELIC roles, it must be the case that if *long* modifies a noun that is variable and measurable in both its FORMAL and TELIC role specifications, then ambiguity should result. Indeed, *book*, as in (3), allows either interpretation of *long*, since nothing prevents us from applying *long* to either the FORMAL (books have physical forms that can be measured) or the TELIC (books are for reading, and reading takes time) quale:

(3)   a long book = 'a book that has a large measurement in one of its physical dimensions'
                   OR
                   = 'a book that would take a large amount of time to read'

GL thus takes a lexical-semantic route to solving the problem of adjective inter-pretation, by formalizing the notions of QUALIA and selective binding and assuming that adjective senses are vague enough to apply to a number of different quales and types.

An alternative approach would be to hold that *long* is polysemous, in that it has separate spatial and temporal senses, and that it is a pragmatic matter to determine which sense of the adjective applies in which case. In that case, we would start from the notion that *long* can describe length in either minutes or inches and rely on our world knowledge of DVDs, rather than the lexical representation of *DVD*, to figure out that it must be the temporal sense that applies in that case.

11.2.2   Evaluating the selective binding solution

The GL selective binding solution works for some, but not all, variations in adjective meaning. In some cases of polysemy, the differences between the meanings cannot be reduced to the modification of different quales. For instance, a person can be *high*, meaning 'above the ground' or 'intoxicated.' In this case, the two meanings of *high* would have to be represented separately, as the difference between physical and metaphorical 'highness' consists of more than applying one notion ('being above') to more than one aspect of a person. Similarly, there is nothing in the representation of the noun *order* that could combine with the notion of 'great height' in order to give an interpretation for *a tall order*. In these metaphorical examples, we can see that there is a motivation for using the adjectives *high* and *tall* in these contexts – a person who is high ('intoxicated') may feel like they are floating high in the air, and *a tall order* is one that is difficult to meet, just as *a tall shelf* is difficult to reach. But the metaphorical reasoning needed to apply these spatial adjectives to abstract experiences is beyond what the mechanics of the GL approach allows, and so complementary approaches are needed to account for metaphorical applications of adjectives.

Puzzle 11–1

Substitute another adjective for *good* in each of the following sentences in order to demonstrate that *good* describes different qualities in each case. Is the interpretation of the adjective ambiguous in any of these sentences?

a.   *Catch-22* is a good book.
b.   I wore my good shoes to the party.
c.   That child needs a good talking-to.

11.3   Absolute adjectives

Adjectives can be categorized in a number of ways. The first way that we'll discuss is whether or not the adjective applies to nouns in an all-or-nothing kind of way. An **absolute** adjective is one that denotes a PROPERTY that something either has or does not have. *Odd* (in reference to numbers),

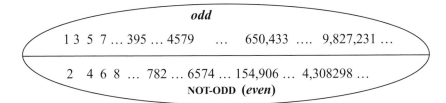

Figure 11.1 *'Oddness' in the domain of numbers*

perfect, and *headless* are all absolute adjectives, in that a number is either odd or it's not, a diamond is either perfect or it's not, and a horseman is either headless or he's not.

In other words, absolute adjectives entail a clear dividing line between the things that have the PROPERTY described by the adjective and those that do not. Let's look at this more closely for the case of *odd*. In the realm of mathematics, an *odd* number is an integer that cannot be evenly divided by two. Any integer can be unambiguously assigned to the category *odd* or *not-odd* – which is to say, *even*. Figure 11.1 illustrates the absolute status of numerical sense of *odd*. The oval is the domain of integers, which divides clearly into the ODD and the NOT-ODD. Some examples of *odd* and *not-odd* (or *even*) numbers are shown in the two sections of the oval, and no number can be on the dividing line between ODD and NOT-ODD.

Because it is clear which numbers belong to the *odd* category, all odd numbers have exactly the same level of ODDNESS. This means that we cannot say that one number is odder than another, as shown in (4). It also means that we cannot use **degree modifiers** with *odd*, since there are not different degrees of ODDNESS within the *odd* category, as in (5) and (6):

(4)   #Five is odder than three.

(5)   #The number five is very/somewhat/extremely odd.

(6)   #Three is completely/absolutely/totally odd.

Other absolute adjectives, like *perfect* and *dead*, are like *odd* in that they sound strange with degree **intensifiers** like *very* and *somewhat*, as shown in (7). But they differ from *odd* in that they can be modified by the types of degree modifiers in (8) and (9) that indicate completeness – we'll call these ones **totality modifiers** (Paradis 2001).

(7)   ??The diamond is very/somewhat perfect.

(8)   That diamond is absolutely perfect.

(9)   The phone line is completely dead.

Adjectives like *perfect* and *odd* are both absolute in that they describe PROPER-TIES that a THING either has or doesn't have. What is different about them – and why it makes sense to use totality modifiers with one group but not the

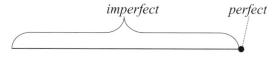

Figure 11.2 *Scale of* PERFECTION

other – is the status of things that do not have the property described by the adjective. Things that are not perfect vary in how close they are to perfect. Contrast this to numbers; no numbers that are not odd are closer to being odd than other numbers. This difference comes through when we use *almost* or *nearly* with the adjectives. *Almost* and *nearly* negate the adjective description, in that something that is *almost* or *nearly perfect* is not perfect. At the same time, they indicate a degree of closeness to the boundary of the PROPERTY denoted by the adjective. So, a diamond with one tiny flaw is *almost perfect*, but one with several big flaws is far from *perfect*. Adjectives like *odd* do not allow negation with *almost* or *nearly*. The number 2.999 is not *almost odd* just because it is nearly 3.

Figure 11.2 shows a way to visualize the meaning of *perfect*, which reflects how it differs from *odd* (compare figure 11.1). Here, 'perfection' is represented as being a particular point on a **scale** of measurements within the **domain** of PERFECTION. Kennedy (1999) refers to scalar adjective meanings as **measure functions** which map an object (the thing described by the adjective) to a measurement on a one-dimensional scale. These scales represent part of how we conceptualize the dimensions that the adjectives describe. In figure 11.2, the scale represents possible measures of how perfect versus imperfect something might be – from having no redeeming qualities to having some flaws to having no flaws at all: 'perfection.' *Perfect* only refers to the maximal value(s) on this scale, but other points on the scale vary in how close or far they are from the *perfect* point.

Thus we can divide the realm of absolute adjectives into two types: **non-scalar absolutes** like *odd*, which are not modifiable, and what we'll call **scalar absolutes**, like *perfect*, which indicate a bounded portion of a scale.

Puzzle 11–2

In chapter 6, we looked at different types of antonymy. Are any of these types particularly associated with absolute adjectives? Consider the absolute adjectives *odd*, *perfect*, *dead*, *square*, and *unique*.

11.3.1   Boundedness

In chapters 8 and 10, we saw that **boundedness** is a useful concept in describing the countability of nouns and the lexical aspect of verbs. Recall that a verb meaning is aspectually bounded [+b] if it is uninterruptible and that a noun meaning is [+b] if it is not divisible. So, for example, if you only get halfway through remembering a fact, you have not remembered it, since remembering is a bounded E V E N T. If you break a table in half, you no longer have a table – or even two tables – because tables are bounded objects. The case can be made that boundedness works similarly for adjective meanings. Following the logic of the noun and verb definitions of bounded, an adjective meaning is [+b] if there is a clear distinction between having the property and not having it. For example, *perfect* is bounded because there is a point at which something is perfect and if it is any less perfect than that, then it is no longer *perfect*. Compare this to *intelligent*. One can be *less intelligent* than someone else, but still be *intelligent*. Absolute adjectives are thus [+b]. The modifiers that can go with scalar absolutes, like *completely* and *absolutely*, are also [+b] in this case.

11.4   Gradable adjectives and semantic scales

Having looked at two varieties of absolute adjectives, let's now turn to adjectives like *tall, angry, green, pleasant*, and *boring*. These are called **gradable** adjectives. Gradable adjectives denote P R O P E R T I E S that can be had at different strengths – which is to say that all tall people are not the same height, all boring people are not equally dull, and so forth. These are the adjectives that can be modified by intensifiers: some people are *somewhat tall*, some *very tall*, some *extremely tall*. And because different instances of T A L L N E S S involve different measurement values, *tall* (and other gradable adjectives) can also occur in **equative**, **comparative**, and **superlative** forms, as well as in the **positive** form, as shown in (10). (Some writers use *gradable* to mean the same thing as *scalar*, but note here that we are not including scalar absolutes in our use of the term.)

(10) a.   Wendy is **tall**. [positive]
    b.   Mick is **as tall as** Jools. [equative]
    c.   Perry is **taller than** Jools. [comparative]
    d.   Wendy is the **tallest** person in the family. [superlative]

Non-scalar absolutes like *odd*, on the other hand, cannot be compared, since they do not have the possibility of different values.

(11)   #Three is odder than five.

Tall also differs from the scalar absolutes, in that it does not make sense to modify it with the same totality modifiers that are used with *perfect* and *dead*, as in (12).

(12)   #Morton is completely/absolutely tall.

Figure 11.3 illustrates the scale for the domain for height. From left to right, the points along the scale represent increasing heights. Three of those points have been labeled here with height measurements and initials, which indicate the

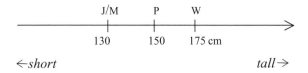

Figure 11.3 *The examples in (10) plotted on the* HEIGHT *scale*

relative placement of the family members mentioned in (10) on the *tall* scale. So Jools and Mick are as tall as each other, Wendy is the tallest, and so forth.

What figure 11.3 doesn't show is how tall is *tall*. Claiming that *tall* refers to a particular section of the scale – for example, from 175 centimeters up – would be a problem, since what counts as *tall* depends on what type of thing is being described as *tall*. For example, in (13)–(15), we would expect that the toddler, man, and giraffe have very different heights, even though each of them is described as *tall*.

(13)   That toddler is tall.

(14)   That man is tall.

(15)   That giraffe is tall.

The measurement value for particular instances of *tall* can vary so much because gradable adjectives are scalar and inherently comparative. When we use gradable adjectives like *tall* in their positive form to describe a THING, we compare the height of the THING to a height value that serves as a **standard of comparison**. A man is *tall* if he is *taller than* some height that we consider to be "unremarkable" for some reference group. In the case of *a tall man*, we might be comparing the man to other men. In that case, we could paraphrase (14) as (16) or (17):

(16)   That man is tall, for a man.

(17)   That man is taller than typical men.

Note that we don't want to say that a tall man is taller than an average man, since that would entail that we measured all men and figured out their average height. The key is what we believe about "typical" or "unremarkable" men's height, rather than the reality of "average" height. Because judgments of TALLNESS are always made with reference to a contextually determined standard, *tall* is said to be a **relative** adjective, as opposed to an absolute one.

It's not the case that *That man is tall* (14) can always be paraphrased by (16) or (17). Given an appropriate context, we could be comparing the man to any number of standards besides 'unremarkable height for a human male.' For example, from the toddler's viewpoint, the man may be tall because her standard of comparison is based on her own toddler height. According to that standard, anyone above three and a half feet counts as *tall*. Similarly, when we say (15) *That giraffe is tall*, we may be comparing the giraffe to animals generally (in which case all giraffes might be considered to be tall) or specifically within the class of giraffes,

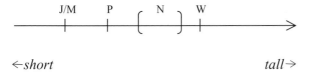

Figure 11.4 *The HEIGHT scale, with neutral range*

in which case the giraffe is tall for a giraffe. In any use of a gradable adjective, determining the standard of a comparison is a pragmatic matter, which requires attention to the context and world knowledge that contributes to deciding which possible standard of comparison is the relevant one in this context.

So in our scalar model, a positive (i.e. non-comparative) use of *tall* compares the value of an object's height and a 'standard' or 'neutral' range of heights for that type of object – marked in figure 11.4 as a bracketed area, labeled 'N' for *neutral*. The neutral range here is the set of heights that are neither *tall* nor *short*. According to figure 11.4, Jools and Perry are *short* – because their heights are shorter than 'neutral' heights. Wendy is *tall* since her height is greater than the set of neutral heights.

One way to approach such adjectives is to think of them as labeling **directions** on the scale, rather than points or sections of the scale. The reason for this becomes clear when thinking about comparison. In the representation of the comparison *Perry is taller than Jools* in figure 11.3, we plotted the values of Perry's height and Jools' height on a scale of TALLNESS, with Perry's height being further in the 'taller' direction on the scale than Jools'. But notice that this does not entail or presuppose that Perry is *tall*; according to figure 11.4, he is *short*, but still *taller* than Jools. Something is *tall* if its measured height is greater than the standard of comparison in the neutral range, but it is *taller* than something else if it has a greater height than the something else, without regard for the neutral standard of comparison. We can represent the meaning of *taller* as (18), where the two arguments of *taller* (the two items being compared) are on either side of the 'greater than' symbol. The subscripted *HEIGHT* tells us the dimension of the adjective. So, if X is *taller than* Y, then X has a greater height measurement than Y. (Another way of putting this is that *taller* describes a **vector** between X and Y – i.e. a direction on a part of a scale.)

(18)   X is ***taller*** than Y: $[_{HEIGHT} \ X > Y]$

The difference between the positive *tall* and comparative *taller* forms is that both of the arguments are explicitly stated in a comparative statement, but, grammatically speaking, a positive adjective does not have two slots in which to express the arguments of its comparison. Still, while *tall* has only one visible argument in a sentence like *Wendy is tall*, semantically it has two arguments: *Wendy* and the standard of comparison in the neutral range. This can be represented for the HEIGHT adjectives as (19) and (20) – *tall* means having a greater height than the neutral range, whereas *short* means having a lesser height than N. We can think of argument N as a default argument, which is used when there are not enough explicit arguments to satisfy the comparative nature of the adjective.

(19)   X is *tall*: [$_{HEIGHT}$ X $>$ N]

(20)   X is *short*: [$_{HEIGHT}$ X $<$ N]

This type of representation can be used for any positive form of a gradable adjective. For example, substitute *WEIGHT* for *HEIGHT* in (19), and you have the meaning of *heavy*.

Puzzle 11–3

So far, we've said that the adjectives *tall* and *short* can be thought of as inherently comparative and directional, in that a comparative form of the adjective indicates a relation between two places on the scale. The point of comparison for a positive use of these adjectives, as in *I didn't expect him to be so tall*, is a contextually 'neutral' set of heights. Test the following adjective pairs in order to determine whether they too are understood in relation to a neutral set of heights. Is there anything different about these, as compared to *tall* and *short*?

>   *tiny/huge*   *cold/hot*

11.5   Properties of scales and types of scalar adjectives

The type of scale for *tall* and *short* in figure 11.4 works for a range of adjectives, like *heavy/light*, *wide/narrow*, and so forth. That scale extends indefinitely toward ever-increasing values – that is, there's no upper limit on how *tall* something can be. But the scale does not continue indefinitely in the opposite direction. Furthermore, the scale makes use of a neutral range and adjectives are associated with both of the directions on the scale. We have already seen one type of scale that looks different from the HEIGHT scale: the *perfect/imperfect* scale in figure 11.2. So, we can assume that scales may have different characteristics. These potential differences include the following, some of which we've already seen illustrated by the differences in figures 11.2 and 11.4:

- Different scales represent different DIMENSIONS.
- A scale may extend indefinitely at one, both, or neither of its ends.
- A scale may include a contextually defined standard of comparison (for a relative adjective) or not.
- Either one or both directions on the scale may be named; if both, then the two adjectives naming the opposite directions will be antonyms.
- Adjectives associated with the scale may involve the entirety of a scale or only a subpart of it.

Our next task is to look at some different type of scalar adjectives that display some of these variations. But how do we know the shape of any scale? In some cases, the denotata give us a clue. For instance, we know that there is no upper limit on how *tall* something can be because we know that, for instance, a stack of books can always be made *taller* by adding another book to it. There is no inherent limit to height. But adjectives may map onto these scales in different ways, so that we need to look at linguistic evidence, such as modification and comparability, which reflect scalar properties. In the following subsections, we see how such evidence can be used in determining the properties of dimensional scales, starting with the question of which end of the scale is 'up.'

11.5.1 Scales and directions

Different adjectives can label the same dimension with reference to scalar directions. It is conventional to represent scales as horizontal lines, so the directions in the illustrations are 'rightward' and 'leftward,' but it is also conventional to understand the right side of the scale illustration as the 'upper' end of the scale and the left side as the 'lower' end. In this case the rightward direction is 'more' and the leftward direction is 'less' of something. So, on a scale of physical measurement, such as HEIGHT (figures 11.3 and 11.4), the range of possible heights is ordered from the lowest heights at the left side to ever increasing measurements on the right side because the rightward direction is toward 'more height.' On a TIME scale, *late* is rightward and *early* is leftward because *later* signals 'more time passed.' Similarly, the 'upper' rightward direction is toward higher temperatures on a TEMPERATURE scale because it signals 'more heat'; this reflects an understanding of heat as a presence and cold as an absence of heat. In all of these cases, the measuring systems that we apply to those dimensions reflect this scalar structure, in that we use higher numbers to represent things that are *taller*, *later*, or *hotter* than others.

But what about more abstract dimensions, which do not have conventional, numerical systems of measurement? Which is the upper and which is the lower end in these cases? Think back to *perfect* and *imperfect* (fig. 11.2), was there a reason why I put *perfect* on the 'upper' end of the scale?

On first glance, one might be able to find some reasons to order the scale in the opposite way, with *imperfect* at the 'upper' end – after all, imperfection involves *more* flaws. But there are other clues that *perfect* is at the upper end of the scale. First, notice that we call it a scale of PERFECTION, rather than a scale of IMPERFECTION. So, just as the upper end of the HEIGHT scale is the end with 'more height' and the upper end of the TIME scale is the one in which 'more time' has passed, the upper end of the PERFECTION scale is the one with 'more perfection.'

Another clue is that *imperfect* is at the opposite end of the scale. In order to describe that end of the scale, we add the negative prefix *im-* to *perfect*. The fact that the opposite of *perfect* is presented with a negative morpheme (but *perfect* itself is not) gives us a hint that *perfect* is the 'positive' quality of the two, and thus is associated with the 'positive' direction on the scale.

You probably didn't need me to point out the negative morpheme on *imperfect* in order to conclude that *perfect* is positive, since we almost always think that *perfect* things are better than *imperfect* things. The linguistic evidence regarding the nominalization and negation of *perfect* reflects the fact that we generally treat 'good' things as involving 'more' of something and 'bad' things as involving 'less' of that good thing – though it would be logically possible for us to do the opposite. It is just a fact of human nature that we tend to look toward 'goodness' and to value it more than 'badness.' So, in general, if one direction on a scale is toward a more positively valued PROPERTY, it will be the 'upper' end of the scale.

11.5.2   Open and closed scales

An end of a scale can be closed or open, in that there may or may not be absolute interpretations of an adjective on that scale. So far, we have seen the *tall* scale with an open upper end and the *perfect* scale with a closed upper end. Kennedy and McNally (2005) list the following possibilities configurations for scales:

*   they can be closed on both ends
*   they can be closed on the upper end but open on the lower end
*   they can be closed on the lower end but open on the upper end
*   they can be open on both ends

If a scale has a closed upper end, for instance, then there may be a scalar adjective that describes the maximal point on that scale. This is the case for *perfect* (figure 11.2); 'perfection' is limited at the upper end – once something can be accurately described as *completely perfect*, there is no room for it to be made more perfect. Notice, however, that the same is not true of the other end of the scale. If we have a very flawed diamond or a very messy piece of knitting, we can probably still make it worse. There is no point at which we would say that something is *completely imperfect*.

For a test of scalar closure, Kennedy and McNally (2005) look at whether the scale can be modified by an expression that indicates completeness (a totality modifier), such as *completely*, *fully*, or *100%*. (Note that these are scalar modifiers, as it would be strange to modify a non-scalar absolute description like *odd number* with them.) Even closed-scale adjectives vary in how "comfortable" they are when collocated with some of these modifiers – for example, we prefer to say *completely perfect* rather than *fully perfect*. But if an adjective can go with one of these modifiers, we can conclude that it has a sense that involves a closed scale. If both members of an antonym pair can go with at least one of these modifiers, then the scale is closed at both ends. Using this modification test, Kennedy and McNally determined the scalar properties of the following sets of adjectival antonyms – in each case the ones with absolute interpretation are shown in bold:

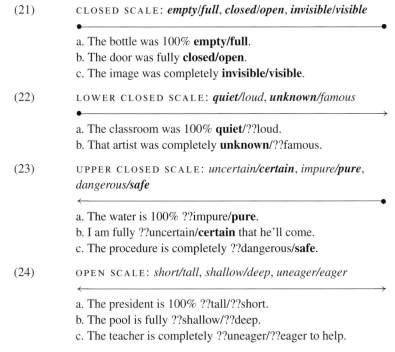

(21)   CLOSED SCALE: *empty/**full**, **closed/open**, **invisible/visible***

      a. The bottle was 100% **empty/full**.
      b. The door was fully **closed/open**.
      c. The image was completely **invisible/visible**.

(22)   LOWER CLOSED SCALE: ***quiet**/loud, **unknown**/famous*

      a. The classroom was 100% **quiet**/??loud.
      b. That artist was completely **unknown**/??famous.

(23)   UPPER CLOSED SCALE: *uncertain/**certain**, impure/**pure**, dangerous/**safe***

      a. The water is 100% ??impure/**pure**.
      b. I am fully ??uncertain/**certain** that he'll come.
      c. The procedure is completely ??dangerous/**safe**.

(24)   OPEN SCALE: *short/tall, shallow/deep, uneager/eager*

      a. The president is 100% ??tall/??short.
      b. The pool is fully ??shallow/??deep.
      c. The teacher is completely ??uneager/??eager to help.

If two adjectives describe the opposite directions on a completely closed scale, then neither will apply to the middle of the scale in a simple, positive adjective use. So, for example, a one-liter bottle filled with just 300 milliliters of wine is not *a full bottle*, but neither is it *an empty bottle*.

(25)   [FALSE]   The bottles in figure 11.5 are **empty/full**.

But we can still tell that these adjectives describe directions on the entire scale, rather than just the end-point of the scale, in that the points in the middle of the scale can be described with either adjective in the cases that (a) the adjective is in the equative, comparative, or superlative form, or (b) the adjective is used with a proportional measurement, such as *half* or *30 percent*. Figure 11.5 shows two one-liter bottles that are each filled with 300 milliliters of wine and scalar architecture that allows for the examples in (26) – with the (a), (b), and (c) meanings labeled.

(26) a.   The bottle of red wine is as full/empty as the bottle of white.
    b.   The bottles are 30% full.
    c.   The bottles are 70% empty.

In contrast, when we say simply that a bottle is *full*, we refer to the upper end of the scale – that is, the **maximum** value in that direction. Likewise, *the bottle is empty* invokes the **minimum** value on the scale. The linguistic paraphernalia

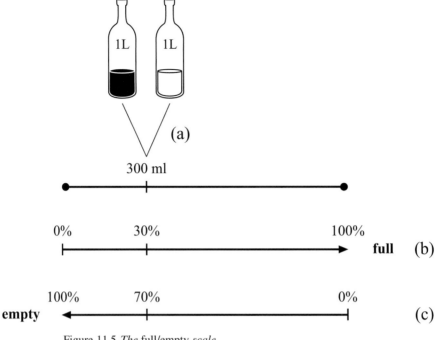

Figure 11.5 *The* full/empty *scale*

of comparisons and proportions in (26) signals that *full* and *empty* are to be understood in some way other than the maximal/minimal interpretation.

(There is a little wiggle room here for a range of maximum values. For instance, a bottle is considered to be *full* at some point before the contents reach the brim. How full any particular thing needs to be in order to be considered *full* is a pragmatic matter, dependent on world knowledge and contextual expectations.)

Thus, *full* and *empty* are scalar absolutes in that they describe an absolute condition in their positive forms and are not interpreted (unlike *tall*) with reference to a neutral standard of comparison. But they do not neatly bisect the domain of 'how full something can be' and they thus make reference to a scale. Note that the comparative or proportional uses in (26) would not have worked with the non-scalar absolute *odd (number)*.

The situation is different for scales that are closed on only one end. In that case, one of the antonyms is absolute and the other not, and proportional modification does not make sense since one needs a fixed start and finish for the scale in order to measure at which point *half* or *most* of the scale has been reached. So, on the upper-closed scale of PERFECTION, *perfect* is absolute, but it makes no sense to say that a diamond is *40% perfect* because the lower end of the scale does not have an exact boundary. Having only one end closed also means that the antonym associated with the open end will have the properties of a gradable adjective. So, *perfect* is an absolute describing the maximum point on a scale, and *unknown* is an absolute on the describing the minimum point on its scale, and each has a complementary (§6.2.4) antonym that can describe any point on the rest of

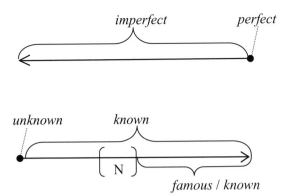

Figure 11.6 *The PERFECTION and FAME scales*

the scale. Unlike the complementary antonym of a non-scalar absolute, however, antonyms of scalar absolutes on a half-open scale can be modified with gradable modifiers like *very* rather than the absolute ones like *completely*:

(27) a.   That diamond is completely perfect/??imperfect.
     b.   That artist was completely unknown/??famous.

(28) a.   That diamond is very imperfect/??perfect.
     b.   That artist was very famous/??unknown.

Figure 11.6 shows how the FAME scale, being closed on the lower end, inverts the properties of the PERFECTION scale. In each case, most of the scale is covered by the gradable member of the antonym pair. The ability to interpret some of the open-ended antonyms as relative (relating to a neutral standard of comparison) gives us **gradable complementary** antonyms (see §6.2.4) *unknown/famous* or *unknown/known* (in the case where there is a minimal standard of fame to meet before something is described as *known*).

The notion of 'closed' and 'open' scales can be shown to correlate with other adjective facts. For example, Stephen Weschler (2005) has argued that resultative constructions of the form Verb–Noun Phrase–Adjective are sensitive to scale openness. Although a lot more goes on in these constructions than I have space to discuss, a quick observation is that durative verbs can take closed-scale adjective results as in (29), but not open-scale ones as in (30).

(29)   CLOSED-SCALE RESULTATIVES
        a. Neil pushed the door closed/open.
        b. Sarah hammered the metal flat/straight.
        c. Arthur wiped the table clean/dry.
        d. Beatrice shook Martin sober.

(30)   # OPEN-SCALE RESULTATIVES
        a. #Sarah hammered the metal curved/bumpy.
        b. #Arthur wiped the table dirty/wet.
        c. #Beatrice served Martin drunk.

Viewing all of the above linguistic facts in terms of open and closed scales is not a completely uncontroversial approach – but it seems to at least describe the facts about adjective modification well.

11.5.3   Neutralization

Among the antonyms that describe measurements on the same scale, we can find differences in how some of those adjectives behave in various types of contexts. For instance, in chapter 1 I mentioned that some but not all adjectives can occur with measure phrases like *six miles* or *30 minutes*.

(31)   The lake is one mile wide.

(32)   #The lake is one mile narrow.

(33)   The concert was 30 minutes long.

(34)   #The concert was 30 minutes short.

Even if the concert lasts just five minutes, we still use the adjective for greater length in describing it as *five minutes long*.

Similarly, if you want to know when a concert will end, you ask a question using *long*, like (35), no matter whether you think the concert will be long or short. In other words, the question can have a **neutral interpretation** – it does not presuppose a particular length.

(35)   How long was the concert? [neutral or committed reading]

On the other hand, you would only ask question (36) in a context in which it has already been established that the concert is particularly short:

(36)   How short was the concert? [committed reading]

In other words, by using *how short* you **commit** yourself to the presupposition that the concert was short. It is also possible to get a committed reading for (35), making that sentence ambiguous between neutral and committed senses of *long*.

In each of these cases, we have two adjectives, one of which indicates the 'upward' direction on the scale – that is, the one with greater measurements – and the other the 'downward' direction. Examples (31)–(36) indicate that the meanings of some adjectives can be **neutralized** with measure phrase modification and in *how* questions.

We can use the "inherent comparison" view of gradable adjective meaning to account for some aspects of neutralization. The single spatial/temporal dimensions like HEIGHT, WIDTH, and LENGTH are asymmetrical, in that one can measure indefinitely in one direction, but not the other. In other words, the lower end of each of these scales provides a starting point from which measurement can be plotted. In this case, when we use a measure phrase, we compare the value of the thing that is being described with that starting point. An adjective can be modified by a measure phrase, then, if it describes the direction from the starting point to the measurement value of the thing. So, on the HEIGHT scale, if Steve is *five feet tall*, his height measures five feet from the starting point of the scale ('zero') in the *tall* direction on the scale. Since we are comparing Steve's height to the starting point on the scale, no comparison is made to the neutral range of the scale, as shown in (37), where '0' marks the scale's starting point. We thus get a neutralized meaning of *tall*, which relates the height measurement only to the starting point and not to the neutral (i.e. "typical") standard of comparison that is used in non-neutral, positive interpretations of *tall*.

(37)   X is *five feet tall*: [$_{\text{HEIGHT}}$ (X = 5 feet) > 0]

$$\xrightarrow{\hspace{4cm} \text{X} \hspace{1.5cm}}$$

feet   0   1   2   3   4   5

We cannot measure Steve's HEIGHT value from the opposite end of the scale and describe him as some number of *feet short* because that end is not fixed – it continues on indefinitely. Since there is no natural place on that end of the scale to start our measurement from, we do not, other than in jest, say that anything is *five feet short*. When we do jest in this way, we have to understand *short* as asserting that *five feet* is shorter than the neutral standard of comparison for HEIGHT.

All this works the same for the neutral *how* questions in (35), in that neutral *how* questions ask for a measurement from the starting point of a scale – i.e. 'how far from 0 on the scale is the value of the measurement?' Committed *how* questions like *How short is he?* ask for a point on the scale to be compared to the neutral range.

If we can say *five feet tall*, why not *??30 kph fast*, *??30 decibels loud*, or *??30 kilos heavy*? It has been observed that the 'zero' points in dimensions like HEIGHT and AGE are not "real" points on the scales, since there is nothing in the physical world that cannot be measured for its spatial extent, nor nothing that can exist without having an age (Kennedy 2001). On the other hand, the SPEED, SOUND VOLUME, and WEIGHT dimensions have zero points at which things can be measured – but the things with zero values on those scales cannot be described by either of the relevant antonyms. Something whose speed is zero kilometers-per-hour is not *slow* or *fast*; it is *still*. Similarly, SOUND VOLUME and WEIGHT have zero-values that are populated by *silent* and *weightless* things, respectively. So, perhaps one can use a starting point as a comparison point for a measurement only if that starting point is not describable by the adjective in question. This helps us to reconcile the evidence for an asymmetrical HEIGHT scale with a starting point with the evidence that the scale is open at both ends (§11.5.2). In this case, we can view the starting point on the HEIGHT scale as mostly irrelevant to *short/tall*, since those adjectives never describe that starting point. The problem with such attempts at explanation, however, is that the data are messier than this. Other languages, like Swedish and German, have no problem with '30 kilos heavy.' And it is not unheard of to say things like *30 decibels loud* in English (Murphy 2006), although most semanticists who have looked at the problem mark this as an impossible phrase.

Puzzle 11–4

There is no starting 'zero' point at either end of the scale of TIME, since our perception of TIME has it extending indefinitely into the past and the future. Nevertheless, it is possible to use measure phrases, like *five minutes*, with the temporal adjectives *early* and *late*:

> *The bus arrived five minutes early*
> *The bus arrived five minutes late*

How is the scale for *early/late* configured such that it is acceptable to use a measure phrase with these adjectives? Do *early* and *late* have neutralized interpretations when they co-occur with measure phrases?

11.5.4   One scale or two?

Many gradable adjectives fall into contrary antonym relations (see §6.2.4), in which there is a "middle ground" that neither adjective describes. For instance, if someone is *not tall*, it does not mean that they are *short*, since they could be neither short nor tall – that is, their height could fall in the neutral range. In a case like *tall/short*, the two opposites describe scalar relations in the HEIGHT dimension, in which some measurements are as *short* and others as *tall*, as compared to the contextually determined neutral range. We can tell that the two antonyms describe the same dimension because the relations between them are reciprocal – *X is taller than Y* entails *Y is taller than X*, and vice versa. In other words, (38) paraphrases (39):

(38)   Jane is shorter than Tarzan.

(39)   Tarzan is taller than Jane.

Not all antonym pairs work in this way, however. Take, for instance, *sweet*, which is used with various opposites: *bitter, sour, savory*. We can tell that *sweet* is gradable because it can be intensified (*very sweet*) and compared (*X is sweeter than Y*). Nevertheless, *sweet* does not act as if it is in the same dimension as *bitter* (or any of the other antonyms here – test them!), as we can tell from the fact that (40) does not entail (41).

(40)   Hugh's cake is sweeter than Hilda's.

(41)   Hilda's cake is more bitter than Hugh's.

This tells us that the scale of sweetness ranges from NOT-SWEET (or *tasteless*) to *sweet*, as in figure 11.7, rather than from *bitter* to *sweet*. So, in the case of *sweet* and *bitter*, the fact that they are (in some contexts) opposite does not mean that

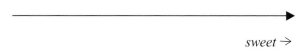

sweet →

Figure 11.7 *The* SWEETNESS *scale*

they describe the same dimensional scale. Instead, each of the taste adjectives describes a distinct dimension of taste.

Puzzle 11–5

For each of the following pairs, determine whether the two opposite terms describe the same or different dimensions:

a.   *red/green* (which are opposites on the color wheel)
b.   *light/dark* (of colors)
c.   *happy/sad*

11.6   Summary and conclusion

This chapter has concentrated on adjectives that are not derived from nouns or verbs, and has given special attention to scalar adjectives. In context, adjective interpretation is greatly affected by the noun that the adjective modifies – both because the adjective can modify different aspects of different noun meanings (e.g. *fast typist* vs. *fast game*) and because many adjectives rely on a pragmatically defined standard of comparison that determines which measurements in a dimension are within the adjective's denotational range. We looked at a range of properties of scales, which serve as ways of representing the semantic differences among adjective types, giving rise to different types of antonymy.

11.7   Further reading

Interest in formal aspects of adjective meaning has seen a boom in the past decade. For reasons of exposition, some aspects of the theoretical positions have been simplified, and so the interested reader is encouraged to consult the readings suggested for a full picture, particularly of the scale structures advocated by Christopher Kennedy and Louise McNally (2005). Scalar treatments of gradable meaning are proposed by Manfred Bierwisch (1989) and Kennedy (1999), with further development of Kennedy's position in the sources cited in §11.5.2. McNally and Kennedy's edited collection *Adjectives and Adverbs* (2008) includes a helpful introduction. Carmen Rotstein and Yoad Winter (2004) have looked in some detail at the semantics of the antonym pairs (developing the notion of **partial** and **total** adjectives introduced by Yoon (1996)) that Cruse (1986; see chapter 6) labeled as gradable complementaries. Carita Paradis (2001) explores the application of BOUNDEDNESS to the adjective category and to the intensifiers and totality modifiers that can modify adjectives from a more cognitivist perspective.

Lehrer 1985 presents a thorough description of adjective neutralization as a symptom of the linguistic phenomenon of **markedness** (mentioned in §9.4.4) – but see also Haspelmath (2006), who disputes the relevance of markedness in explaining such phenomena.

11.8   Answers to puzzles

11–1

a.   *A good book* is typically an *interesting* book or a *well-written* book. This relates to the function of a book (to be read) and, in turn, the function of reading (either for information or for entertainment). But given a context like *That's a good book if you need to prop open a door*, another interpretation is available in which the physical form, rather than the content, of the book is relevant.

b.   There are at least two possible interpretations of *my good shoes*:
- *my dressy/fancy/special shoes* (i.e. the ones I save for special, dressy occasions)
- *my functional shoes* (i.e. the ones that don't have holes in them)

c.   *A good talking-to* is usually a *severe* or *thorough* talking-to. It is possible to imagine contexts in which it could mean 'an eloquent talking-to,' among other things, but since *a good talking-to* is an idiom meaning 'a scolding,' it is less likely than the other examples to be interpreted compositionally (and thus ambiguously).

11–2

Absolute adjectives typically have complementary antonyms, for example *odd/even*, *perfect/imperfect*, *dead/alive*. For those, the negation of one entails the assertion of the other, and vice versa. So, *I am perfect* entails *I am not imperfect*, and *I am imperfect* entails *I am not perfect*. Some non-gradable adjectives are part of larger contrast sets, rather than antonym pairs. For example, *square* is contrasted with *round*, *rectangular*, *triangular*, and so forth. These could be considered complementary sets (see example (19) in chapter 6). Some adjectives – absolute or not – do not have conventionalized antonyms, and *unique* seems to be in that group. However, one might propose various antonyms for it, including *non-unique* or *common*. *Unique* is not in a complementary relation with *common* since some things are *rare* rather than *unique* or *common*. In this case, *unique* is a scalar absolute (something can be *almost unique*) and so it could have either contrary antonyms that are at the opposite end of the scale (*common*) or complementary antonyms (like *non-unique*) that cover all of the scale that is not described by *unique*.

11–3

Each of these adjectives is a relative adjective, interpreted with relation to a neutral point. We can know this because the size of *huge* or *tiny* things varies according to the type of things they are, and the temperature of *hot* or *cold* things varies in a similar way. For example, a *huge mouse* will not be as big as the minimal size requirements for a *huge mountain*, and a *hot stove* is probably a lot cooler than a *hot nuclear reaction*. These pairs are a bit different from *tall/short*, however, in that they denote extremes, rather than the whole scale. So, for example, in the HEIGHT dimension, something can be *taller* than something else while still being *short* (recall Perry and Jools in figure 11.4). It doesn't work, however, to say that one cold thing is *hotter* than another or one huge thing is *tinier* than another. *Hot/cold* and *tiny/huge* thus involve partial subscales of the TEMPERATURE and SIZE scales. In contrast, *cool/warm* and *little/big* or *small/large* describe the entirety of the TEMPERATURE and SIZE scales.

Despite its context-sensitivity, *huge* does not act like a gradable adjective, since it is odd with intensification or in the comparative form, while it is OK with the totality modifier *absolutely*:

a.   ?The elephant is very huge.
b.   ??The elephant is somewhat huge.
c.   ??The whale is more huge than the elephant.
d.   The elephant is absolutely huge.

I'll leave it to you to decide whether *tiny* follows the same pattern. (My own intuitions on it are mixed.) *Hot* and *cold*, by contrast, are happier with intensification (*very hot*) than with totality modification (*?absolutely hot*), and both can be compared (*hotter, colder*).

11–4

Late and *early* measure time from a particular point on the TIME scale, although that point is not at one end of the scale. Instead, they measure time from a contextually determined time somewhere along the TIME scale – in the examples here, the time at which the bus was scheduled to arrive.

11–5

In each of these cases, we want to test adjective 1 and adjective 2 by asking: "If X is more *adjective-1* than Y, then is Y more *adjective-2* than X?" If the answer is "yes," then the two adjectives operate in the same dimension.

a.   If your shirt is *redder* than your hat, it doesn't mean that your hat is *greener* than your shirt. Thus, these must be on separate scales.
b.   If your green shirt is *lighter* than your green hat, then your green hat is *darker* than your green shirt. Thus, these are on the same scale.

c.   If Ruth is *happier* than Rachel, it does not necessarily mean that Rachel is *sadder* than Ruth – Rachel instead could be more angry or upset rather than sad. Thus, *happy* and *sad* are on separate scales.

11.9   Exercises

Adopt-a-word

If your word is an adjective, determine its properties using the diagnostics presented in this chapter (occurring with intensifiers or totality modifiers, comparison, interpretation in *how* questions and so forth). If it is a scalar adjective, sketch a scalar representation for it, paying particular attention to whether the scale is open-ended and whether the adjective shares its scale with its antonym (if it has one).

General

1.   Determine whether the following adjectives are absolute or relative (or both). Give evidence in favor of your answer.
   a. frequent
   b. daily
   c. afraid
   d. sober (in the sense 'not intoxicated')
   e. purple

2.   For each of the following adverb+adjective combinations, determine whether the adverb is an intensifier or a totality modifier and give evidence in favor of your conclusion.
   a. fast asleep
   b. quite angry
   c. dead certain
   d. deeply concerned
   e. stark naked

3.   For each of the following pairs, determine whether they map to a scale that is open, closed on one end (which end?), or completely closed. If any of the pairs is polysemous in such a way that it has more than one scale structure, be clear about which scale structure goes with which senses of the adjectives.
   a. conscious/unconscious
   b. comfortable/uncomfortable
   c. useful/useless
   d. clean/dirty
   e. weak/strong

References

Aitchison, Jean (2003). *Words in the Mind*, 3rd edn. Oxford: Blackwell.

Allan, Keith (2007). The pragmatics of connotation. *Journal of Pragmatics* **39**, 1047–1057.

Aristotle (1941). Categories (trans. E. M. Edghill). In Richard McKeon (ed.), *The Basic Works of Aristotle*. New York: Random House, 7–39.

Bach, Emmon (1986). The algebra of events. *Linguistics and Philosophy* **9**, 5–16.

Barner, David and Jesse Snedeker (2005). Quantity judgments and individuation: evidence that mass nouns count. *Cognition* **97**, 41–66.

Barsalou, Lawrence W. (2009). Ad hoc categories. In Patrick Colm Hogan (ed.), *The Cambridge Encyclopedia of the Language Sciences*. New York: Cambridge University Press, 87–88.

Battig, W. F. and W. E. Montague (1969). Category norms for verbal items in 56 categories. *Journal of Experimental Psychology Monograph Supplement* **80** (3, Part 2), 1–46.

Becker, C. A. (1980). Semantic context effects in visual word recognition. *Memory and Cognition* **8**, 493–512.

Béjoint, Henri (2000). *Modern Lexicography*. Oxford University Press.

Bennett, Paul (2002). *Semantics*. Munich: Lincom.

Biber, Douglas, Stig Johansson, Geoffrey Leech, Susan Conrad, and Edward Finegan (1999). *Longman Grammar of Spoken and Written English*. London: Longman.

Bierwisch, Manfred (1989). The semantics of gradation. In Manfred Bierwisch and Ewald Lang (eds.), *Dimensional Adjectives: Grammatical Structure and Conceptual Interpretation*. Berlin: Springer, 71–261.

Bloomfield, Leonard (1933). *Language*. New York: Holt, Rinehart, and Winston.

Bolinger, Dwight (1965). The atomization of meaning. *Language* **41**, 555–575.

Booij, Geert (2007). *The Grammar of Words*. Oxford University Press.

Carroll, Lewis (1865). *Alice's Adventures in Wonderland*. New York: McLoughlin Brothers.

Charles, Walter G., Marjorie A. Reed, and Douglas Derryberry (1994). Conceptual and associative processing in antonymy and synonymy. *Applied Psycholinguistics* **15**, 329–354.

Chierchia, Gennaro. (1998). Plurality of mass nouns and the notion of 'semantic parameter.' In Susan Rothstein (ed.), *Events and Grammar*. Dordrecht: Kluwer, 53–103.

Church, Kenneth W., William Gale, Patrick Hanks, Donald Hindle, and Rosamund Moon (1994). Lexical substitutability. In B. T. S. Atkins and A. Zampolli (eds.), *Computational Approaches to the Lexicon*. Oxford University Press, 153–177.

Clark, Herbert H. (1970). Word associations and linguistic theory. In John Lyons (ed.), *New Horizons in Linguistics*. Baltimore: Penguin, 271–286.

Clark, Herbert H. and Eve V. Clark (1979). When nouns surface as verbs. *Language* **55**, 767–811.

Collins Concise English Dictionary, 3rd edn. (1992). Glasgow: HarperCollins.

Concise Oxford Engish Dictionary, 8th edn. (1990). Oxford University Press.

Comrie, Bernard (1976). *Aspect*. Cambridge University Press.

Coseriu, Eugenio and Horst Geckeler (1981). *Trends in Structural Semantics*. Tübingen: Narr.

Croft, William and D. A. Cruse (2004). *Cognitive Linguistics*. Cambridge University Press.

Cruse, D. A. (1986). *Lexical Semantics*. Cambridge University Press.

(2000a). Aspects of the micro-structure of word meanings. In Ravin and Leacock (2000), 30–51.

(2000b). *Meaning in Language*. Oxford University Press.

Crystal, David (2003). *A Dictionary of Linguistics and Phonetics*, 5th edn. Oxford: Blackwell.

Dahl, Hartvig (1979). *Word Frequencies of Spoken American English*. Detroit: Verbatim.

Dixon, R. M. W. (1982). *Where Have All the Adjectives Gone?* The Hague: Mouton.

Dowty, David (1979). *Word Meaning and Montague Grammar*. Dordrecht: Reidel.

Encarta World English Dictionary (1999). New York: St. Martin's.

Evans, Vyvyan and Melanie Green (2006). *Cognitive Linguistics*. Edinburgh University Press.

Fellbaum, Christiane (1998a). A semantic network of English verbs. In Fellbaum (1998b), 69–104.

Fellbaum, Christiane (ed.) (1998b). *WordNet*. Cambridge, MA: MIT Press.

Field, John (2003). *Psycholinguistics: A Resource Book for Students*. London: Routledge.

Fillmore, Charles J. and B. T. S. Atkins (2000). Describing polysemy: the case of *crawl*. In Ravin and Leacock (2000), 91–110.

Fillmore, Charles J., Paul Kay, and Mary C. O'Connor (1988). Regularity and idiomaticity in grammatical constructions: the case of *let alone*. *Language* **64**, 501–538.

Fodor, Jerry A. (1975). *The Language of Thought*. Hassocks, Sussex: Harvester.

Fodor, Jerry A., Merrill F. Garrett, Edward C. T. Walker, and Cornelia H. Parkes (1980). Against definitions. *Cognition* **8**, 263–367.

Frawley, William (1992). *Linguistic Semantics*. Hillsdale, NJ: Erlbaum.

Frege, Gottlob (1892). Über Sinn und Bedeutung. *Zeitschrift für Philosophie und philosophische Kritik*, 22–50. Reprinted as 'On sense and nominatum' (trans. P. Geach and M. Black), in Martinich (ed.) (2005), 199–211.

Geeraerts, Dirk (1993). Vagueness's puzzles, polysemy's vagaries. *Cognitive Linguistics* **4**, 223–272.

Geurts, Bart (1997). Good news about the description theory of names. *Journal of Semantics* **14**, 319–348.

Gillon, Brendan S. (1992). Towards a common semantics for English count and mass nouns. *Linguistics and Philosophy* **15**, 597–640.

Givón, Talmy (1979). *On Understanding Grammar*. Orlando, FL: Academic Press.

(1984). *Syntax*, vol. I. Amsterdam: John Benjamins.

Goddard, Cliff (1998). *Semantic Analysis*. Oxford University Press.

(2001). Review: Language, logic and concepts: essays in memory of John Macnamara, ed. by Ray Jackendoff, Paul Bloom, and Karen Wynn. *Journal of Linguistics* **37**, 205–210.

(2009). A piece of cheese, a grain of sand: the semantics of mass nouns and unitizers. In Francis Jeffry Pelletier (ed.), *Kinds, Things and Stuff*. New York: Oxford University Press, 132–165.

(2010). The natural semantic metalanguage approach. In Bernd Heine and Heiko Narrog (eds.), *The Oxford Handbook of Linguistic Analysis*. Oxford University Press, 459–484.

Goddard, C. and Anna Wierzbicka (eds.) (1994). *Semantic and Lexical Universals – Theory and Empirical Findings*. Amsterdam, John Benjamins.

(2002). *Meaning and Universal Grammar: Theory and Empirical Findings*. Amsterdam: John Benjamins.

Goldberg, Adele (1996). Construction Grammar. In Keith Brown and Jim Miller (eds.), *Concise Encyclopedia of Syntactic Theories*. New York: Elsevier, 68–71.

Goldberg, Adele E. and Ray Jackendoff (2004). The English relative as a family of constructions. *Language* **80**, 532–568.

Grimshaw, Jane (1990). *Argument Structure*. Cambridge, MA: MIT Press.

Gruber, Jeffrey (1965). *Studies in Lexical Relations*. Doctoral dissertation, Massachusetts Institute of Technology, published by Indiana University Linguistics Club.

Hamm, Friedrich (2009). Frame Semantics. In Patrick Colm Hogan (ed.), *The Cambridge Encyclopedia of the Language Sciences*. Cambridge University Press.

Harley, Heidi (1999). Denominal verbs and Aktionsart. Papers from the UPenn/MIT Roundtable on the Lexicon (*MIT Working Papers in Linguistics* **35**), 73–85.

(2006). *English Words: A Linguistic Introduction*. Oxford: Blackwell.

Harris, Roy (1973). *Synonymy and Linguistic Analysis*. Oxford: Blackwell.

Haspelmath, Martin (2006). Against markedness (and what to replace it with). *Journal of Linguistics* **42**, 25–70.

Hoffman, Joshua and Gary S. Rosenkrantz (1997). *Substance: Its Nature and Existence*. London: Routledge.

Hopper, Paul J. and Sandra A. Thompson (1985). The iconicity of the universal categories "noun" and "verb." In John Haiman (ed.), *Iconicity in Syntax*. Amsterdam: John Benjamins, 151–183.

Horn, Laurence R. (2001). *A Natural History of Negation*, revised edn. Stanford: CSLI.

Huddleston, Rodney and Geoffrey K. Pullum (2002). *The Cambridge Grammar of the English Language*. Cambridge University Press.

Jackendoff, Ray (1976). Toward an explanatory semantic representation. *Linguistic Inquiry* **7**, 89–150.

(1983). *Semantics and Cognition*. Cambridge, MA: MIT Press.

(1990). *Semantic Structures*. Cambridge, MA: MIT Press.

(1991). Parts and boundaries. In Beth Levin and Steven Pinker (eds.), *Lexical and Conceptual Semantics*. Oxford: Blackwell, 9–46.

(1997). *The Architecture of the Language Faculty*. Cambridge, MA: MIT Press.

(2002). *Foundations of Language*. Oxford University Press.

(2006). On Conceptual Semantics. *Intercultural Pragmatics* **3**, 353–358.

(2007). Conceptual Semantics and Natural Semantic Metalanguage Theory have different goals. *Intercultural Pragmatics* **4**, 411–418.

Jackson, Howard (1988). *Words and Meaning*. London: Longman.

Katamba, Francis and John Stonham (2006). *Morphology*, 2nd edn. London: Palgrave.

Katz, Jerrold J. (1972). *Semantic Theory*. New York: Harper and Row.

Katz, Jerrold J. and Jerry A. Fodor (1963). The structure of a semantic theory. *Language* **39**, 170–210.

Katz, Jerrold J. and Paul M. Postal (1964). *An Integrated Theory of Linguistic Descriptions*. Cambridge, MA: MIT Press.

Kennedy, Christopher (1999). *Projecting the Adjective: The Syntax and Semantics of Gradability and Comparison*. New York: Garland Press.

   (2001). Polar opposition and the ontology of degrees. *Linguistics and Philosophy* **24**, 33–70.

Kennedy, Christopher and Louise McNally (2005). Scale structure and the semantic typology of gradable predicates. *Language* **81**, 345–381.

Kneale, William (1962). Modality *de dicto* and *de re*. In Ernest Nagel, Patrick Suppes, and Alfred Tarski (eds.), *Proceedings of the 1960 Conference on Logic, Methodology and Philosophy of Science*. Stanford, CA: Stanford University Press, 622–633.

Kripke, Saul (1972). *Naming and Necessity*. Dordrecht: Reidel.

Labov, William (1973). The boundaries of words and their meanings. In Charles-James Bailey and Roger W. Shuy (eds.), *New Ways of Analyzing Variation in English*. Washington, DC: Georgetown University Press, 340–371.

Lakoff, George (1987). *Women, Fire, and Dangerous Things: What Categories Reveal about the Mind*. University of Chicago Press.

Landau, Sidney I. (2001). *Dictionaries: The Art and Craft of Lexicography*, 2nd edn. Cambridge University Press.

Langacker, Ronald W. (1987). Nouns and verbs. *Language* **63**, 53–94.

Laurence, Stephen and Eric Margolis (1999). Concepts and cognitive science. In Eric Margolis and Stephen Laurence (eds.), *Concepts: Core Readings*. Cambridge, MA: MIT Press, 3–81.

Leech, Geoffrey (1981). *Semantics*, 2nd edn. Harmondsworth: Penguin.

Lehrer, Adrienne (1974). *Semantic Fields and Lexical Structure*. Amsterdam: North Holland.

   (1985). Markedness and antonymy. *Journal of Linguistics* **21**, 397–429.

Levin, Beth (1993). *English Verb Classes and Alternations*. University of Chicago Press.

Levin, Beth and Malka Rappaport Hovav (2005). *Argument Realization*. Cambridge University Press.

Lieber, Rochelle (2004). *Morphology and Lexical Semantics*. Cambridge University Press.

Löbner, Sebastian (2002). *Understanding Semantics*. London: Arnold.

Lucy, John (1992). *Grammatical Categories and Cognition*. Cambridge University Press, 37–69.

   (1996). The scope of linguistic relativity: an analysis and review of empirical research. In John Gumperz and Stephen C. Levinson (eds.), *Rethinking Linguistic Relativity*. Cambridge University Press.

Lycan, William G. 1999. *Philosophy of Language: A Contemporary Introduction*. London: Routledge.

Lyons, John (1977). *Semantics* (2 vols.). Cambridge University Press.

(1995). *Linguistic Semantics*. Cambridge University Press.

Martinich, A. P. (ed.) (2005). *The Philosophy of Language*, 5th edn. Oxford University Press.

McCawley, James D. (1975). Lexicography and the count–mass distinction. *Proceedings of the Berkeley Linguistic Society* **1**, 314–321.

(1992). Justifying part-of-speech assignments in Mandarin Chinese. *Journal of Chinese Linguistics* **20**, 211–246.

McNally, Louise and Christopher Kennedy (2008). *Adjectives and Adverbs: Syntax, Semantics, and Discourse*. Oxford University Press.

Mel'čuk, Igor (1996). Lexical functions. In Leo Wanner (ed.), *Lexical Functions in Lexicography and Natural Language Processing*. Amsterdam: John Benjamins, 37–102.

Meyer, Charles F. (2002). *English Corpus Linguistics*. Cambridge University Press.

Mill, John Stuart (1867). *A System of Logic*. London: Longman.

Morris, Michael (2007). *An Introduction to the Philosophy of Language*. Cambridge University Press.

Muehleisen, Victoria L. (1997). Antonymy and semantic range in English. Doctoral thesis, Northwestern University, Evanston, IL.

Murphy, M. Lynne (2003). *Semantic Relations and the Lexicon*. Cambridge University Press.

(2006). Semantic, pragmatic and lexical aspects of the measure phrase + adjective construction. *Acta Linguistica Hafniensia* **38**, 78–100.

Newmeyer, Frederick J. (1986). *Linguistic Theory in America*, 2nd edn. San Diego: Academic.

Nunberg, Geoffrey, Ivan A. Sag, and Thomas Wasow (1994). Idioms. *Language* **70**, 491–538.

Olsen, Mari Broman (1997). *A Semantic and Pragmatic Model of Lexical and Grammatical Aspect*. New York: Garland.

Özçalişkan, Seyda (2004). Typological variation in encoding the manner, path, and ground components of a metaphorical motion event. *Annual Review of Cognitive Linguistics* **2**, 73–102.

Palmer, F. R. (1971). *Grammar*. Harmondsworth: Penguin.

Papafragou, Anna (2005). Relations between language and thought: individuation and the count/mass distinction. In H. Cohen and C. Lefebvre (eds.), *Handbook of Categorization in Cognitive Science*. Oxford: Elsevier, 256–277.

Paradis, Carita (2001). Adjectives and boundedness. *Cognitive Linguistics* **12**, 47–65.

Pustejovsky, James (1991). The generative lexicon. *Computational Linguistics* **17**, 409–441.

(1993). Type coercion and lexical selection. In James Pustejovsky (ed.), *Semantics and the Lexicon*. Dordrecht: Kluwer, 73–94.

(1995). *The Generative Lexicon*. Cambridge, MA: MIT Press.

Quirk, Randolph, Jan Svartvik, Geoffrey Leech, and Sidney Greenbaum (1985). *A Comprehensive Grammar of the English Language*. London: Longman.

Ramchand, Gillian (1997). *Aspect and Predication: The Semantics of Argument Structure*. Oxford University Press.

Ravin, Yael and Claudia Leacock (eds.) (2000). *Polysemy*. Oxford University Press.

Reeves, Lauretta M., Kathy Hirsh-Pasek, and Roberta Golinkoff (1998). Words and meaning. In Jean Berko Gleason and Nan Bernstein Ratner (eds.), *Psycholinguistics*, 2nd edn. Orlando, FL: Harcourt Brace, 157–226.

Romaine, Suzanne and Deborah Lange (1991). The use of *like* as a marker of reported speech and thought: a case of grammaticalization in progress. *American Speech* **66**, 227–279.

Rosch, Eleanor (1973). On the internal structure of perceptual and semantic categories. In Timothy E. Moore (ed.), *Cognitive Development and the Acquisition of Language*. New York: Academic, 111–144.

(1975). Cognitive representations of semantic categories. *Journal of Experimental Psychology: General* **104**, 192–233.

(1978). Principles of categorization. In Eleanor Rosch and Barbara B. Lloyd (eds.), *Cognition and Categorization*. Hillsdale, NJ: Erlbaum, 27–47.

Rotstein, Carmen and Yoad Winter (2004). Total adjectives vs. partial adjectives: scale structure and higher-order modifiers. *Natural Language Semantics* **12**, 259–288.

Saeed, John I. (2003). *Semantics*, 2nd edn. Oxford: Blackwell.

Saint Dizier, Patrick (ed.) (2006). *Syntax and Semantics of Prepositions*. Dordrecht: Springer.

Saussure, Ferdinand de (1959/1915). *Course in General Linguistics* (ed. Charles Bally and Albert Sechehaye; trans. Wade Baskin). London: Peter Owen.

Sinclair, John (1998). The lexical item. In Ella Weigand (ed.), *Contrastive Lexical Semantics*. Amsterdam: John Benjamins, 1–24.

Sowa, John F. (2005). Building, sharing, and merging ontologies. Available at: www.jfsowa.com/ontology/ontoshar.htm.

Stilman, Eduardo (translator) (2003). *Aventuras de Alicia en el pais de las maravillas* (*Alice's Adventures in Wonderland*, by Lewis Carroll). Buenos Aires: Longseller.

Stubbs, Michael (2002). *Words and Phrases: Corpus Studies of Lexical Semantics*. Oxford: Blackwell.

Talmy, Leonard (1985). Lexicalization patterns. In Timothy Shopen (ed.), *Language Typology and Syntactic Description*, vol. III. Cambridge University Press, 57–149.

(2000). *Toward a Cognitive Semantics*, vol. I. Cambridge, MA: MIT Press.

Taylor, John R. (1993). Prepositions: patterns of polysemization and strategies of disambiguation. In Cornelia Zelinsky-Wibbelt (ed.), *The Semantics of Prepositions: From Mental Processing to Natural Language*. Berlin: Mouton de Gruyter, 151–175.

(2003). *Linguistic Categorization*, 3rd edn. Oxford University Press.

Tenny, Carol (1987). Grammaticalizing aspect and affectedness. Doctoral dissertation, Massachusetts Institute of Technology.

Thomasson, Amie (2004). Categories. In Edward N. Zalta (ed.), *The Stanford Encyclopedia of Philosophy*, Fall 2004 edn. Available at: http://plato.stanford.edu/archives/fall2004/entries/categories/.

Trask, R. L. (2000). *The Penguin Dictionary of English Grammar*. London: Penguin.

(2004). What is a word? *University of Sussex Working Papers in Linguistics and English Language*, LxWP11/04. Available at: www.sussex.ac.uk/linguistics/1–4–1–2.html.

Tuggy, David (1993). Ambiguity, polysemy and vagueness. *Cognitive Linguistics* **4**, 273–290.

Tyler, Andrea and Vyvyan Evans (2003). *The Semantics of English Prepositions*. Cambridge University Press.

Vendler, Zeno (1957). Verbs and times. *Philosophical Review*, **66**(2), 143–160.

Verkuyl, Henk J. (1993). *A Theory of Aspectuality*. Cambridge University Press.

Wechsler, Stephen (2005). Resultatives under the event–argument homomorphism model of telicity. In Nomi Erteschik-Shir and Tova Rapoport (eds.), *The Syntax of Aspect-Deriving Thematic and Aspectual Interpretation*. Oxford University Press, 255–273.

Westerhoff, Jan (2005). *Ontological Categories*. Oxford: Clarendon.

Wierzbicka, Anna (1972). *Semantic Primitives*. Frankfurt: Athenäum.

(1985). Oats and wheat. In John Haiman (ed.), *Iconicity in Syntax*. Amsterdam: John Benjamins, 311–342. (Also reprinted in Wierzbicka 1988, 499–560.)

(1986). What's in a noun? (or: How do nouns differ in meaning from adjectives?). *Studies in Language* **10**, 353–389. (Also reprinted in Wierzbicka 1988, 463–498.)

(1988). *The Semantics of Grammar*. Amsterdam: John Benjamins.

(1990). "Prototypes save": on the uses and abuses of the notion of 'prototype' in linguistics and related fields. In S. L. Tsohatzidis (ed.), *Meanings and Prototypes*. London: Routledge, 347–367.

(1996). *Semantics: Primes and Universals*. Oxford University Press.

(1997). *Understanding Cultures through their Key Words*. New York: Oxford University Press.

(2007a). Theory and empirical findings: a response to Jackendoff. *Intercultural Pragmatics* **4**, 399–409.

(2007b). NSM semantics versus Conceptual Semantics: goals and standards (a response to Jackendoff). *Intercultural Pragmatics* **4**, 521–529.

Wittgenstein, Ludwig (1958). *Philosophical Investigations*, 3rd edn (trans. G. E. M. Anscombe). New York: Macmillan.

Wolf, Michael P. (2006). Philosophy of language. In James Fieser and Bradley Dowden (eds.), *The Internet Encyclopedia of Philosophy*. Available at: www.iep.utm.edu/l/lang-phi.htm

Yoon, Youngeun (1996). Total and partial predicates and the weak and strong interpretations. *Natural Language Semantics* **4**, 217–236.

Index